AF412130

VIZZION
ARCHITECTS

THE MASTER ARCHITECT SERIES

VIZZION ARCHITECTS

Foreword: Şefik Birkiye · Introduction: Michael J. Crosbie · Texts and coordination: Georges Binder

images Publishing

Published in Australia in 2009 by
The Images Publishing Group Pty Ltd
ABN 89 059 734 431
6 Bastow Place, Mulgrave, Victoria 3170, Australia
Tel: +61 3 9561 5544   Fax: +61 3 9561 4860
books@imagespublishing.com
www.imagespublishing.com

National Library of Australia Cataloguing-in-Publication entry:

Title:	VIZZION Architects.
Publisher:	Mulgrave, Vic. : Images Publishing Group, 2008.
ISBN:	978 186470 065 7 (hbk.)
Notes:	Includes index.
Subjects:	VIZZION Architects.
	Architectural firms – Europe.
	Architecture – Europe – 21st century.
Dewey Number:	720.94

Coordinating editor: Andrew Hall
Image and graphics selection advisors: Frédéric Doerflinger, Muriel-Laurence Lambot
Firm profile texts: VIZZION Architects
Firm profile translation from French: ALIAS Languages sprl
Additional support: Sabine Gaudissart

Designed by The Graphic Image Studio Pty Ltd, Mulgrave, Australia
www.tgis.com.au

Pre-publishing services by Splitting Image Colour Studio Pty Ltd, Australia

Printed by Everbest Printing Co Ltd., Hong Kong/China

Contents

Foreword
by Şefik Birkiye

Throughout our education at La Cambre in Brussels in the beginning of the 1970s, we learned to regard the city as a socioeconomic fabric and the quality of such urban fabric as a social connecting and well-being factor. Since the beginning of our professional practice, our approach of architectural creation was not that of a personal exercise in style, but rather the contribution to a shared language, which is ruled by every country or area's own established practices. We thus discovered the endless possible ways to practice architecture.

Early on, we were able to set up teams that could meet the expectations of diversified programs offered by the various real-estate actors. As we acquired professional practice, we simultaneously gained the conviction that it is nowadays possible to build with originality and diversity, without a backward-looking attitude, whilst being respectful of traditions and contributing to a place-specific architecture that meets the local population's expectancies. Through our achievements, we contributed to repairing some cities or building city districts, keeping in line with tradition, which we reconsider, renew and revive, sustained by both imitation and innovation in formal combinations.

However, given that there are public and private partners who are motivated by other standards and shifting place-related contexts, it can sometimes be tough for an architect to convince or to let his fundamental choices on the city, mixed-use, width or variety of programs be heard when other people get to take the decision.

With VIZZION Europe, we funded our ambitions by organising the financial aspect of the investments needed to realise all our projects. This structure allows us to completely manage all decision-making, to increase the number of projects and to better meet the needs that we sense all around Europe and the world. We can thus be attentive to opportunities, choose the sites where we get involved, define the programs and find investors in order to carry out our architectural mission and endorse a creative role in accordance with our convictions.

Architecture, like many other creative spheres, has had to adapt to and create more appropriate conditions in a financial context that has become worldwide and international. However, architecture never gave up its cultural and social responsibilities that are deeply rooted in particular local backgrounds, each time different, and from which as architects we draw inspiration.

In every country where we are involved, VIZZION Europe has a network of correspondents, staff members and partners. Therefore, the projects we offer are consistent with the local reality. All those achievements nevertheless benefit from the efficiency of an international structure, one that is able to elude unforeseen context-related events, thus allowing us to consider duration as a core component, for both the financial partners and end-users. The interest and comfort of the end-user of the buildings obviously remains the main concern of our architecture.

This monograph is of particular significance to the practice of our profession, standing as a turning point between the past and the future of our mission, from architect to investor-architect.

Şefik BIRKIYE, Town planner architect
Founding Partner, VIZZION Architects
President, VIZZION Europe

Brussels is booming. The seat of the European Union is changing its skyline with new government complexes and corporate headquarters. In the heart of the European Union district, the Berlaymont building, constructed in 1970 and rejuvenated in 2004, shimmers in the night. To the north, more construction projects crowd the horizon with cranes as new phalanxes of office towers rise. The city has always been welcoming to those with a spirit of construction, who want to make their mark in the world by placing brick upon brick. Rather than the grand city vision that is Haussmann's Paris, Brussels' urban mass is made up of the thousands of individual, entrepreneurial efforts of its architects and builders over the past two or three centuries. The rich mix of architectural styles, heavy with ornament and building craft, reflects the polyglot nature of Brussels – a city where conversations in French, Flemish and German can be overheard on its streets. Rather than a signature architectural style, Brussels' identity is comprised of a bit of classicism, doses of various vernacular flavors echoing the blend of cultures, and the wonderful bouquet of Art Nouveau and Art Deco that can be discovered in almost any city block.

Brussels is also the home of VIZZION Architects, formerly known as Atelier d'Art Urbain, arguably one of Europe's most creative, committed and prolific architecture firms. The practice was founded in 1979 by principal Şefik Birkiye. Shortly after, he was joined by colleague Dominique Delbrouck and then by Christian Sibilde and Grégoire de Jerphanion, who became partners as well. In 2006 Şefik

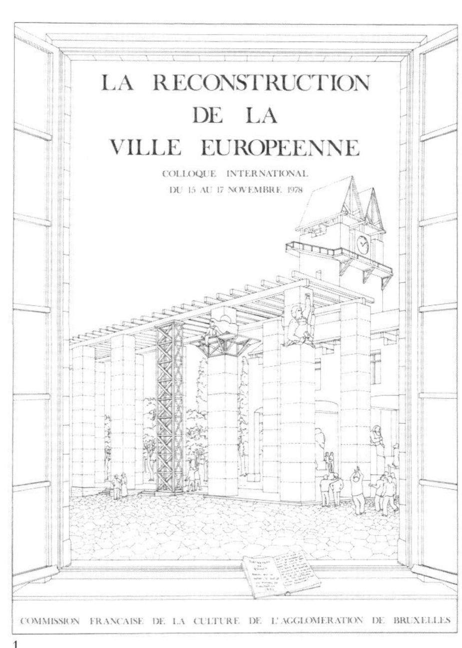

1

Birkiye struck out in a new direction without his three partners to pursue an architectural practice that includes development, all under the umbrella of VIZZION Europe.

The architectural practice is now attracting recent architectural graduates from around Europe as VIZZION expands from a primarily Belgium-based practice to projects around the globe – buildings that range from the modest to the grandest scale, entailing sensitive details and urban precincts that magnify and celebrate the life of the city.

VIZZION's organisation and structure is a radical departure from conventional architectural practice. After nearly 30 years of such convention, Şefik Birkiye could readily see its limitations on the architect. The

architect's role continued to shrink within the development team, and as it diminished, so did the quality of design. In 2006 Şefik Birkiye made the bold move to reassert the architect's role as the master builder – the one who conceives the project, assembles the project team, secures financing, executes design and construction, and oversees completion and commissioning. 'It's wonderful to no longer have clients,' Şefik Birkiye confessed to me over dinner one evening in Brussels, meaning that he himself is now his one and only client, conceiving the developments as well as designing the architectural solutions. The first year, VIZZION Europe financed projects valued at 600 million euros in seven different countries. For 2008–09, the firm anticipates 2.2 billion euros for projects in 10 countries, with a projection of nearly 3 billion euros in projects by the end of the decade.

A studio for city-building

VIZZION Architect's founding name, Atelier d'Art Urbain, means literally 'urban art workshop', and it is impossible to understand and appreciate the firm's practice without basing it in its urban context. Although the firm has designed projects in nearly a dozen countries – among them Switzerland, Luxembourg, France, the Netherlands, Monaco, Egypt and Turkey – its sensitive approach to urban presence, human scale, material richness, exacting detail and studied composition was wrought first in Brussels. Şefik Birkiye believes that an appreciation of this city's wealth of architectural variety and the attention to detail in even the most unassuming buildings has made

Introduction
by Michael J. Crosbie

VIZZION Architects attuned to the local architectural traditions and craft anywhere in the world, and has enabled them to translate them into new designs.

'The wealth of examples of architecture here in Brussels makes one more aware of the range of possibilities in style, design, and character,' explains Şefik Birkiye. 'We are similarly attuned to the architectural traditions and styles when we build in other places. We can pick up on what is special to a place, any place in the world, and that influences the buildings we create.'

Theory based in the life of the city

Şefik Birkiye studied architecture at La Cambre in Brussels in the 1970s. The Modern movement, with its disregard for history, was still very much part of the academy at that time, but students were turning against it. They could see how whole parts of cities were being destroyed for the construction of new projects that were alien to the existing urban fabric. Such architecture was anti-urban, and some architecture students and young architects of the time (including Şefik Birkiye) reacted very strongly against it. Şefik Birkiye saw in the work and theories of such visionaries as Léon Krier and Maurice Culot a way of designing in the city that possessed universal value in the existing context, yet reacting to that context with pragmatic solutions that were particular to a place, a time, and to the people who would use the buildings.

'This was during the period of Brutalism, when additions to the city were often hostile to the urban fabric,' explains Şefik Birkiye. 'We wanted to make the urban fabric better, instead of always starting from scratch – typically the modern approach.' Students made counter-proposals in reaction to insensitive, destructive projects from the city planning office. They saw design as 'renovation' of what was already there, inserting new buildings into the pattern of use that pre-existed, which would strengthen neighbourhoods and reinforce their sense of place. They saw designing in the city as a political act – a belief that continues to guide the work of VIZZION Architects around the world.

The firm's work is deeply connected to the city. Indeed, it is difficult to imagine the firm's architecture in anything other than an intense urban context. VIZZION Architects values and is quite comfortable working in the realm of ideas – of philosophy, art, craft and ornament, which it also pursues through publishing, exhibition and debate in the public arena. Its work is not cut off from the life of the city, and it is not 'ivory tower' architecture. It has a grand vision of the possibilities of architecture in the public sphere, how the spaces and buildings that it creates add depth and richness to the civic life of every citizen of

2

3

the city. But its vision is always grounded in the city's reality – in the circumstances of building codes, zoning, height limits, setbacks, access, scale and transportation – through which it realises its architecture. VIZZION Architects does not reject or ignore the reality of the design problem, but meets it head on, on the problem's own terms, with the goal of transcending the pragmatic to create a metropolitan art.

Design as a collaborative effort

VIZZION Architects operates somewhat like an architectural atelier from earlier times. Instead of apprentices, the practice attracts new graduates from architecture programs all over Europe and schools farther afield. For them, VIZZION Architects is a 'graduate school' that will teach an approach to architectural design that places emphasis on every building's urban connections, architectonic logic and material expression. The group VIZZION occupies several floors of the Lloyd George 7 building, a 1970s-era Brutalist building on Avenue Lloyd George that was renovated and revived by the firm in 1997. The office tends to have a low rate of turnover – those who share the values of the firms and want to pursue work that is faithful to those values are generally welcome to work there for as long as they wish.

Şefik Birkiye is involved at multiple levels – conceiving the project, finding the land, putting together the financing, bringing his expertise in planning, design, detailing, construction and project administration. Every project team includes the project architect from the very start, so that the design's guiding ideas in terms of site design, plan function and architectural character are understood and can be elaborated as the project moves closer to completion.

Şefik Birkiye and his team members work together closely, set the direction of each in terms of how to organise the site, the themes and ideas to be explored in the project, and how to make connections to the fabric of the city. The majority of the projects completed to date have been in Belgium, and the architectural imagery springs from that twilight between the end of Beaux-Arts classicism and the rise of Modernism. The transition point between these two very strong architectural movements is what attracts Şefik Birkiye, because it was a time when architecture was reinvented. Before Modernism's free plans and functionalism, designers were trying to fit with the past but also be Modern. This period of transition is exciting even today, because it is rich in examples of different alternatives between Classicism and Modernism. VIZZION Architects attempts to see the world as these designers did, as a bridge between the past and the future. It tries to perceive Classicism as Otto Wagner might have. Not quite Beaux-Arts and not quite Modern: a space in-between that remains rich in possibilities for an architect today.

But it would be erroneous to view VIZZION's architecture as a revival of historical styles. The stylist or the copyist is timid, creating work that does not venture further than the tried and true. In a confusing or threatening world, architectural revivals are welcome because they offer us something familiar to hang on to. However, such architecture is ultimately hollow, and the society satisfied with such a built environment is like a hermit crab, appropriating empty shells created for a once-vibrant but now dead culture.

VIZZION Architects' approach is very different. Their buildings and public spaces attempt to mend the rupture of civic life that is the debris of Modernism. It is as if during the middle half of the 20th century, the Modern world entered

4

5

6

a Dark Age where the knowledge of authentic city building was lost, and architects no longer could manipulate the tools of architecture to create such urban places. It is as if the language of architecture became lost, and architects became mute in describing through design a place where people could live lives with a fully civic dimension. It is as if architecture had become divorced from the human body, and we found that we could no longer relate physically to the environments that were being created in the name of a brave new world. Instead, architecture appeared to become the product of machines, and its scale relationship more suitable to the needs and whims of the efficient state or smooth-flowing commerce. Perhaps most disastrous of all, Modernism appeared to have jettisoned architecture's

function as a shelter for the human soul. In stripping architecture of its nurturing role through the cheapening or wholesale elimination of art, craft, colour and ornament (as a means to express emotion, memory, dreams and aspirations) Modernism reduced architecture to nothing more than a functional container for the detritus of human life. In the process, the physical city became a poverty of inhospitable plazas, deadened street life, horrifically scaled buildings, crumbling materials, environmental sinkholes and obliterated neighbourhoods.

It is this context of alienation, and the threat of more to come, that activated young architects all over the developed world in the 1960s to reject Modernism and to grope their way to create

architecture in which human beings would matter. Şefik Birkiye did this, first, by exploring how to conceive of new pieces of the city that would link to the old. Some of the firm's earliest projects in the late 1970s and early 1980s focused on the planning and design of public spaces and urban precincts in such cities as Paris, New York, Chicago and Cleveland.

Hotels as miniature cities

Şefik Birkiye first pursued hotel projects (including a cruise ship on the Nile River), multifamily housing, office buildings and renovations of existing buildings. Most of these projects were in Belgium, but one of its first significant projects was located in Istanbul. The 308-room Klassis Resort Hotel was the product of a design competition. Located on the shore

7

8

of the Sea of Marmara, the hotel is very urban in its scale, an amalgam of building elements rendered in the spirit of Ottoman architecture and composed as a small city cascading down a hill, embroidered with staircases, loggias and bridges. Şefik Birkiye worked closely with the local builders to design ornamental details rendered in indigenous materials. The complex invites one to meander down winding paths, through gardens, around across terraces. Glimpses of the sea and new perspectives of the Klassis Resort Hotel present themselves at every turn. It is a variegated and rewarding collection of public, semi-public and private spaces open to discovery, framing the guest's experience of the hotel and its surrounding environs.

The Klassis Resort Hotel sets the stage for another of Şefik Birkiye's important projects from the late 1980s and early 1990s. The Radisson SAS Royal Hotel is located in the heart of downtown Brussels on the corner of a winding street. The narrow thoroughfares girding the site and the existing surrounding buildings make for an intense urban density, in which the design of the Radisson revels. Where the Klassis Resort Hotel creates its own city enclave, the Radisson SAS asserts its place in the city with anthropomorphic certitude. The composition of the entire building block is clearly rendered with base, middle and top. The base is a rusticated dark grey limestone, upon which rests a light-coloured limestone. For the top, the mass steps back at the final two floors of smooth limestone and stamped green metal siding that integrates with a mansard roof. Regulating the building horizontally are bays that carry through from top to bottom, divided at the top by three-storey-tall light-bearing pylons with rounded Art Deco-like bases (early in the building's life the bases supported slender evergreens that have since, unfortunately, disappeared). Negotiating the building's transition at the corner is an astonishing quarter-round bay that stands with its arms lifted to the city, its shoulders and railing-crowned head rendered in green metal. It surmounts the intersection, with street-level bays of shops framing it on either side.

The hotel's vehicular entry on Rue Fossé-aux-Loups leads to a gracious lobby and a central courtyard with walls expressing the same city scale as the exterior, but with a more measured palette of materials. Here, in miniature, is a ground floor for exploration, akin to the entire site of the Klassis Resort Hotel, including the remnant of an excavated medieval wall.

Şefik Birkiye's success with the Klassis Resort Hotel and Radisson SAS led to other hotel projects, which also suggest miniature cities. The Monte-Carlo Bay Hotel & Resort in Monaco, completed in 2005, is like an island of blue pools and green palms, populated by diminutive temples framed by a gracious hotel of materials and colours sympathetic to the context. The scale of Monaco contributes to its feel of a village built on a promontory over the sea. Developed by the Société des Bains de Mer, the Monte-Carlo Bay Hotel & Resort is constructed on land reclaimed from the sea, on a dramatic site facing the water. The architects were inspired by the Mediterranean architecture of the great houses and palaces to be found along the Côte d'Azur in designing this 334-room hotel on eleven floors. The four-star resort hotel is conceived to accommodate very different types of clientele – business, leisure, Spa lovers – without them having to run into one another. An interior swimming pool prolonged by a series of lagoons covering some 1716 square metres

on a sand base, along with 8000 square meters of landscaped terrace, create a unique environment, not to mention the casino built into the hotel, of which more than 75 percent of the rooms take advantage of an ocean view.

In France, the Dream Castle Hotel just outside Disneyland Resort Paris appears as a community of classically inspired forms. In Egypt, the new 552-room Fairmont Cairo hotel, inspired by the region's traditional architecture, has recently been completed. The sand-coloured towers overlooking the Nile simultaneously appear contemporary and timeless – a heroic presence which will be joined by other VIZZION Architects' projects in the Nile City development.

Between land and water

In projects that followed the Radisson SAS Royal Hotel over the next few years, Şefik Birkiye continued to build upon the idea of

creating multifaceted urban environments that embodied a sense of the city's memory, joining the chorus of older structures with a voice clearly in a contemporary key. Perhaps the best example of the firm's work in this vein is the Canal Front in Brussels. This landmark development is found along the banks of the city's canal and includes a number of individual projects: a bank headquarters, an office complex and several apartment houses. These projects are complex and bold, with strong ties to the city and its history.

The KBC Bank Headquarters, the first project completed, is a grand gesture. The minute you approach Place Sainctelette over the canal, the headquarters loom behind a scrim of trees along the canal to the right. A brick base wraps the first three stories of the building, save for the central entry at mid-block that faces the canal, which is rendered in dark green metal and semi-mirrored glass. This central element

9

10

appears to be an older element in the block development and it possesses the architectonic power that one often finds in bank buildings of a century or more ago. It is temple-like, with a suggested pediment and columns. The main entrance is wreathed by an arch that springs gracefully over a bank of revolving doors. Viewing this façade from the canal, one at first might imagine the arch as a gateway into a park beyond, as the trees in front of the entry are mirrored in the glass and appear to occupy the courtyard inside. But what one finds inside is even more spectacular: an urban room of colossal proportions.

The public lobby of the headquarters recalls the great 19th-century banking halls. It is a fitting setting for the home of an international financial concern. The plan is simple in its layout, with the lobby at the centre and offices wings surrounding it to form a 'U'. The walls of the hall are composed with a base, middle and top, appearing as interior façades, with the multistorey corridors of the halls appearing as streets. This imagery is reinforced by the fact that the interior of the hall is illuminated through glass roofs, which give the illusion that the interior streets are open to the sky. Trees and greenery are abundant throughout the hall, with garden terraces and fountains suggesting city parks in miniature. Decorative details and ornament throughout the building reinforce the refined human scale and the visual richness of this urban environment.

The lessons learned at KBC Bank Headquarters were revisited in the European Union at Eudip Three in Brussels. New interiors weave a number of existing buildings together, joined by several urban-scaled events within. The welcoming, multistorey lobby with its gracious staircase is much smaller than that at KBC Bank Headquarters, but it is the produce of the same vision: making an urban space within the building, upon which office workers can look and gain views and daylight. A second spatial event is another wide, open staircase (the floors of the existing buildings were are a variety of levels that needed careful negotiation), this one rendered in warm wood tones, which delivers you to an elevator bank. An employee cafeteria looks out onto this carefully scaled space. Most surprising of all is the new roof garden, which also helps to tie the building together, and allows distant views within the heart of the office complex.

11

12

Another project of Canal Front is worth commenting on, for it opens another vein of VIZZION Architects' virtuosity. The city's regional planning office requires developers of office complexes to build affordable housing as well. Just northwest of the KBC bank building (and linked to it) is Le Jardin des Fonderies, the Garden of the Foundries, which incorporates an existing 19th-century brick stove works. The older building was cleaned, gutted and fitted with new apartment units. On the back side of the foundry are three new majestic entry stair towers with balconies that overlook a garden shared with two other apartment buildings designed by the firm: Residence Van Meyel and Le Lorrain. The architects picked up on the scale, rhythm, proportion, materials and ornament of nearby housing blocks and incorporated them into the design of the new residential buildings, making them feel as though they have always been part of the city's fabric.

The sensitivity in the design of Le Jardin des Fonderies to scale, colour and materials, and the symbiotic relationship of indoor and outdoor space, carries through other residential projects by the firm. The 'Les Jardins Victoriens' housing development outside of Disneyland Resort Paris establishes a sense of urban density while providing generous open space inside the complex for the enjoyment of the residents. Soft, inviting colours and stylised classical details recalling a time between Art Nouveau and Modernism give Les Jardins Victoriens a wonderful scale and sense of place. These architectonic elements are also present in other projects that the firm has

13

designed for and around Disneyland Resort Paris, such as its administrative headquarters building, which was obviously influenced by the work of Otto Wagner.

A more sophisticated handling of urban scale and the stitching together of ragged ends of the city into a new neighbourhood is seen at Euro Village in Brussels, near the European Union Parliament Building. The light-coloured brick with striped accent lines appear to make the apartment blocks nearly weightless, along with the eroded building corners that allow for balconies. Rounded elements at one end of the complex provide a grand scale as the complex faces a thoroughfare. Plazas that weave through Euro Village allow pedestrian pass-through to a nearby commuter rail station

and towards the parliament, tying the complex into the life of this precinct.

Mending with revitalisation and rebirth

The poise with which VIZZION Architects creates whole new segments of the city is due to the lessons learned on dozens of urban projects in which older structures have been transformed into a fabric that forms part of a greater urban garment. In many cases, VIZZION Architects is undoing the damage wrought by poorly designed projects from a generation ago (when Şefik Birkiye was an architecture student). In this sense, his spirited protest against Modernism's anti-urbanism continues today, as it mends the city through renovation.

14

15

On the Avenue d'Auderghem, two buildings with anonymous Modern façades are joined together with a newly designed skin of stone and glass that provides a hierarchy of entry, better urban scale and a crisply detailed lobby. On block after block throughout Brussels, one finds Şefik Birkiye at work turning sow's ears into architectural silk purses.

City Center, a refurbishment of and addition to the Art Deco-era Le Bon Marché store in the heart of Brussels on Boulevard du Jardin Botanique is a deft piece of city-making. The old 1928 store had been added onto years later with a shopping mall, but the entire block was dilapidated. The architects revitalised the Le Bon Marché for office space, extending its façade and mansard roof to fill the site along

the boulevard. Behind the preserved and new façades is a new office building organised around two courtyards. Behind this new building, an existing 1970s-era shopping mall was renovated and expanded by Şefik Birkiye, with larger atria and a new third level, stretching back into the block to create a pedestrian enclave, with a new entrance under a glass canopy at an interior corner of the site. Inside, the new mall is spacious and light-filled with a glass roof. New public spaces lead to offices and shopping, plus a parking garage and five storeys of new housing.

VIZZION Architects' newest projects extend the lessons of its work in urban regeneration to a new level – the creation of urban centres on sites around the world. For example, in

Istanbul, VIZZION Architects is currently engaged in designing an urban centre in the midst of a booming business district. Oyak Towers will tower above the European shore of the city, joining other developments that are populating Büyükdere Avenue, which is becoming Istanbul's major financial district. Oyak Towers will comprise office, meeting and fitness facilities in addition to a retail centre, with all construction above a garage with parking for hundreds of cars. But the shimmering glass envelopes, which will range in height from 16 to 37 storeys (depending on the development scenario used), are also well placed to take advantages of Istanbul's existing and expanding transportation infrastructure. The Büyükdere Avenue, along with being a hub for entertainment and retail activity, is directly linked to the city's highway network. An underground subway station will also serve the site, and Oyak Towers will also offer proximity to two major shopping malls, Metrocity and Kanyon.

On another site in the very heart of Turkey, an ambitious project is a study in the creation of a variegated city district. The Kayseri project will be a transformation of the city's major stadium into a place of civic life in the heart of the metropolis. The development will bring together a shopping and leisure mall, a luxury hotel, a conference centre and two multifamily buildings. There is a vital mix of shopping, leisure activities, cinemas, restaurants and even gardens on the roof. All of this will be supported with parking for more than 5000 cars.

Set within a park with public gardens, Kayseri will take its building design cues from the region's architectural language. VIZZION Architects has studied traditional Selcukide architecture, reinterpreting it with a contemporary accent. Some of the forms have been inspired by the voluptuous Cappadoce landscape. Through its architecture and urban planning, Kayseri is poised to be a landmark in the polis that will bring new life to the city.

VIZZION Architects' design for Anka Hill, in Ankara, Turkey, likewise takes its inspiration for the natural forms of Cappadoce, to dramatic effect. As is the case for the other projects in Turkey, this project is designed to create a vibrant city centre and a landmark on the Ankara skyline. The development includes a shopping mall, entertainment, a health centre, multifamily housing towers and a hotel tower.

One of the most exciting VIZZION Architects projects on the horizon is Green Square in Brussels, which continues the firm's work in the realm of multipurpose centres that form a lively city core. The project is planned for a corner block at the intersection of Boulevard Général Jacques, Boulevard du Triomphe and Chaussée de Wavre, right across the street from the Université Libre de Bruxelles campus.

This project has had an interesting evolution. The site was once occupied by an ice house, the remnants of which are protected by the local historical society. The scheme is more than a simple multi-use building. It builds a new neighbourhood where none before existed. Green Square integrates serviced residences with conventional apartments quality services, accommodation, housing for senior citizens, a health centre and local retail shops. In the heart of the district, a new private mews will be built and a park laid out for the enjoyment of all residents.

Green Square is an architectural proposition that it is possible to create an inner city development that celebrates nature. The architectural language allegorically refers to nature, using its smooth curves and evocative shades of colours, and the design encourages density and proximity to everything a person needs for urban living. The development supports the concept of a sustainable city, and the buildings include ecological materials and techniques that offer high performance levels in thermal comfort, acoustics, energy conservation and water management. Specific attention has been paid to the global conception of greenery: green façades, a private interior garden, green roofs and vegetation throughout Green Square.

17   Green Square, Brussels, Belgium
18   Istanbul seaside, North of Istanbul, Turkey

Green Square is an example of VIZZION Architects' emphasis on socially conscious architecture. VIZZION Architects is now pursuing more projects with a focus on sustainability: conserving natural resources and creating buildings with greater user comfort. This aspect is discussed further in the chapter on VIZZION's High Environmental Value architecture.

Preserving the 'useless'

This introduction to the architecture of VIZZION Architects provides a context for appreciating the firm's work as a piece of a greater whole. This portfolio of projects reveals that VIZZION Architects' design focus is not only on the building itself, but includes what is just beyond the building site: the block, the neighbourhood, the district, the city, the history, the culture. Ultimately, architecture exists in relation to everything else around it.

New projects just being designed promise to take VIZZION's architecture to a new scale, in which entire towns and settlements take shape. For example, in the north of Istanbul, VIZZION Architects is designing and developing a new town, Istanbul seaside, which will lie on the banks of the Black Sea. The architects have carefully studied the vernacular architecture of the region, incorporating salient features that will ground this community in the architecture of this part of the world. Density and vitality are the watchwords here – the very lessons that Şefik Birkiye has learned in his decades-long love affair with the city as a setting for the civic life. These lessons Şefik Birkiye now explores in the Istanbul seaside project, with its compact neighbourhoods, marketplaces, cultural centres, plazas and recreational places – all mixed together so that the life of the city is constantly charged and energising its citizens. Such a place as Istanbul seaside is only possible if the architect controls all aspects of the project. Every thread of this new city is woven to create the magic that has distinguished cities for thousands of years.

Reflecting on the works presented here, what can we conclude about VIZZION Architects and its values? Clearly, it is against the grain of contemporary mass-media culture. VIZZION Architects presents a counter view. Its architecture values the public realm over that of the private, it demonstrates a preference for the civic over the personal. There is an

17

18

emphasis on the function of the exterior compared to that of the interior, which is hidden from view. It values architecture that is decorative rather than unadorned. It values the particular over the universal, and prefers the humane over the merely utilitarian. VIZZION Architects chooses art over entertainment and values historical consciousness. Human scale is more important than the monumental. VIZZION Architects knows that value is more important than cost.

Ultimately, and paradoxically, VIZZION Architects values the 'useless' in the sense that architecture does not need to exist in order to provide shelter. The philosopher Hannah Arendt articulated the value of the 'useless' – music, literature, art and architecture – as those elements that civilise us, because they are not necessary for us to survive as a species. Architecture is not the servant of the useful, in the way we normally consider function and utility. Architecture is part of that great collection of human artefacts that we take delight in, through which we express ourselves, which reflects our spirit and is passed on to future generations. Architecture is the thing that lasts long after utility has left the building. It is the reason why the Parthenon is still architecture, even if its roof and most of its walls have vanished. The society that values utility and function above all else is not capable of assessing the value of such 'useless' artefacts as architecture and art, literature and music, history and legacy. But these are ultimately the things that last after all, and upon which tomorrow is built. They last

longer than we do and they make us intelligible to those who will come after.

Şefik Birkiye and the architects of VIZZION Architects know that the architect's ultimate responsibility is to ensure the transfer of the 'useless' to generations beyond his or her own – to communicate a culture of value

that will tell people in the distant future who we were and what we cared about. That is the value of the architecture that VIZZION Architects creates.

19

20

It is the insight of the VIZZION Group to link its vertical organisation to the goal of sustainability. The connection might not seem obvious at first, but architects can attest to the important role that the development team can play in achieving sustainability. The real challenge of designing and building a sustainable, energy-conserving environment is in the coordination of the hundreds of decisions that must be made. If the decisions are made by a plethora of parties who do not value sustainability, or assess its importance to varying degrees, then true sustainability is difficult to achieve. Sustainability demands that the project be conceived as environmentally sensitive before the first design decisions are made. Development and financing must aid in the creation of buildings with high environmental value.

For example, few commercial developers today appear to have a genuine commitment to sustainability. But if the developer is also the architect, the case for sustainability does not have to be made to the client. Those who finance, design and oversee the project have the shared value of sustainability. Thus, financing can be structured that promotes sustainable solutions, sometimes with higher up-front costs and longer payback periods. A development team that understands the contribution that sustainability can make to a project's financial success will be more willing to champion its green features. The developer will build sustainably because by doing so, a project's long-term costs can be reduced, for instance, through the use of more durable materials that require fewer replacements and are lower in cost to maintain. Better performance in energy conservation will reduce

operating costs, thus adding to the developer's return on investment. Interior environments that have better indoor air quality and rely on natural light for illumination result in fewer instances of employee absence, which adds to the company's bottom-line performance. Such environments have been shown to improve employee productivity.

The developer with sustainability in mind will find ways to maximise the building's efficiency through the performance of the heating and cooling systems, thanks to better insulation, high-performance windows and glazing, proper solar orientation and alternative or renewable fuels. This can be realised with the specification of smaller heating plants, the elimination of certain cooling equipment or the use of lower-cost fuels. This in turn contributes to lower first costs (construction costs) and lower life-cycle costs. A sustainable building can add value to the developer's real estate portfolio, and should show a greater return on investment. We can see this happening now in multinational firms around the world, which are turning to sustainable building design and construction not because they want to save the Earth, but because it makes financial sense from a long-term business point of view. It makes sense to the parties involved: the developer, the client and the architect. The vertical structure of project organisation – from development, financing, marketing and communication, to design, documentation, construction management and commissioning, to sales and management – is thus the only rational way to achieve sustainability, without conflicting goals and values. Sustainability can also be promoted

at greater scale – that of towns and communities – which allows economies of scale to make some high-cost technologies and sustainable strategies, such as photovoltaic systems, more economically viable.

An intellectual framework for sustainability

Because the VIZZION Group is organised to pursue large, urban-scaled projects, the commitment to sustainability becomes even more important. It is part of the firm's intellectual makeup and part of its long history. While many architects in developed countries have by now pledged commitment to the principles of sustainability, VIZZION Architects' founding firm, Atelier d'Art Urbain, has since its founding in 1979 promoted what can be described as a sustainable approach to architecture and design: to create contemporary buildings that respect the environment and integrate their surroundings and history, thus lending to their durability. Urban living and working solutions are the best answer to our impending global environmental crisis. Reducing commuting distances, revitalising urban centers, sharing infrastructure and public transportation and accentuating density are all strategies that support sustainability. Multi-use buildings are more sustainable, with a combination of functions to serve a multiplicity of users – the condition one finds in every city and town that also promotes social integration. Through project selection, development, design and construction it is possible for VIZZION to maximize the effectiveness of architecture that creates a dialogue between the traditions of the city and its citizens.

Towards a sustainable world:
VIZZION's High Environmental Value architecture
by Michael J. Crosbie

VIZZION Architects recognises the importance of construction and building science in realising its goal of sustainability. The company has assembled an ensemble of experts in building construction and performance who can quantify the effects of various sustainable strategies and technologies. Materials are chosen for their durability and long-term performance, their low 'embodied' or 'grey' energy (the energy expended in making them), their appropriateness to the context, their ability to be recycled, the content of recycled materials used, the reduction of carbon dioxide, their contribution to indoor air quality and low toxicity. VIZZION Architects also has a commitment to identify new materials and technologies as they are brought to market that might offer new solutions.

Energy conservation is part of any serious commitment to sustainability, but one must also change the mindset of seeing the Earth as a 'horn of plenty', with natural resources that are to be used without regard to long-term effects. Alternative fuels and sources of energy generation are a key part of the equation. How might the architecture reduce a dependence on fossil fuels – not just for a single building, but also at the scale of the city and for society at large? Does wind power offer a viable alternative to replace conventional forms of energy, or to reduce the dependence on fossil fuels? How can sources that are part of the natural cycles of the earth (geo-thermal energy, water-power, bio-fuels, tidal movement, solar generation) be incorporated into mainstream use?

1

What is HEV?

The concept of sustainability that constitutes VIZZION Group's approach to architecture is described as 'High Environmental Value', or HEV. The HEV concept is purposely open-ended to accommodate the group's broad horizon of operations. The focus here is not a particular technology, product or end-all solution, but rather an orientation to problem-solving that attempts to keep the manmade and nature environment in balance.

VIZZION Group describes HEV primarily as an approach to project management and execution, in which the quality of the building as an environment for sustaining a high quality of life is first and foremost. The goal of HEV is to limit the impact of the project on the environment while also ensuring buildings that are comfortable, high-performance and life affirming. The approach is holistic, not focused on one aspect such as energy conservation or recycling, but on the entire environment and its affect on every scale, from the immediate neighbourhood to the entire planet. Such effects are minimised through the informed choice of construction materials, through proper function and maintenance of the building, with the eventual scenario of the building's dismantling and recycling.

The VIZZION Group's orientation to HEV is found in four realms of activity that help shape a project. At a large scale, VIZZION

SITE DEVELOPMENT

- Respect for regional typologies and quality of public and private spaces.
- Integration of the buildings into the city, the site, the land parcel.
- Optimised application of bioclimatic principles.
- Minimal disturbance caused to animal and plant life.

ENERGY

- Reduction of energy needs and establishment of energy interactions between the different functions.
- Reinforcement of the external wall insulation.
- Installation of heat recovery for air and water.
- Use of renewable energies.

MATERIALS

- Use of low environmental impact materials.
- Significant use of regional recycled materials.
- Use of responsibly managed materials.
- High quality of implementation.

POLLUTION

- Use of materials that are non-toxic and listed according to the REACH regulation.
- Reduction of work site pollution.
- Waste sorting.
- Limitation of pollutant production.

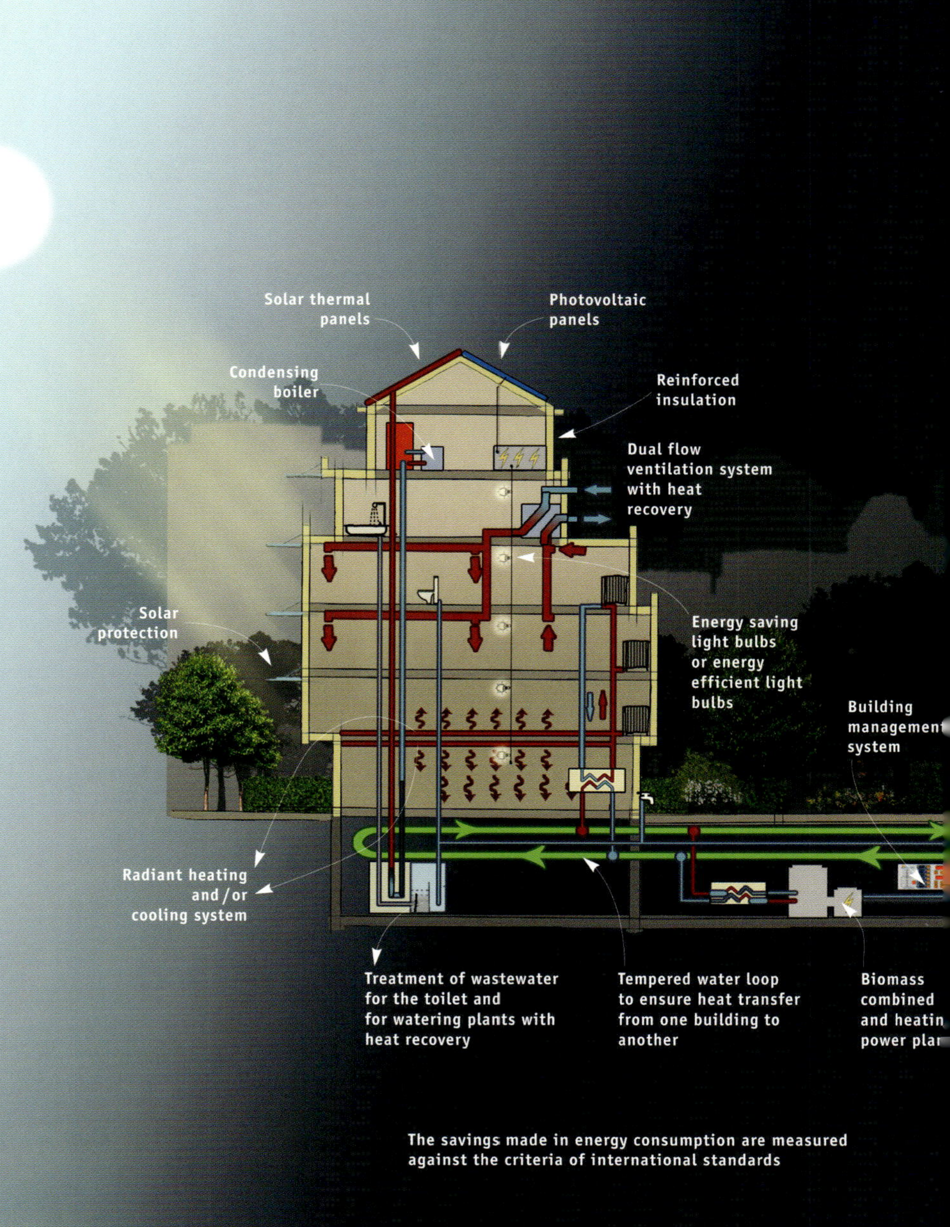

The savings made in energy consumption are measured against the criteria of international standards

2

THROUGH ITS INTEGRATED APPROACH, VIZZION EUROPE CREATES A SUSTAINABLE ENVIRONMENT

TRANSPORT

- Diversity of functions on the neighbourhood scale.
- Development of 'soft mobility'.
- Extension of the public transport networks.
- Development of a transport plan.

HEALTH AND WELL-BEING

- Natural lighting and outside views ensuring visual comfort.
- Installation of double flow ventilation system.
- Temperature control adjusted by the occupant.
- Provisions to support persons with reduced physical abilities.

MAINTENANCE

- Establishment of centralised technical installations.
- Long-term design of installations.
- Train, inform and check.
- Control of environmental risks from the maintenance systems.

WATER MANAGEMENT

- Sparing utilisation of drinking water.
- Rainwater recovery for watering and upkeep.
- Waste water sanitation.
- Installation of a leak detection system.

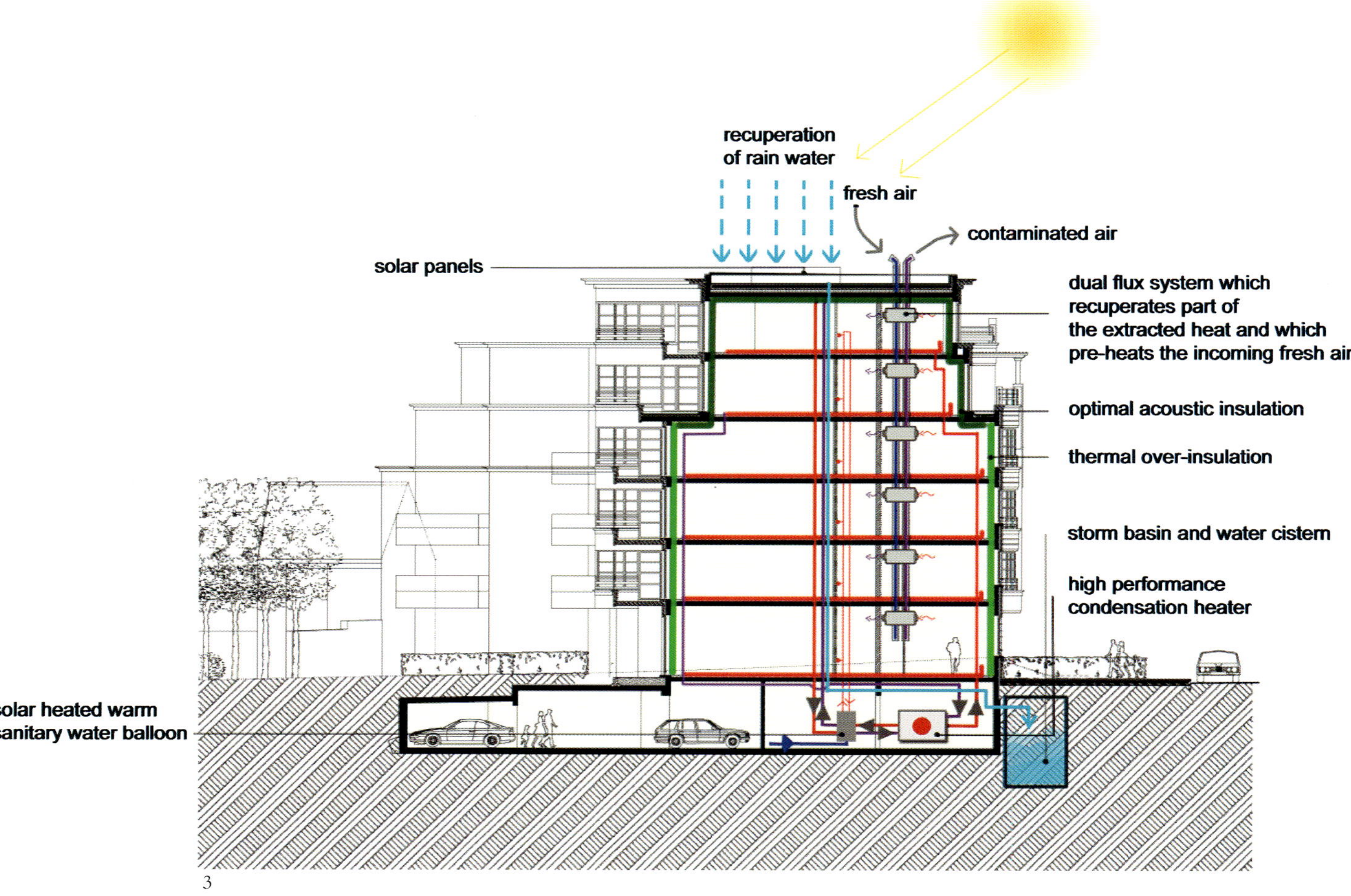

links city planning and the environment. It recognizes that what makes a city vibrant and lively is also what makes it sustainable: rich and complex spaces where many aspects of people's lives unfold. For instance, VIZZION Europe investigates the site's immediate agencies, understanding how a new building might connect into the ongoing life of the city and its myriad networks. How can the project contribute to the diversity of the site? How does it interface with public transportation, walkways, rail and bus lines, canals and cycling paths, and what opportunities might there be to expand these networks? What opportunities are there to mix living, working, learning and entertainment? Also essential is to determine how the project will tread lightly in the neighbourhood – how does it respect the existing context and not deplete the quality of life that already exists there?

The second realm is an architectural conception and 'build-ability' that is sustainable. A large part of this approach includes architecture's bioclimatic qualities. This requires not ready-made solutions, but design responses that are special to the microclimate, the building traditions and opportunities to preserve natural resources. The microclimate suggests ways that the building should be oriented, how it might offer shade, how it captures the sun's warmth, or channels cooling breezes. Compactness of form helps contribute to bioclimatic performance. The building envelope should insulate from heat or cold, it should preserve a comfortable environment inside, and it should help conserve energy. In many ways, in the various parts of the world where VIZZION Architects designs, this bioclimatic architecture is closely tied to the vernacular tradition. Often the answers to the question of how one should build are found in the abundance of

4

native genius that has, over hundreds of years, found ways to heat and cool buildings with minimal environmental damage. In this way, VIZZION Architects' interest in vernacular architecture extends far beyond aesthetics. It is a basis for designing environments that are in harmony with nature. Often, vernacular architecture helps in the choice of sustainable building materials that reduce carbon emissions (manufactured locally, from local materials). Products made of recycled materials, which are are easily recycled themselves, or are highly durable, are sustainable choices. New, high-performance materials also merit attention.

The third realm is the preservation of natural resources. Ways to help achieve this are alternative or renewable fuels, energy conservation, high-performance equipment and sophisticated building management systems. Depending on the project's location, renewable and alternative energy sources might present themselves: wind energy on a seaside coast, hydrothermal energy near underground sources. Not using fossil fuels also helps avert damages to the environment through spills and leaky underground containers (which can damage water sources). VIZZION Architects and VIZZION

Engineering pay close attention to HVAC systems, which should be calibrated to the building's location and function. Integrity of the building envelope and designed ventilation can lead to smaller-sized systems. Exhaust from heating or cooling systems can be used to power other building functions. Natural resources such as water should be carefully monitored and managed. For instance, monitoring user behaviour and instituting changes in how resources are consumed can often lead to dramatic reductions in water as well as energy.

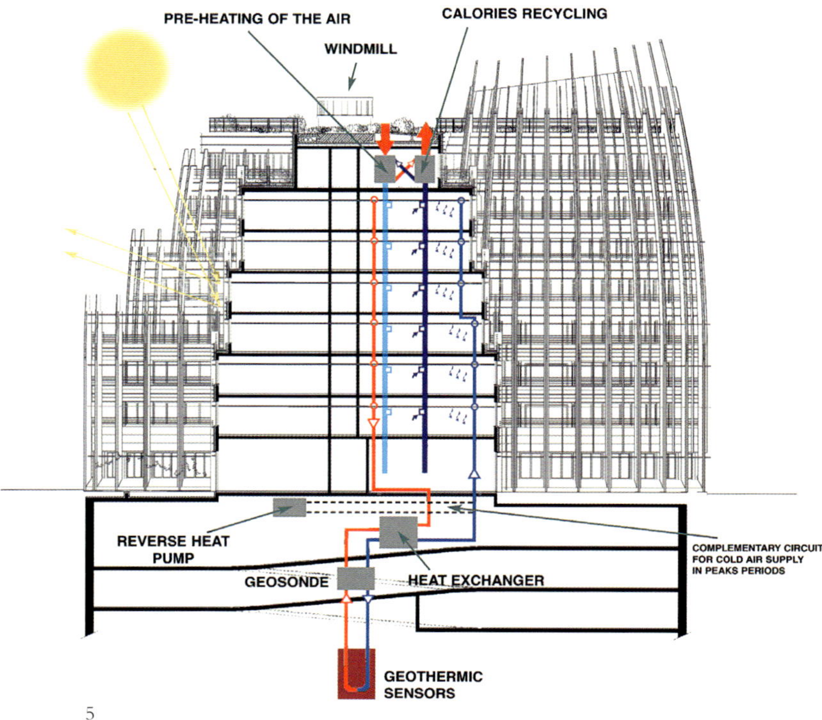

5

The fourth realm of the VIZZION Group's commitment to HEV is ensuring the quality of the environment for human use and habitation. Here, the focus is on comfort – thermal, acoustic, visual and olfactory. There is also attention to building waste and its disposal, and techniques to avoid environmental contamination. The success of any work of architecture depends on what it adds to human life – how it helps us to forge connections with other human beings and provides appropriate settings for the grand play of life. How convenient does the architecture make the thousands of daily personal interactions? Is the environment convivial to life's civic, social and productive dimensions? Are the environments accessible to the wide range of physical abilities one finds among people?

These are all questions of environmental quality to which VIZZION Architects is attentive in its architecture.

From theory to practice

VIZZION's intellectual framework for HEV is translated into architecture that does not appear 'green' or overly 'techy'. The projects do not wear sustainability as a costume, but integrate it into a project's very fabric – from its very conception to its commissioning, occupation and management. Several projects now in process show the depth of this commitment.

For example, two new residential projects recently completed in Brussels, La Belle Chanson and Les Trois Mâts, exhibit the trademark VIZZION design flair while incorporating such sustainable features as solar-heated hot water, rainwater collection and recycling, heat recovery for pre-heating fresh air, heavy thermal and acoustical insulation, and high-performance mechanical equipment.

Another project, the Arlon 65–67 in Brussels, now completed, is a showcase of renewable energy systems (in fact the building is the headquarters of the European Renewable Energy Council). Among the innovative technologies employed is a 80 kW wood-pellet boiler fuelled with a renewable alternative to fossil fuels; a ground-source heat pump that takes advantage of the earth's steady-state temperature; solar cooling, a system that uses solar panels to heat water for a storage tank,

6

which in turn drives cooling machinery; an air-handling unit with adiabatic cooling; and a photovoltaic systems used to generate part of the building's electricity.

Green Square is perhaps VIZZION's most dazzling sustainable project to date. Located on a prominent full-block site near a university in Brussels, the 30,676-square-metre project includes apartments and serviced residences and some commercial retail space and a health club. The project goals were impressive: cut energy use by half for the HVAC system compared to what a typical building of this size would consume, eliminate mechanical cooling and maximise the use of alternative energy options. VIZZION boosted the building's insulation and specified high-performance low-

emissivity, argon-gas filled windows. It also designed a high-performance ventilation scheme with a heat-recovery wheel system. Adiabatic cooling is specified, along with a ground-source heat pump for heating. Green Square will use concrete thermal mass floors and ceilings for radiant heating and cooling. The building will also incorporate wind turbines on the roof to help power ventilation; its vertical architectural expression recalls a forest, reaching to the sun.

Far from Brussels, in the north of Istanbul, VIZZION Architects is now designing Istanbul seaside, an entire city that will occupy the banks of the Black Sea. It is an opportunity for VIZZION Architects to explore the creation of a total living environment based on sustainable principles, such as using vernacular

Turkish architecture as an inspiration for bioclimatic design. Green spaces will be preserved and created anew, while transportation routes, nodes and hubs will be concentrated to promote density and shared infrastructure between population centres.

These projects and others on the drawing boards of VIZZION Architects constitute an approach to sustainability that grows from the architect's total control of the process, one that places the harmonious coexistence of the man-made with the natural world – a vision of environmental architecture aligned with the natural rhythms of the Earth.

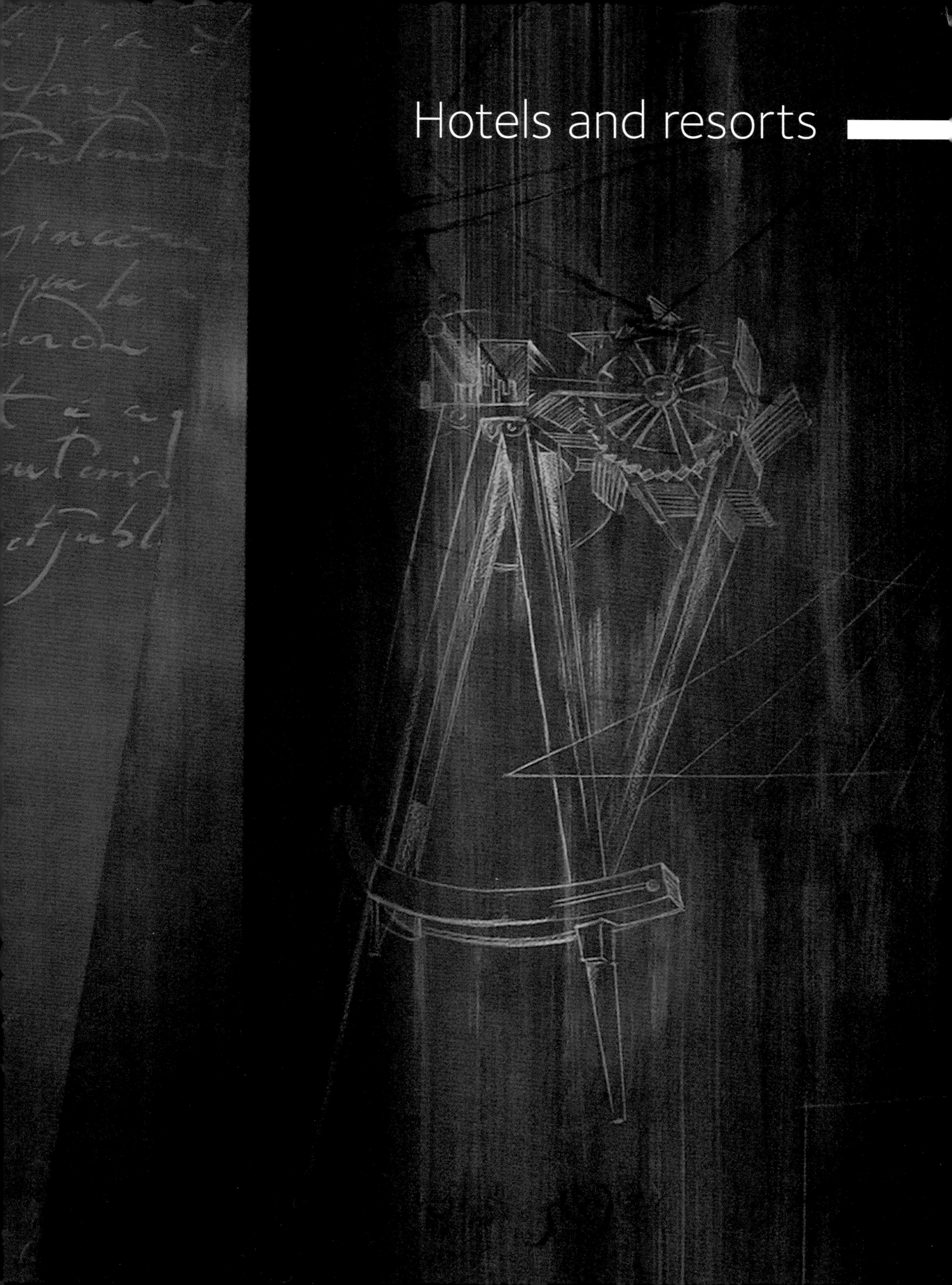

Hotels and resorts

1

Monte-Carlo Bay Hotel & Resort
Monaco, Principality of Monaco

Client: Société des Bains de Mer
Above ground area: 42,000 square metres
Completion: 2005
Awards: Competition-winning project;
MIPIM Awards 2006, finalist in the
hotels and tourism resorts category

Developed by the Société des Bains de Mer, the sea-facing Monte-Carlo Bay Hotel & Resort was constructed on a 4-hectare site that was reclaimed from the sea.

The architecture of the hotel, which comprises 334 rooms on 12 floors, is inspired by the Mediterranean architecture of the great houses and palaces to be found along the Côte d'Azur. In addition to the standard rooms and suites, the resort features 24 furnished apartments for long-term residents.

The luxury resort hotel is conceived to accommodate different types of clientele – business, leisure, spa lovers – without them having to run into one another.

An interior swimming pool, prolonged by a series of sand-based lagoons covering some 1716 square metres, along with 8000 square metres of landscaped terrace, create a unique hotel environment that also features a casino. Many of the hotel's rooms are extended with a terrace, and more than 75 percent of the rooms take advantage of an ocean view.

This Mediterranean-style hotel is without doubt the only one to have been built in Monaco in decades that offers the original character of the Monte-Carlo Palaces, those grand buildings that gave rise to the mythical imagery of the Principality of Monaco.

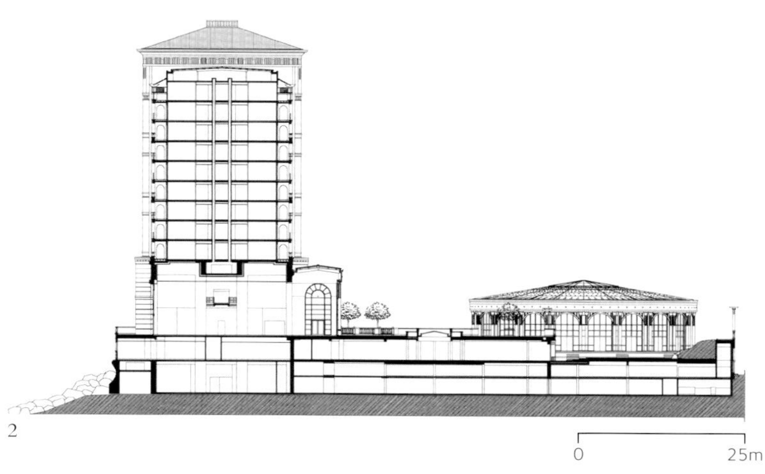

2

0   25m

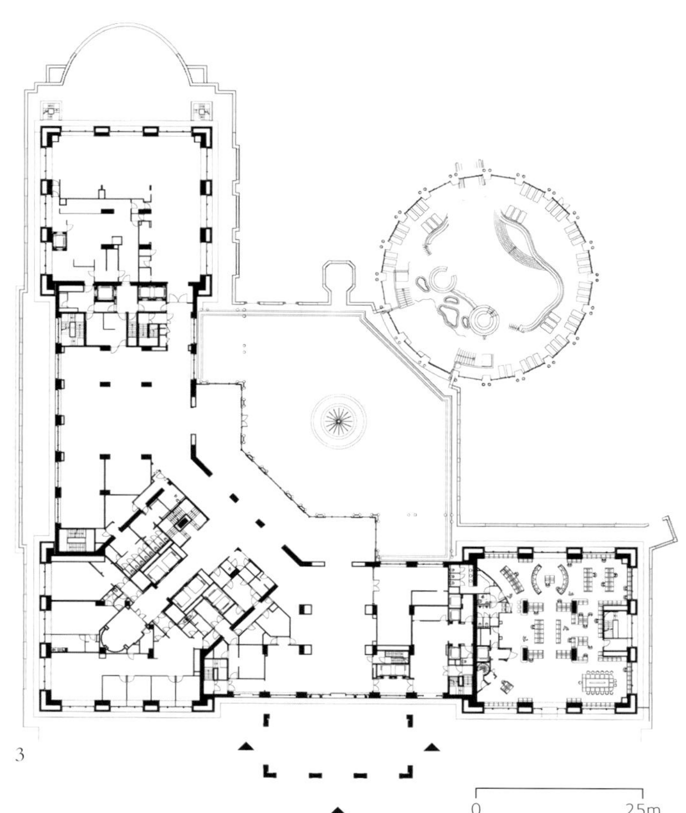

3

0   25m

1   Aerial view
2   Section
3   Ground floor plan

4

5

6

7

8

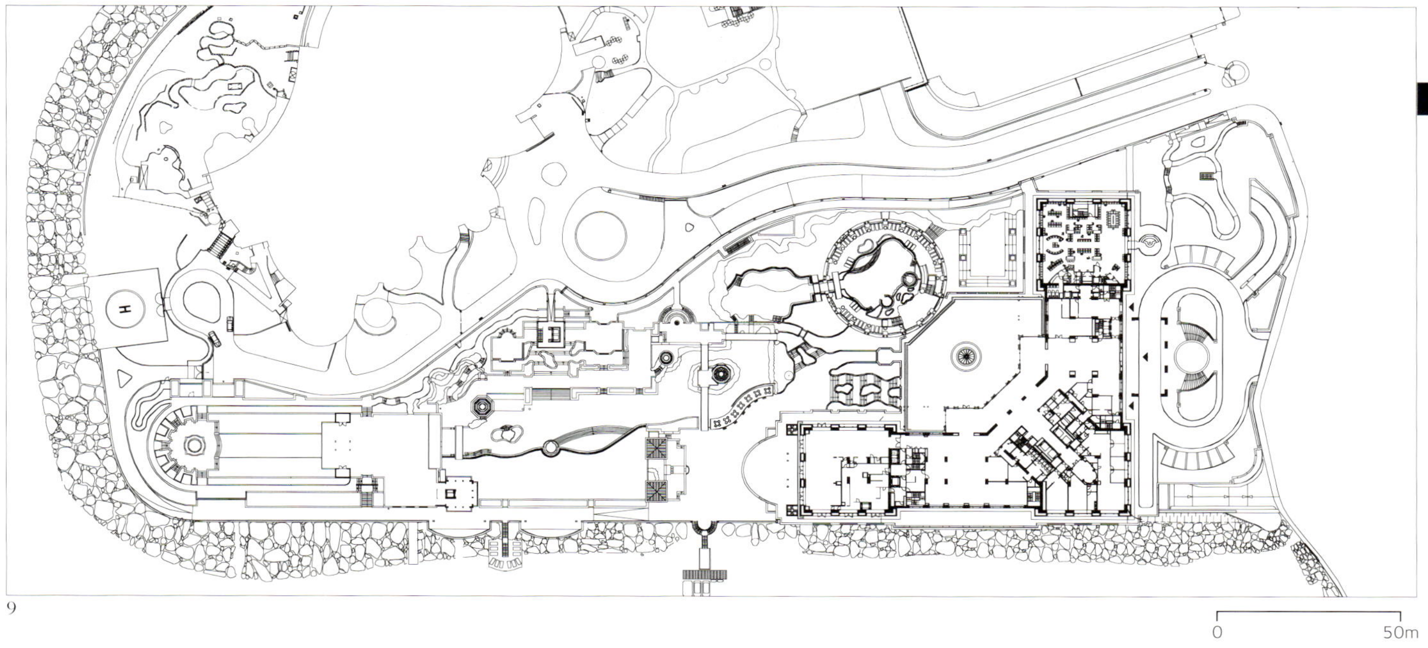

9

5   *Façade detail*
6   *Garden*
7   *View to the lagoon*
8   *Entrance detail*

9   *Master plan*
10   *Main façade, night view*
Following pages:
    View across swimming pool

10

Hotels and Resorts
Klassis Resort Hotel
Silivri (Istanbul), Turkey

Client: Klassis Turizm
Gross building area: 40,000 square metres
Completion: 1989
Award: Competition-winning project

Opposite   Health club
*   2   Villas*
*   3   Master plan*
Following pages:
*   General view*

The Klassis architecture, inspired by the Anatolian civilisations, is a harmonious synthesis of Greek, Roman, Seljuk and Ottoman styles. The 308-room resort hotel opens up onto the Sea of Marmara and is organised around a valley-like arrangement. The openness allows easy and pleasant access and a visual opening onto the sea. In order to be even more in keeping with the area, excavated earth has been used for the production of bricks, allowing the resort to feature a village-like appearance.

The resort's unique indoor and outdoor pools are filled with seawater, and the glass-covered indoor pool has a tropical garden atmosphere. In addition to a casino and an array of sports and recreational services available on site, the hotel also provides seven different halls with a capacity of 1500 people for all types of conventions and events.

The diversity of architectural elements such as loggias, balconies, pergolas and the overhanging roofs are in sharp contrast with hotels built according to the international style, as was most often the case in the area prior to the completion of this resort hotel.

2

3

1 Entrance pavilion			
2 Villas	8 Lobby		
3 Tennis courts	9 Administration	14 Restaurant terrace	
4 Service entrance	10 Service courts	15 Swimming pool	18 Amphitheatre
5 Conference centre	11 East wing guestrooms	terrace	19 Gardens
6 Hotel entrance	12 West wing guestrooms	16 Swimming pool bar	20 Marmara Sea
7 Casino	13 Lobby terrace	17 Villas	21 Samong Harbour

5

5 *Lobby lounge*
6 *Lobby foyer*
7 *Swimming pool*
8 *Detail*
9 *Patio*

6

7

8

9

Radisson SAS Royal Hotel
Brussels, Belgium

Client: SAS International Hotels
Above ground area: 23,500 square metres
Completion: 1990

The 281-room Radisson SAS Royal Hotel is one of the early projects designed by VIZZION Architects. The success of the project demonstrated the architect's ability to design monumental buildings in keeping with the character of the City of Brussels and its architectural history. In addition to the architecture inspired by the eclectic and Art Deco architecture of the Brussels boulevards with their abundance of rich details, the design approach was to create an architecture which blends in with surrounding structures, such as the 1950s-completed major financial headquarters building located across the street.

Façade elements such as bow windows reveal the residential character of the hotel nestled in an area surrounded by administrative buildings. A solid two-level base made of blue stone, a material often used in Brussels, is followed by three levels, then a storey emphasized by banding, then a strong cornice punctuated with consoles, and finally two setback attic storeys. Being located at the corner of the city block, the curved building corner itself is treated as a major event with its crowning glass cupola, while the main façade of the hotel helps re-establish a sense of urban unity on a location previously used for a parking lot.

This was the first building in Brussels to feature atrium architecture with glass-enclosed elevators on a grand scale. Of special interest are the remains of medieval ramparts that have been preserved and integrated into the overall interior design, connecting the restaurant and coffee shop in the atrium lobby, which comes equipped with pools, cascades, rocks, plantings and meandering pathways. The glassed roof brings light into the atrium and the rooms facing the lively inner volume.

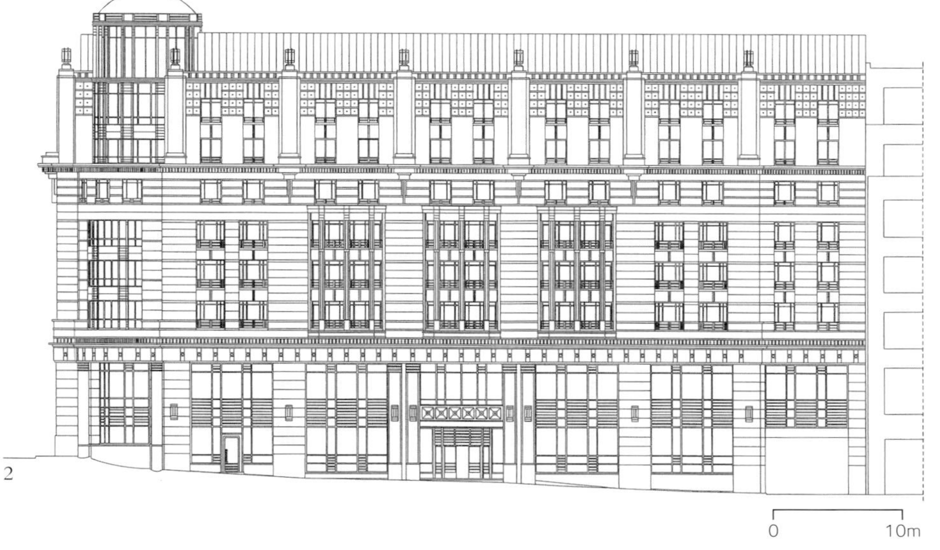

2

Opposite   Main corner elevation
2   Elevation

3

4

5

3   Atrium, glass roof
4   General view, night view
5   Façade detail

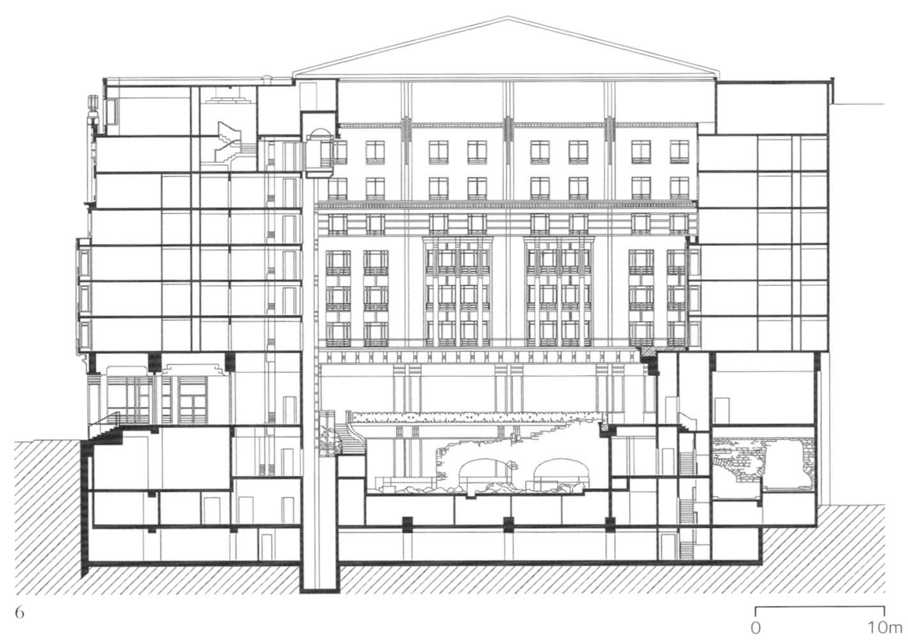

6

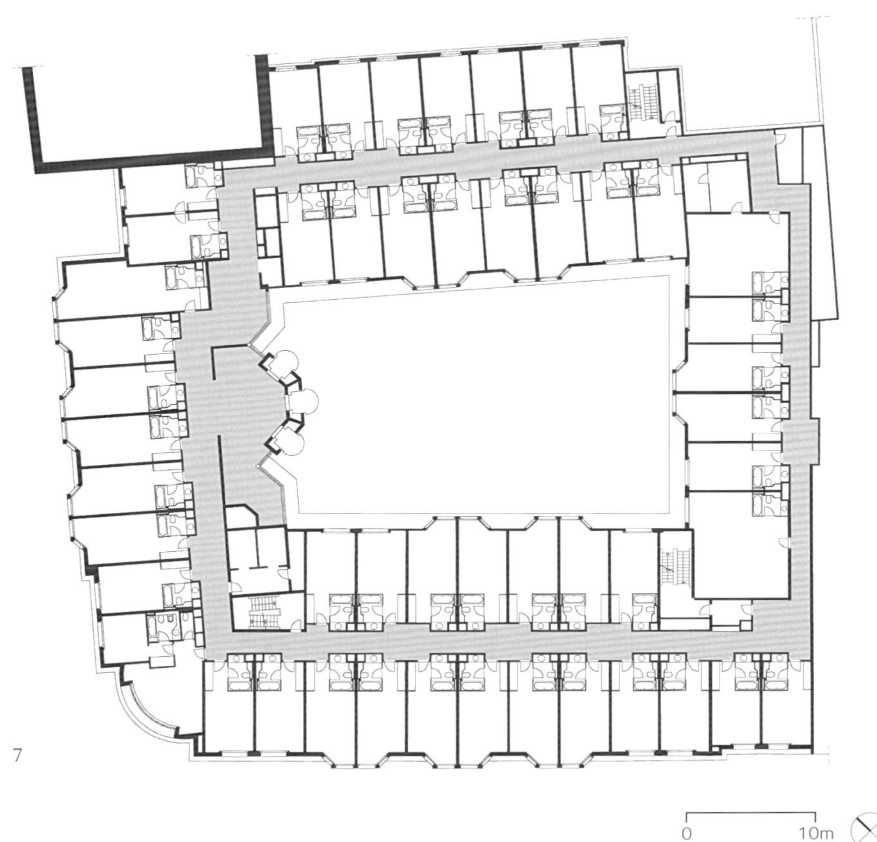

7

Novotel Brussels Centre Tour Noire
Brussels, Belgium

Client: Accor Hotels Belgium
Above ground area: 13,883 square metres
Completion: 1999

At the time of completion, Novotel Brussels Centre Tour Noire was the only new major hotel built in the central boulevards of Brussels for some years. The client for this project was not a developer, as it is often the case, but a leading French hotelier and owner of the Novotel chain, Accor.

The property occupies a full block in the historical centre of Brussels. Despite its historical location, the hotel is surrounded by very large, tall blocks typical of 1950s and 60s architecture, designed without any consideration for the culture and the history of the location. The design of the project aimed to recreate a sense of refinement in this important part of the city.

The hotel property is now a major link between the traditional market square-type Place Sainte-Catherine and the Haussmann-style Boulevard Anspach. The façades of the triangular-shaped hotel, with its cut corners, present a series of details usually only found in deluxe properties. The strength of the design principles that govern all of the architect's projects allowed the design of refined classical details with low-cost materials such as brick and concrete; mouldings and band mouldings, elements that jut out and set backs are just a few of the tools that create a façade with depth, and the lines and decor are linear or geometrical.

The brown brick-clad hotel façade became a jewel box for the Tour Noire, a historical Brussels landmark that remains on site. The Tour Noire was part of one of the original 12th-century Brussels City Walls, and the 17.9-metre-high monument has been a listed landmark since 1937. The 217-room hotel comprises all modern hospitality amenities such as conference and fitness centres and, of course, a restaurant, bar and brasserie.

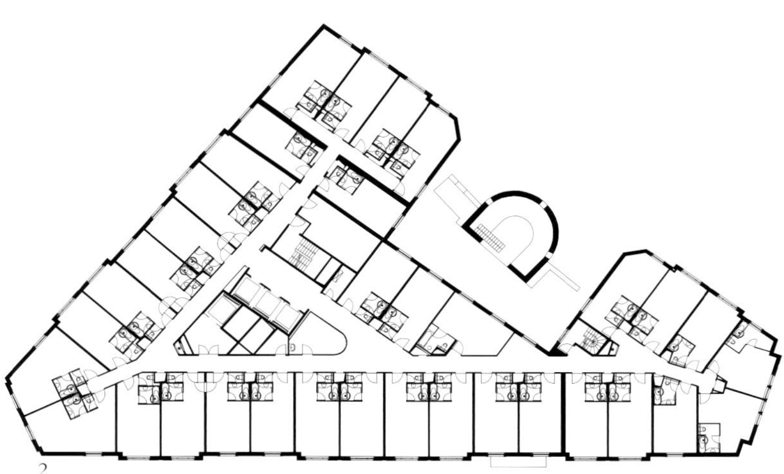

2

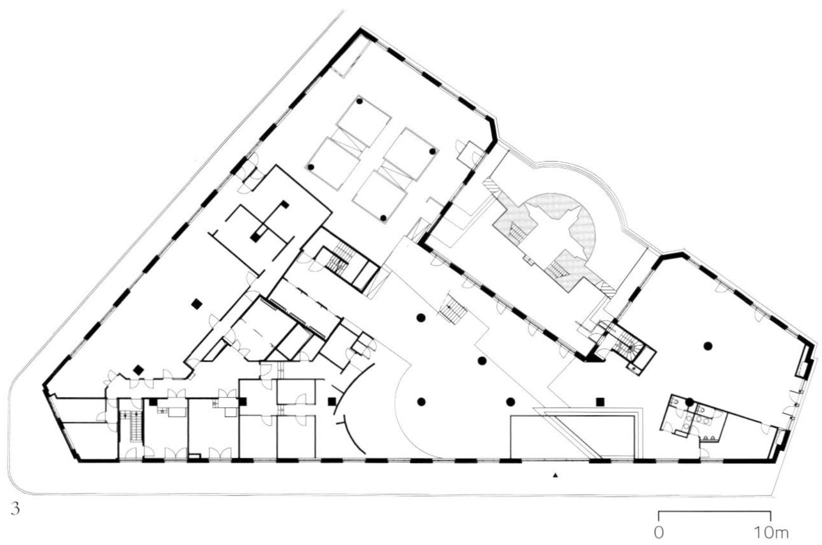

3

0   10m

Opposite   Corner elevation
   2   Typical plan
   3   Ground floor plan

4 *Elevation*
5 *The hotel and the 'Tour Noire'*
Opposite *Façade detail*

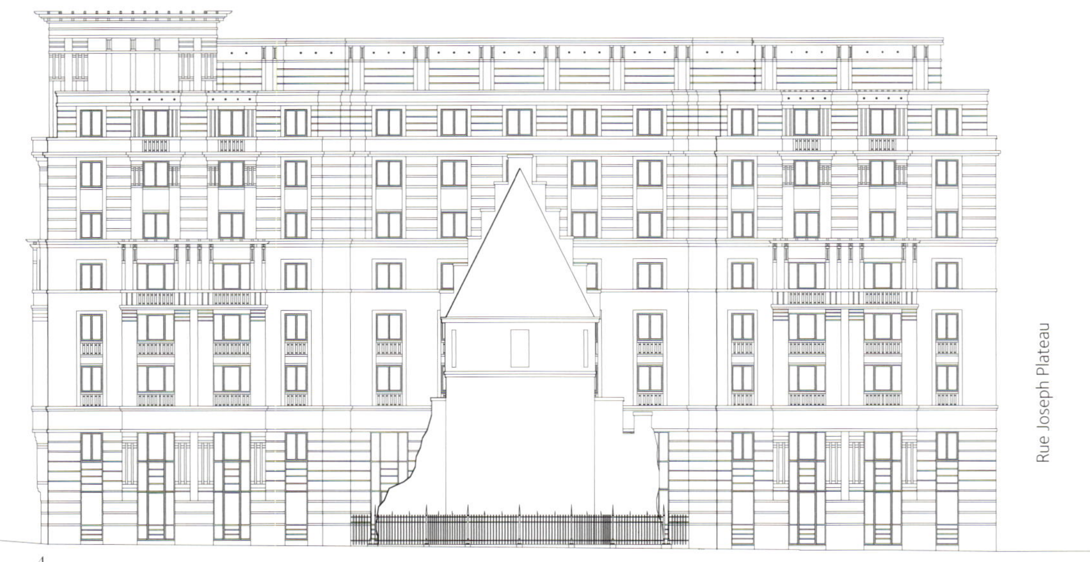

4

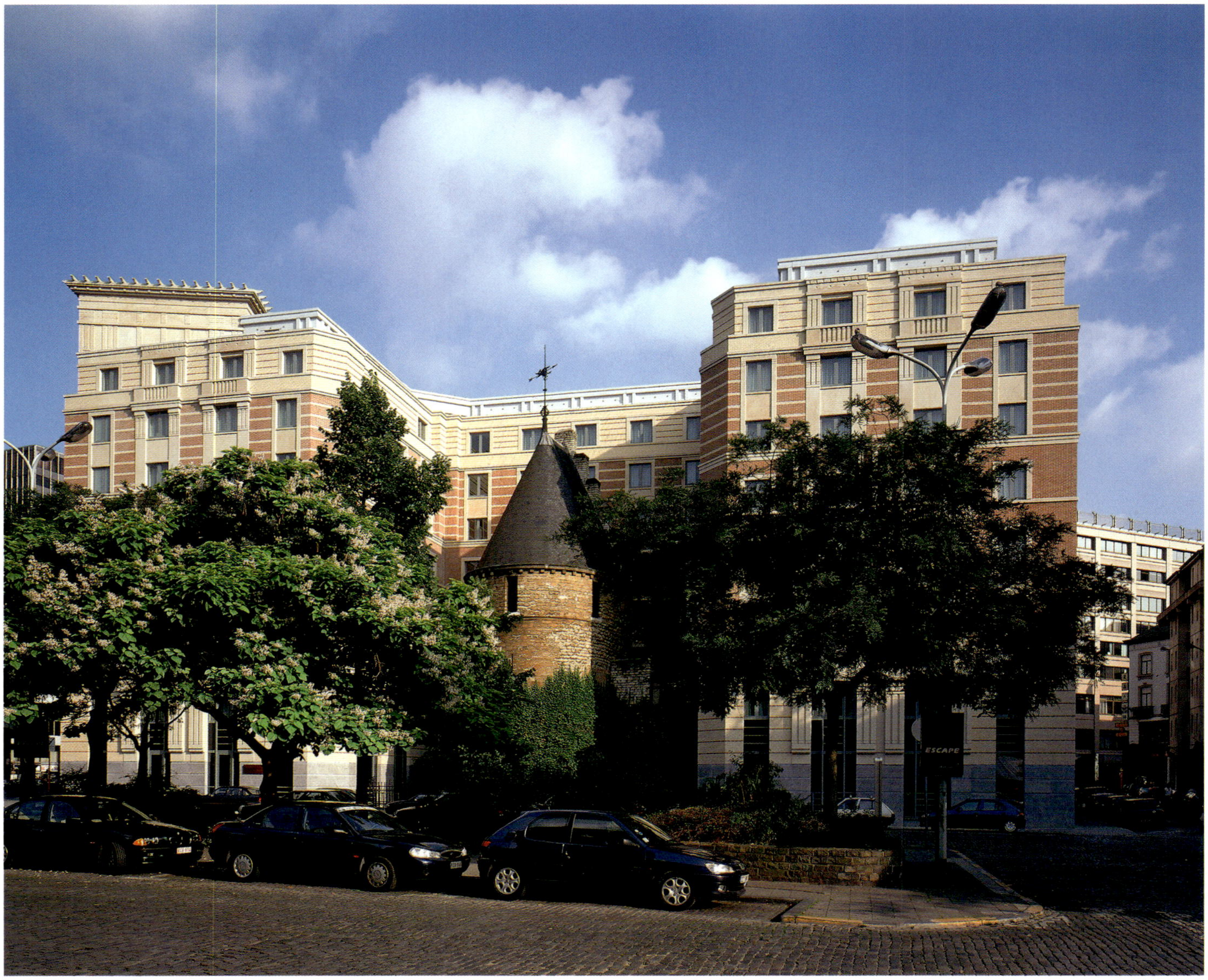

5

1

2

Kempinski Hotel Dukes' Palace
Bruges, Belgium

Client: P&V
Above ground area: 10,027 square metres
Completion: 2008

1 General view seen from the garden, digital rendering
2 Aerial view, photomontage
3 Renovated existing castle accommodating the most luxurious rooms

The distinctive Kempinski Hotel Dukes' Palace comprises a former convent and an historical castle, located in the heart of Bruges's medieval centre, which is recognised by UNESCO as a World Heritage Site. Bruges is often called the Venice of the North, well known for its exquisite water canals. The hotel is situated in the most picturesque part of the city, near the marketplace with its famous clock tower, the Belfort, and is close to all major attractions. The gable and stone architecture of the hotel is inspired by the area's old town vernacular.

The project is composed of two main units: the castle and the new adjoining wing. The castle has been preserved, renovated and brought back to its former glory following thorough historical studies, which included the participation of the Sites and Landmarks Commission. In several cases, two rooms have been transformed into magnificent suites in order to keep the original framework and interior details visible. The newly built wing, contemporary in style, respects the hierarchy of volumes and the architecture of the existing urban fabric. The façades of the new wing are composed of stone and wood, accentuated with wooden window frames.

The hotel has 80 rooms and 15 suites, one specialty restaurant for fine dining, a bar, two lounges and an undergound garage for aproximately 130 cars. There is also a ballroom and several meeting rooms with state-of-the-art equipment for conferences, meetings and special events. In addition, the hotel features a fitness and wellness centre for relaxation and rejuvenation, as well as an historical wedding chapel and its own park. The hotel is surrounded by a vast, landscaped garden providing an unexpected, expansive atmosphere in the centre of a town otherwise densely built on tiny land parcels.

3

Dream Castle Hotel at Disneyland Resort Paris
Marne-la-Vallée, France

Client: PORR Group
Above ground area: 24,668 square metres
Completion: 2004

The Dream Castle Hotel is a part of the hotels and resorts expansion program linked to the development of Disneyland Resort Paris. The 400-room resort, although designed as a mid-range hotel, provides comfort and luxury through the use of rich architectural details, spacious public spaces and vast gardens. The hotel is located in Magny le Hongre in Marne-la-Vallée. The above ground surface area is 24,668 square metres and the resort is located in a landscaped park of more than 46,000 square metres.

The architecture of the hotel explicitly refers to the Manors of the region; the design of the façades respects the hierarchy of classic architecture, while the choice of colours and materials is inspired by the historical residences of the Ile de France area. The hotel façades are richly detailed and avoid the monotony of the rigid grid often found in large-scale projects.

Dream Castle Hotel invites you to live an unforgettable experience in a typically French-style castle with charm, character and mature French gardens. All around, references to European cultural heritage are present, including architecture, literature and legends. A wide range of views overlooking the lake, garden or countryside can be enjoyed, and the spacious rooms are air-conditioned and equipped with anti-allergy bedding. The peaceful surroundings make the Dream Castle Hotel the ideal place for a family holiday or a business trip or function.

Opposite Façade looking towards the garden, detail
2 Landscaped terrace overlooking the garden
3 Landscaped terrace

Located immediately adjacent the Disneyland Resort Paris, local urban guidelines required that at this location the architecture of the project becomes an integral part of the land and site situation in such a way that it preserves the natural elements of the surrounding countryside. The location of the hotel facing the water retention reservoir is the result of careful analysis from the local authorities; everything built on this site is built on piles, so as to have the minimal impact of the natural environment.

4   Main entrance, night view
5   Typical floor plan
6   Garden elevation
Following pages:
    View from the garden

4

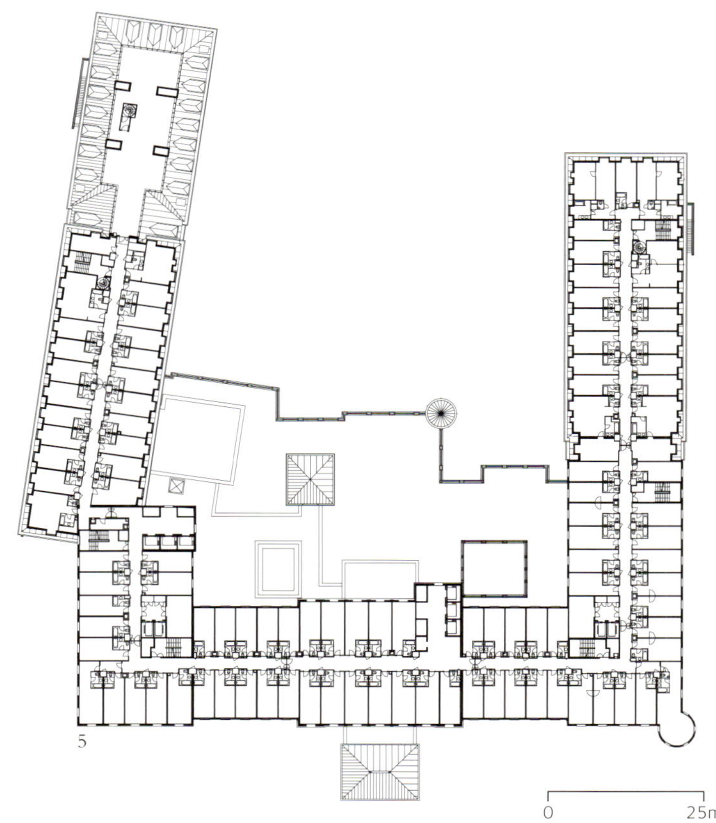

5

0   25m

The Fairmont Cairo at Nile City
Cairo, Egypt

Client: Nile City Investments
Above ground area: 52,757 square metres
Completion: 2008

The Fairmont Cairo at Nile City is located on a prime site overlooking the Nile River, 30 minutes from the Pyramids of Gizeh. The hotel forms the third and final tower of Cairo's most prestigious office and retail development in the Nile City complex. The luxury 26-storey, 552-room hotel comprises 704 bays for a total built-up area of 52,757 square metres. The twin 143-metre office towers and the 100-metre, V-shaped Fairmont Cairo hotel stand in the heart of the Egyptian capital, opposite the island of Zamalek.

The base is common to all three towers and houses the separate entrances to the offices, the shopping galleries and the hotel. The hotel features vertical divisions and large glazed panels, which, along with the hotel's positioning, has been designed with a distinctive shape allowing guests to have sweeping views of the Nile.

The first floor features an impressive double-height main lobby accessible by two vehicle ramps and staircases. The second floor accommodates a business centre, meeting rooms of different sizes, a 480-person ballroom and hotel administration offices, while the third floor accommodates an array of restaurants, private dining areas, lounges and two outdoor terraces. Some of the more dramatic hotel features include the outdoor, rooftop swimming pool equipped with a fitness centre and a large leisure area with dining facilities. The rooftop offers splendid views of the serene banks of the Nile, the sophisticated island of Zamalek and the Pyramids of Gizeh.

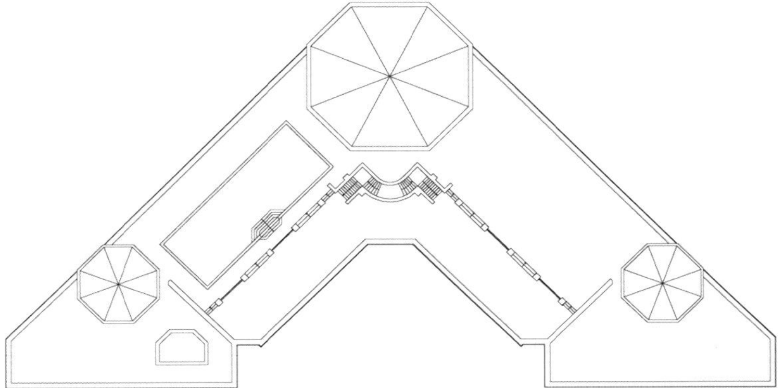

2

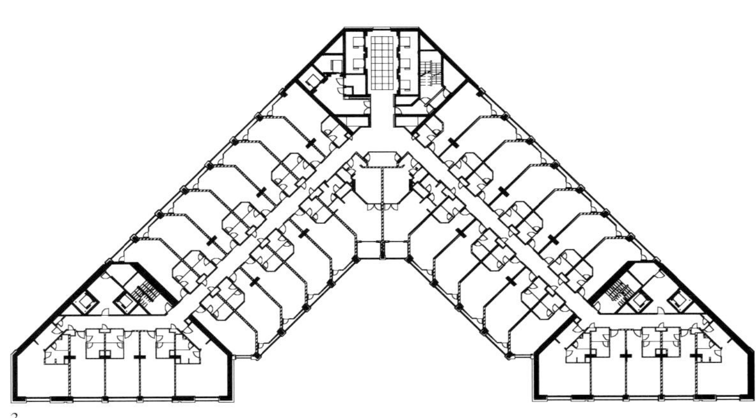

3

Opposite   General view
2   Roof plan
3   Typical floor plan

4

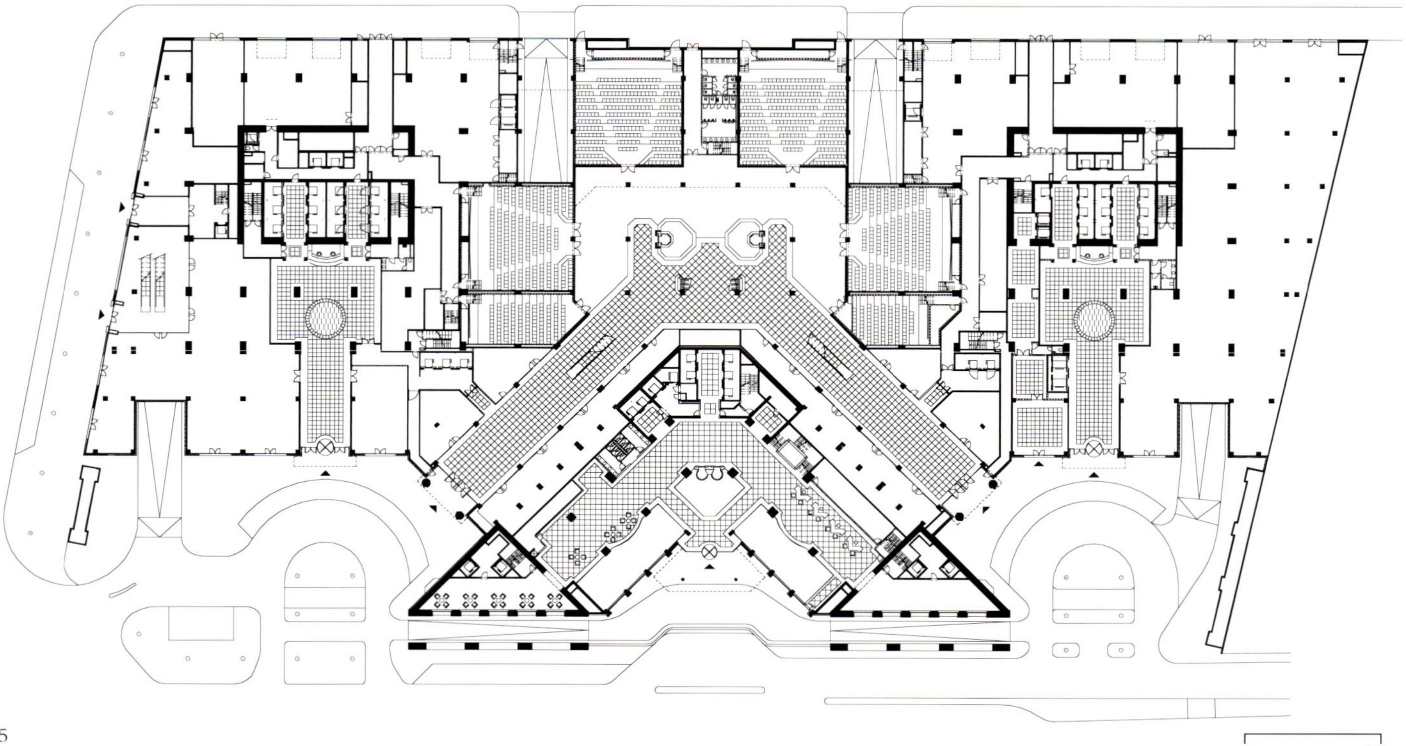

5

0   20m

6

7

1 *Aerial view showing the hotel glass-enclosed atrium, rendering*

Le Parc
Villars-sur-Ollon, Switzerland

Client: VIZZION Europe
Above ground area: 43,263 square metres
Completion: 2012

Nested in a wooded park in the heart of Villars-sur-Ollon, a renowned winter location, Le Parc covers a 9-hectare site. Integration into the surrounding environment is one of the project's main objectives.

The resort comprises a luxurious 96-room hotel equipped with a conference centre, a wellness centre and several high-end apartment buildings as well as single-family chalets; the resort also benefits from south-facing views over the *Dents du Midi*.

The Grand Hôtel du Parc is the centrepiece architectural landmark around which the project will evolve. The 1932 main building is being renovated and transformed into a state-of-the-art congress centre and hotel, which will include a wellness centre equipped with outdoor lagoon and indoor swimming pool. The hotel also comprises three restaurants. One face of the hotel will feature the renovated listed façade of the original hotel, while the side facing the mountain will feature a large, undulating, glass-enclosed atrium. It will become the hotel focal point and the three glass-enclosed panoramic elevators will add visually animated drama.

Arranged around the hotel are 92 serviced apartments; the four apartment buildings each comprise 16 units, while the 32 four- to five-room chalets are designed according to five different typologies. Mindful of integration, the architecture of each building will enhance the Villars' style, inspired by local architecture and featuring natural materials such as stone and wood. The project is faithful to VIZZION Architects' High Environmental Value attitude. The selected materials respect the rules and processes that guarantee the sustainability of the building, quality of the environment and in a further stage prove to be highly recyclable when submitted to renovations, while various technical solutions are designed to control the consumption of energy resources and to promote the use of renewable energy.

The global concept developed throughout the whole site is based on the notion of 'well-being', which materialises through the outstanding setting, carefully chosen fittings and exceptional services, all contributing to create a genuine art of living.

3

2 *General view*
3 *Master plan, photomontage*
4 *The Residences, general view*

2

Headquarters and administrative centres: renovations

Headquarters and administrative centres: renovations
Loi 62
Brussels, Belgium

Client: Fortis / Compagnie Immobilière de Belgique
Above ground area: 6755 square metres
Completion: 1997

The eight-storey project was originally built in 1965 and is typical of the modern office buildings that were popular in that period in Brussels. From the original building, only the concrete structure remains.

This rather small building is located in the major thoroughfare of the central business district and faces a huge, recently built building. The non-loadbearing façades have been demolished to allow for construction of new ones that are characterised by new prefabricated red curved brick facings applied to the concrete columns.

The two new corner façades are therefore meant to give character and more visual prominence to the speculative Loi 62 project. The design gives some rhythm to a rather monotonous boulevard in the European district, with the red columns providing sharp contrast to the horizontal white stone bands.

Raised floors and air-conditioning have been implemented and the structure was slightly modified in order to provide a double-height entrance porch. As in all other projects designed by the firm, interior finishes are refined using a selection of marbles and woods in the main lobby as well as in the elliptical-shaped elevator lobby area.

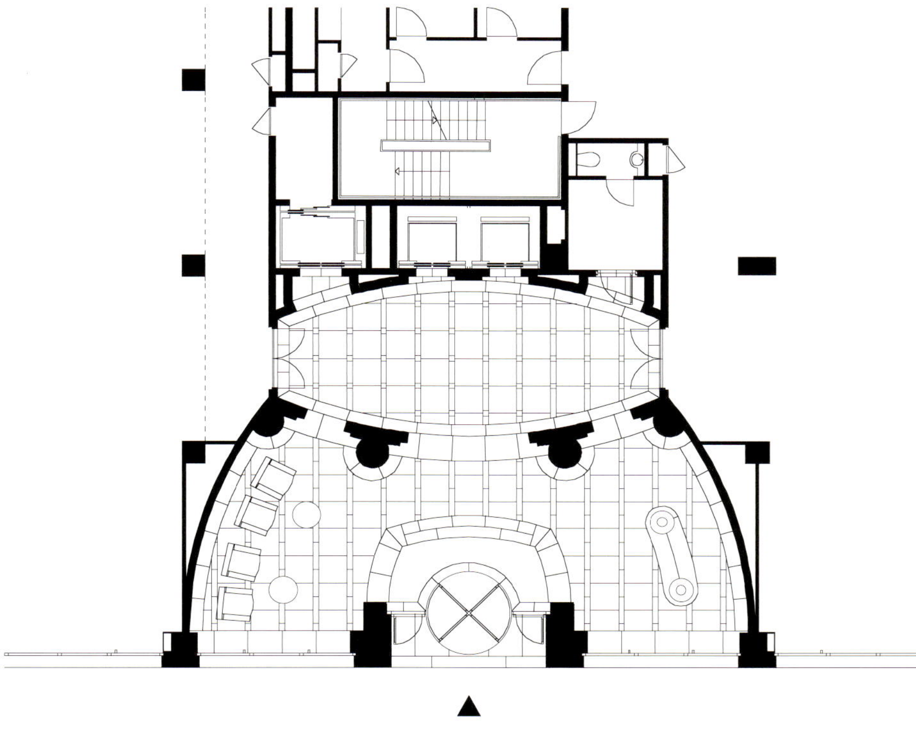

2

3

Opposite   General view
2   Lobby plan
3   Elevator foyer in the lobby

The European Union at Eudip Three
Brussels, Belgium

Client: Banimmo
Above ground area: 16,220 square metres
Completion: 2001

Opposite   Eudip Three, main atrium lobby
2   Eudip Three, ground floor plan
3   Eudip Three, section

Eudip Three leads the way in terms of urban regeneration in the European district of Brussels. The Brussels central business district, built between the early 1960s and the mid-1970s, was originally a series of relatively small office buildings averaging 6000 to 7000 square metres. The requirements of the European Union, one of the major anchor occupiers in the area, currently occupy buildings comprising more than 25,000 square metres.

Providing 16,220 square metres of office, Eudip Three is the major component of a larger urban administrative ensemble designed by the architect; the ensemble consists of several different renovated buildings and provides state-of-the-art contemporary administrative quarters. These different building units were renovated in different phases due to the fact that they were previously owned by different companies. Renovated by different developers and completed between 2003 and 2006, they include Park Avenue, the Pavilion and City Garden, the only newly built building of this vast urban ensemble.

The heart of Eudip Three features man-scaled atria allowing easy and friendly communication between the project's different wings. The project also encompasses a French-style garden. The rhythm of the stone-clad façades, the cornices, the bands and the mouldings are reminiscent of the typical classical buildings located in the city's central boulevards.

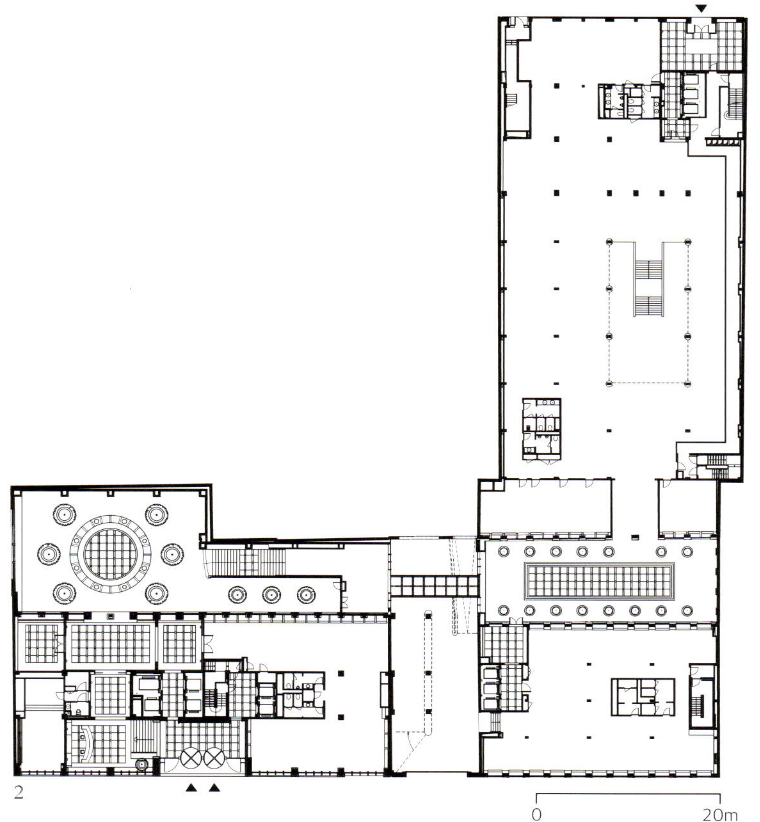

2

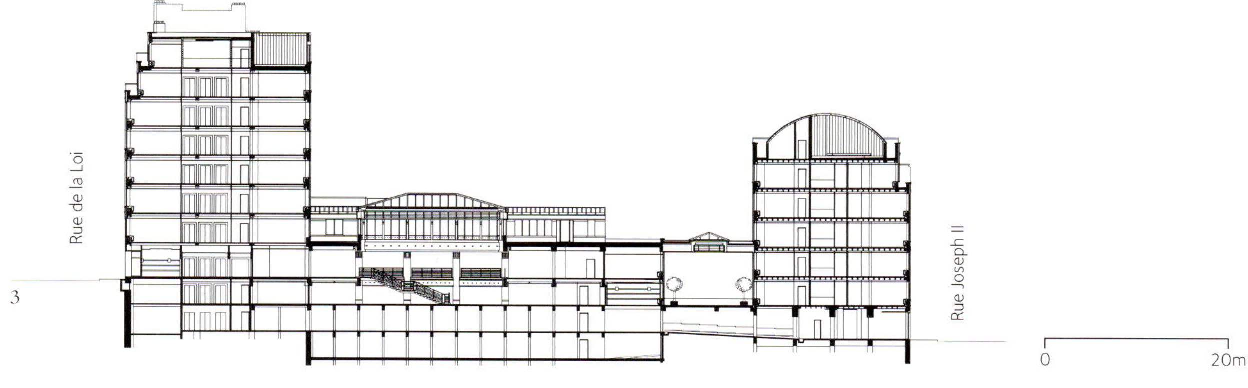

3

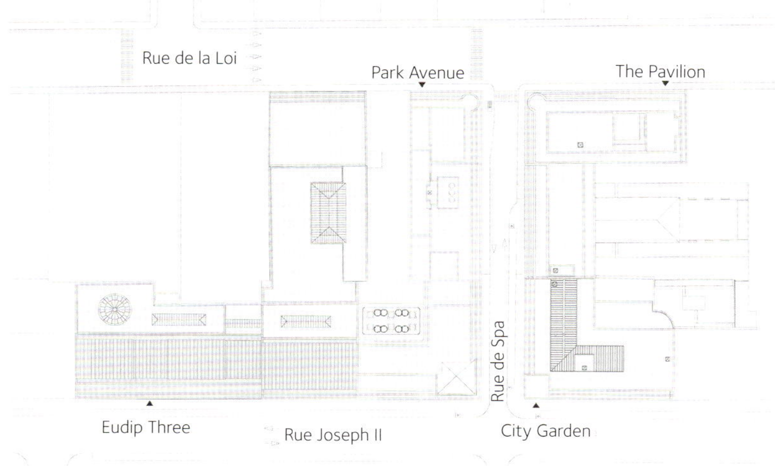

4   *Eudip Three, main entrance*
5   *Eudip Three, Atrium 1*
6   *Eudip Three, Atrium 2*
7   *Eudip Three, glass-enclosed skyway*
8   *Eudip Three, Joseph II Street*
9   *General master plan*

10, 11, 12   The Pavilion and Park Avenue, details
13   City Garden, night view

1

2

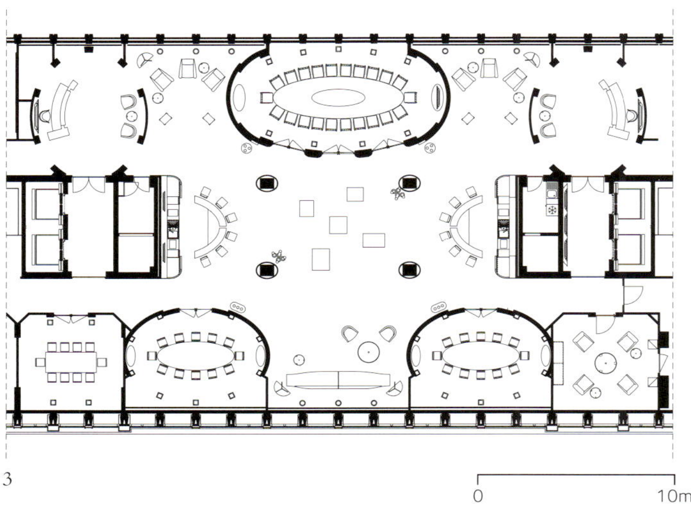

3

0   10m

4

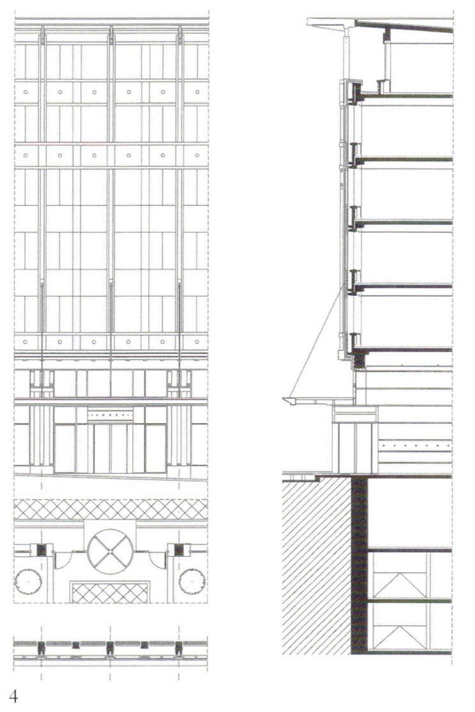

5

Headquarters and administrative centres: renovations
Lloyd George 7
Brussels, Belgium

Client: Zurich Assurances
Above ground area: 13,319 square metres
Completion: 1997

Facing the main city park in uptown Brussels and originally completed in 1975, the building is made of prefabricated concrete elements. By the mid–1990s, Zurich Assurances asked the architect to create a brand new corporate identity for their new headquarters that would not involve major structural changes to the existing building. In response to this request, the architect designed a new glass, metal and stone skin to be applied to the existing load-bearing façade.

This renovation radically transformed the once boring, very long concrete façade, and the main entrance is now clearly advertised by the shining metal and glass section in between the two stone and glass sections on each side of the entrance.

In terms of office units, some of the original 1.8-metre modules were modified to obtain a new 2.7-metre modulation in order to comply with the needs of the client and the current office market. Today, the building is also home to the VIZZION Group's headquarters, which are housed on several levels.

1   *General elevation*
2   *Main entrance*
3   *VIZZION Europe meeting rooms plan*
4   *Façade, plan and section*
5   *Main entrance at night*

Headquarters and administrative centres: renovations
Dexia Bank at Galilée Building
Brussels, Belgium

Client: Dexia Bank
Above ground area: 34,100 square metres
Completion: 2001
Award: Competition-winning project

The Galilée Building, originally completed in 1971, has now become one of the three main administrative buildings of the Belgo-French Dexia Bank in Brussels. It is one of the most ambitious renovations ever completed in the city involving the removal of asbestos. The design of the renovated ensemble takes into account the architecture of an adjacent, well-known, 1957 office building, and since the architect aims at rebuilding city centres in a more human way, the goal was to produce a project with new façades that are reminiscent of nearby buildings but are in no way derivative.

At the base, stone, pergolas, terraces and a unique lighting system give the Dexia Bank building both a sense of urbanity and newfound nighttime visibility. The partly recessed podium features a grand, newly built, double-height, glass-enclosed lobby that transforms a former low-profile, speculative building into a major bank building.

The building's everyday use has been entirely rethought in terms of energy and circulation. For instance, each elevator takes passengers to selected floors only after maximizing the calls sent before entering the cabs. The large floor plates accommodate a mix of open-floor and partition plans and provide in their centre an area used for meeting, socialising and resting.

The renovation work has created one of the most energy efficient buildings in the city through the use of an active double-skin façade. The building's active façade is coupled with a radiant air-conditioning system and provides an optimal visibility towards the outside, an internal comfort without draughts or unwanted noise, a negligible maintenance of the radiant ceilings and, above all, a very low overall cost. The curtain wall is made from an innovative double skin approximately 15 cm wide that contains motorised, perforated, horizontal blinds.

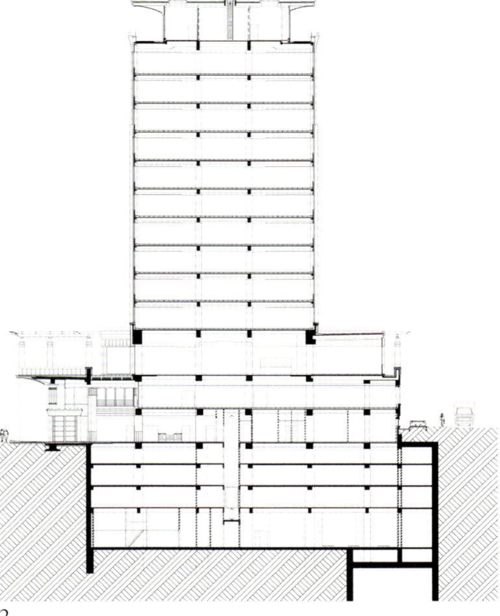

2

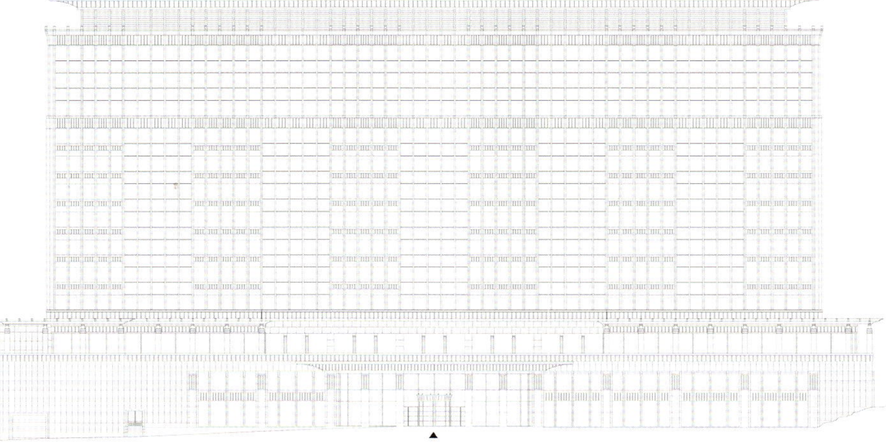

3

Fresh air enters the offices through grilles next to the lights in the ceilings. After being drawn across the offices, the air is then extracted through the double-skin façade, creating a thermal barrier to the exterior and interior glass surface at ambient room temperature and eliminating the need for radiators or air-conditioning along the façade. This in turn provides comfort for the occupants and more space for work areas.

4

5

4   Upper level detail
5   Main lobby
6   Main entrance

   Dexia Bank at Galillée Building

Headquarters and administrative centres: renovations
Dexia Management Headquarters
Brussels, Belgium

Client: Copropriété 1 Square de Meeûs/Dexia Bank
Above ground area: 5660 square metres
Completion: 2000

Although Dexia Holding has traditionally been based in the heart of Brussels, the company chose to relocate their headquarters to this newly renovated building because of its prime location in the European district and also for the building's striking aesthetic.

From the building originally erected in 1966, only the concrete structure remains. All circulation and mechanical elements have been entirely rethought and rebuilt. The project includes a new curtain-wall-type façade that is made of powder-coated aluminium, glass and cast iron elements. The regular rhythm of the columns and the sense of grandeur generated add a sense of quietness to the public green square it faces.

Two levels are entirely devoted to the office of the presidents and the boardroom. Other facilities include the welcome lounge and the dining room as well as a video-conference centre equipped with translation equipment.

Noble materials such as wood, wood flooring and 'stuccato veneziano' plaster as well as detailed lighting studied for each room confirm the attention to detail regarding both the exterior and the interior spaces.

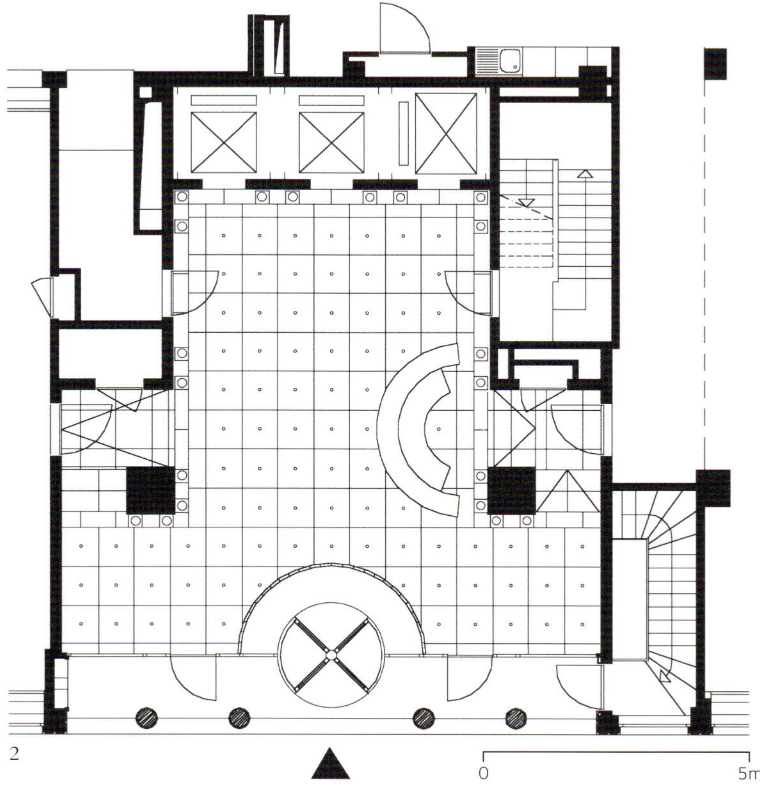

2

0   5m

Opposite   Façade detail
2 Lobby floor plan

3

3   Façade detail
4   Main lobby
5   Conference room
Opposite   General view

4

5

DEXIA
DEXIA

Headquarters and administrative centres: new constructions

Headquarters and administrative centres: new constructions
Canal Front
Brussels, Belgium

Clients: Allfin, BESIX, Immomills-Louis De Waele, Investissements & Promotion, Kredietbank (now KBC), NCC Group, SDRB

Above ground area: 151,488 square metres, office; 23,377 square metres, housing

Completion: 1994–2010

Awards: Competition-winning project (KBC Bank Headquarters); 1998 Prix Européen Philippe Rotthier de la Reconstruction de la Ville, mention; MIPIM Awards 1998, winner in the residential developments category (Le Jardin des Fonderies); MIPIM Awards 2000, winner in the business centres category (Green Island); RICS Awards 2005, finalist in the regeneration award category (Canal Front)

More than just a line of buildings with a similar architectural presentation, Canal Front represents a real waterside frontage alongside the canal in Brussels, a frontage which recalls not only the industrial architecture of the surrounding district but also the typically eclectic style found throughout Brussels. Besides the three main Canal Front office buildings – KBC Headquarters (formerly known as Kredietbank Headquarters), the Admiral Building, a competition-winning project also used by the bank, and the award-winning Green Island – other office buildings and a series of housing projects have also been newly built and a former industrial building has been transformed into the award-winning housing project Le Jardin des Fonderies (see page 140).

The Canal Front area and its glorious past have been carefully studied and an architectural style was created to blend in with the rich industrial past of an area dedicated to light industries. In the early 1990s, the period the industrial zone was living out its last years, the Kredietbank, now the KBC Bank, the largest 100 percent Belgian-owned bank, decided to build a new headquarters and centralise its employees previously working in several locations. The decision of the KBC Bank to settle in the decaying former industrial zone gave a socio-economic boost to the area when the bank building was completed in December 1994. The KBC headquarters was followed by the Green Island building, partly occupied by the KBC Bank and partly occupied by the Henkel chemical company, whose previous headquarters was located at that location. More than other Canal Front projects, the

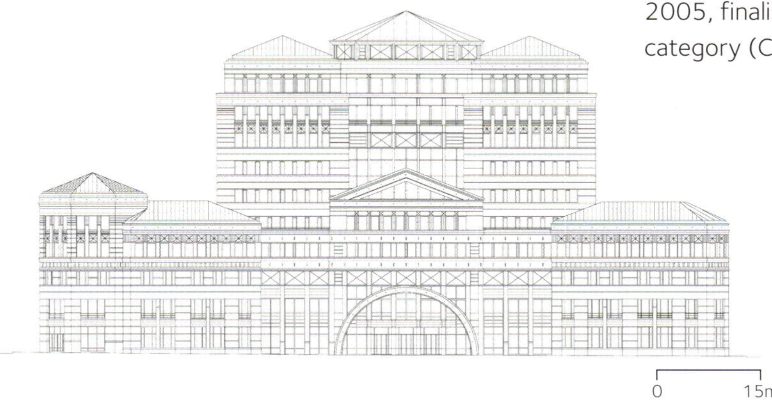

2

3

architecture of the Green Island projects is inspired by the industrial architecture of the next-door Tour & Taxis buildings. Green Island is actually designed to house both office spaces and light industries, with the entire underground section designed to allow trucks to manoeuvre inside the basement. The building also has a wing built behind listed façades. Green Island received a MIPIM Award in the business centres category in Cannes (France) in 2000. This followed another MIPIM Award, this time in the housing category in 1998, for the Jardin des Fonderies, a residential project mentioned above.

The Canal Front acted as a catalyst for the regeneration process of the whole area. Once the Canal Front project was well underway, the city decided to rebuild the banks along the canal, and the banks fronting the Canal Front buildings have been designed as public areas, which are particularly popular in summer. The fact that the area has been studied and imagined as a whole and not as the sum of individual buildings most probably led to the general renewal of the district we can now observe.

5

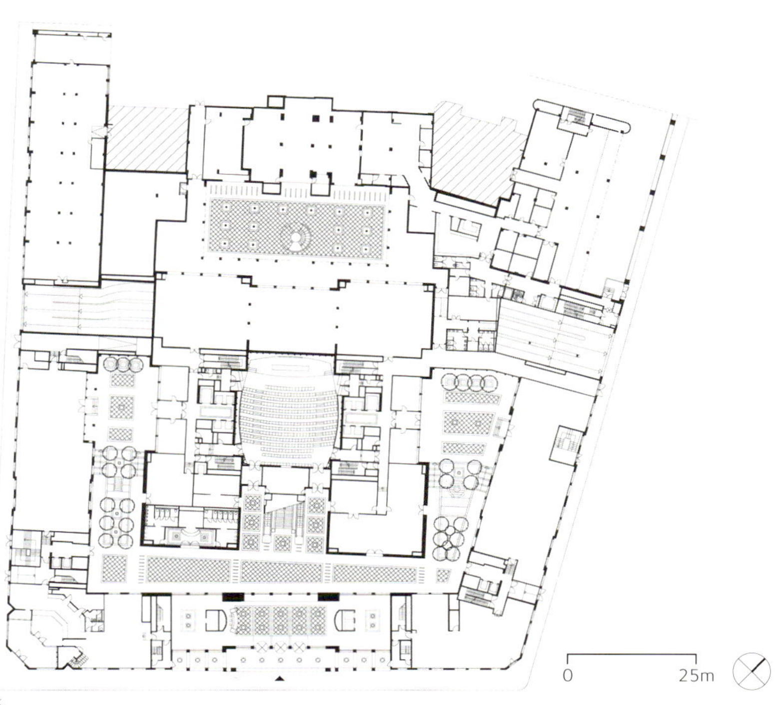

6

Previous pages:
*General view from the canal: KBC Bank
Headquarters, Admiral Building and Green Island*
5   *KBC Bank Headquarters, lobby foyer*
6   *KBC Bank Headquarters, ground floor plan*
7   *KBC Bank Headquarters, side atrium*

7

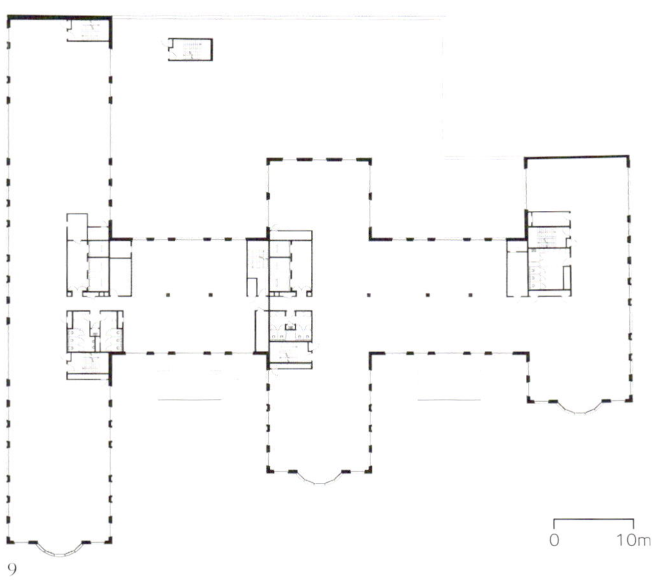

9

Opposite   Admiral Building, tower
9   Admiral Building, typical floor plan
10   Admiral Building, general view from the canal

10

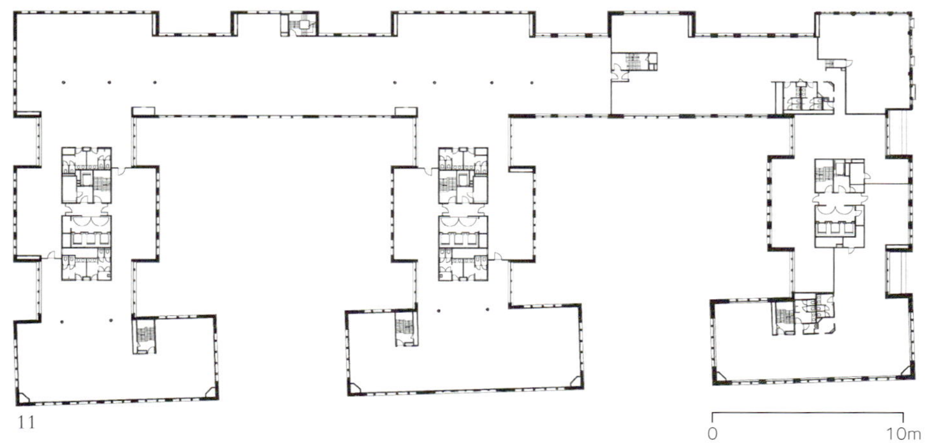

11

12

13

14 Green Island, entrance
15 Green Island, new construction and renovated building
Opposite Green Island, gable detail

14

15

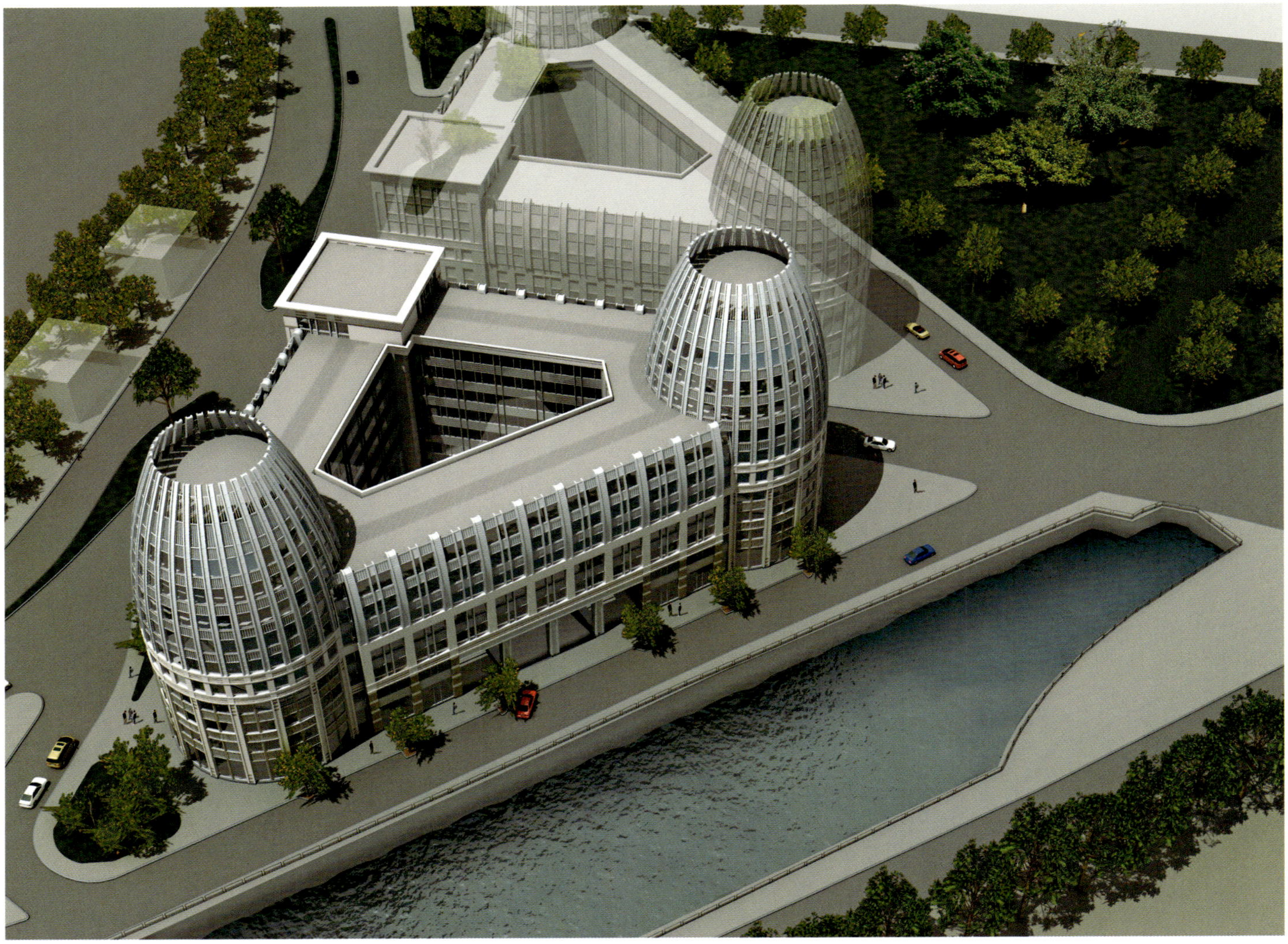

17

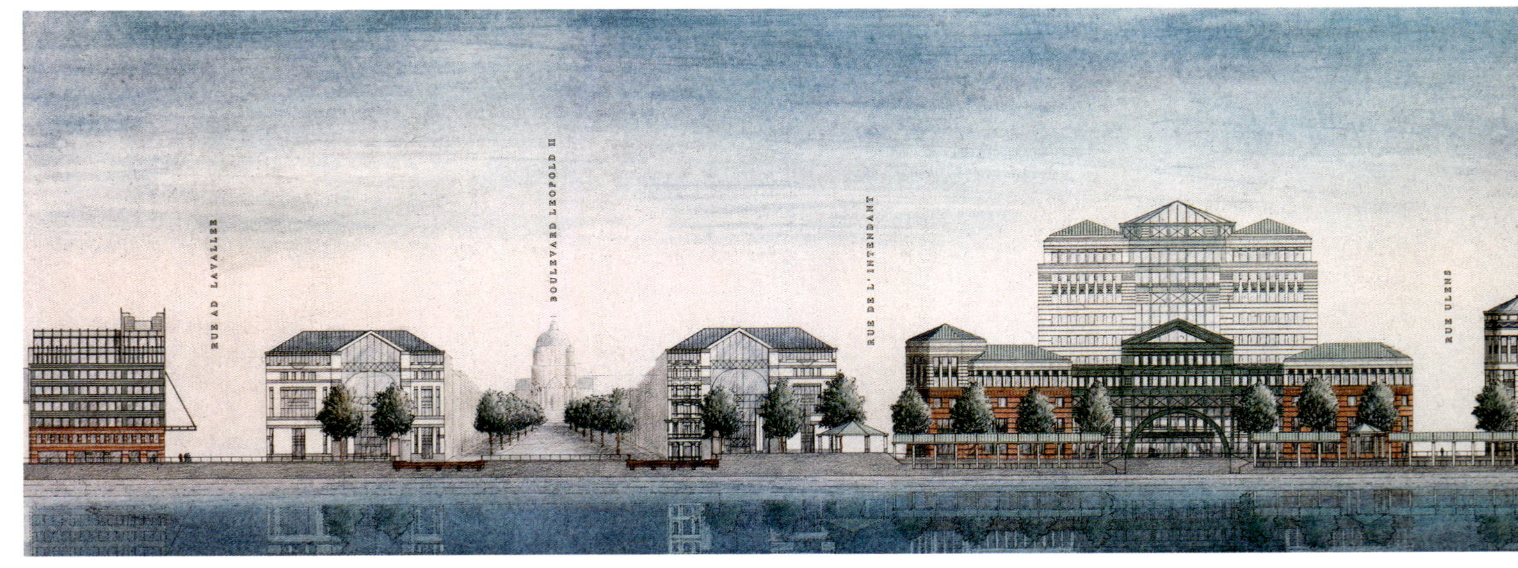

RUE AD LAVALLEE
BOULEVARD LEOPOLD II
RUE DE L'INTENDANT
RUE ULENS

18

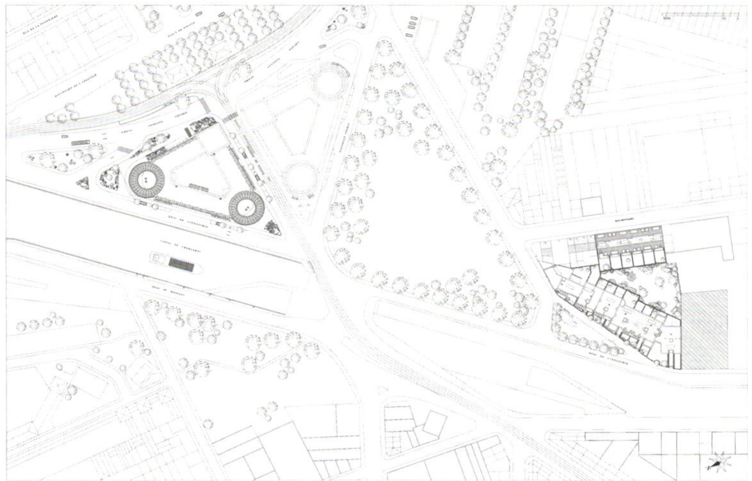

19

17 *Porte de Ninove, early axonometric study,
    digital rendering*
18 *Les Terrasses de l'Ecluse, rendering*
19 *Porte de Ninove and Les Terrasses de l'Ecluse,
    master plan*
20 *Canal Front, rendering*

20

Headquarters and administrative centres: new constructions
French Consulate
Brussels, Belgium

Client: CEPIM–SEPEC–IBF
Above ground area: 10,644 square metres
Completion: 1993

Opposite   Main entrance
2   Elevation
3   Penthouse levels, detail

Located in the heart of Brussels, near the city's early financial and administrative area erected at the beginning of the 20th century, the project is built on a difficult curved, sloping site. The developer's brief was for a building with a monumental character that would accommodate the medieval remains within the block.

The curvilinear project has a solid base that allows the building to stand proudly from any perspective along the sloping site, while the centrally located entrance is marked by a dramatic, recessed, five-level porch characterised by two majestic columns standing guard.

The project faces the huge 1960s state administrative centre, which was designed according to the International Style standards, and although rather small in stature when compared to this neighbouring building, the powerful nature of its architectural unity led the French Embassy to transform this building – originally designed as a speculative project – into the Brussels French Consulate.

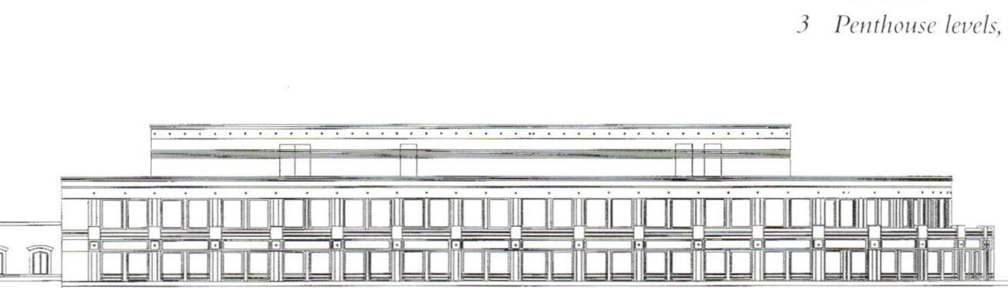

2

3

Business Center Glacis
Luxembourg, Grand Duchy of Luxembourg

Client: WACO – DIC (Deutsche Immobilien Chancen)
Above ground area: 20,320 square metres
Completion: 2004

Business Center Glacis, developed in Luxembourg by Frankfurt-based DIC (Deutsche Immobilien Chancen), houses the Crédit Agricole Investor Services Bank Luxembourg and Loyens & Loeff, the attorneys and tax lawyers. The 17,935-square-metre, 7-storey office project comes together with a 2190-square-metre housing project and 195 square metres of retail space.

The scale and the architectural expression of the office project allow a grand, unified gesture facing the Glacis Place. The design creates a landmark-type building along the Allée Scheffer; the three-unit building is designed to present different appearances, yet in a unified way. The office ensemble has three main entrances and comes equipped with a 135-car garage.

Soon after the first stone was laid out in 2002, two units were acquired by German institutional investors and the third unit by a private investor from the Grand Duchy of Luxembourg.

2

Opposite   Corner view
2   Hall entrance
3   General view seen from the place

3

1   General view from the Escaut River: Riverside Square and Residentie Alphee

1

Riverside Square
Antwerp, Belgium

Client: Exmar
Above ground area: 10,200 square metres
Completion: 1990

The Riverside Square design had to take into account both the exceptional site, located along the bank of the Escaut River in Antwerp, and tight financial constraints. The long side of the site, facing the river and situated in between two street corners, encouraged the architectural concept of breaking the project into different parts. It is therefore made up of a central section housing the entrance and is flanked by a wing on either side. The octagonal five-storey pavilion creates an original transition with the next-door building separated by an inner driveway.

A strong, two-level base topped by large bays crowned by an attic level turns Riverside Square into an imposing urban element, yet the structure is still in keeping with the existing city fabric.

Riverside Square is part of a multi-unit ensemble that includes other buildings behind it. It is worthy of note that there is no difference in the quality of treatment for the front, rear or side façades of the building.

In 1997, the completion of the Residentie Alphee, developed by Reslea, added to Riverside Square an eight-storey residential unit characterised by a brick and white stone façade topped by a metal roof. Together, the office and residential building units have created a major mixed-use ensemble along the bank of the Escaut River.

2 *R. S. Office, main elevation*
3 *R. S. Office, ground floor plan*
4 *The Residentie Alphee*
Opposite *General view from the street*

2

3

4

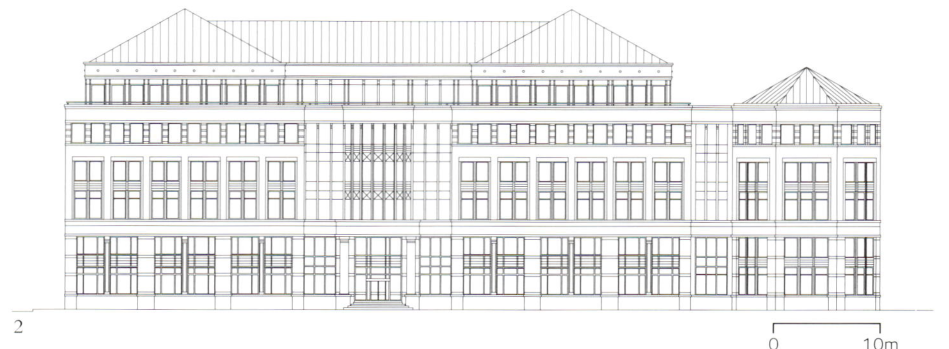

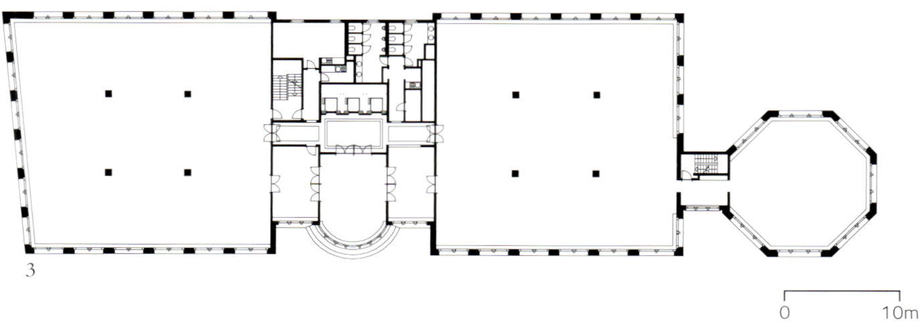

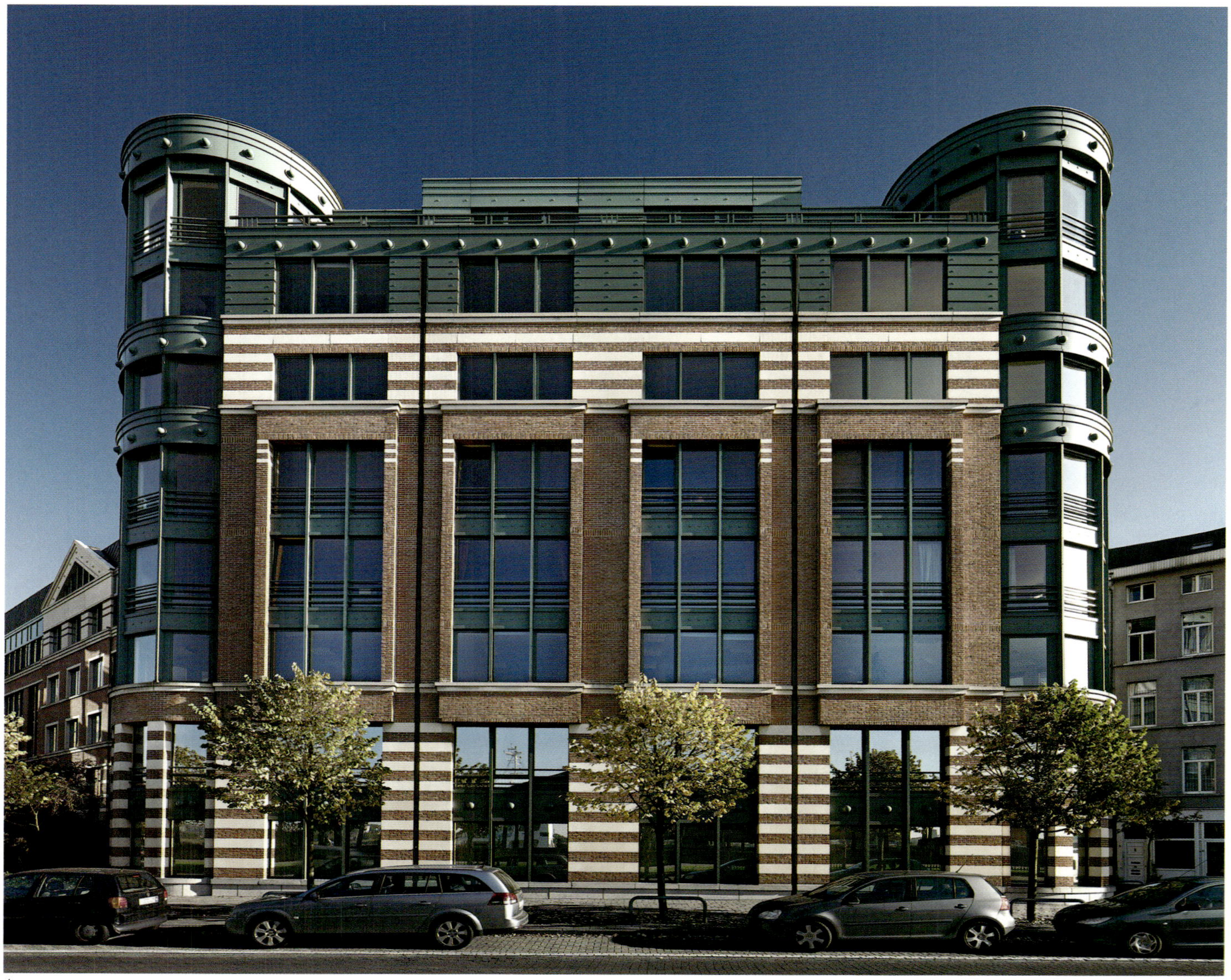

1

Headquarters and administrative centres: new constructions
Mechelen Campus
Mechelen, Belgium

Client: U-PLACE
Above ground area: 56,104 square metres
Completion: 2005

The Mechelen Campus is located between Brussels and Antwerp, along one of Belgium's busiest thoroughfares. The 11-building business park comprises 10 five-level buildings arranged around a 14-storey, 15,400-square-metre tower nestled in a landscaped site. The tower is one of Belgium's tallest buildings completed in the last three decades outside an urban zone. Automobile circulation routes are located at the periphery of the site, while two landscaped squares create a sense of urbanity within this suburban project.

One of the striking characteristics of the business park is that instead of the usual high-tech approach, the architect aimed at recreating an urban typology using bricks of two different colours in a unified way, while still affording each building its own identity. The central element of two low-rise buildings, one in the form of an octagon and the other one in the form of a cylinder, create a monumental gate entrance to the office park. All in all, touches of elegance and urbanity have been used by the architect in organising this so-called business park.

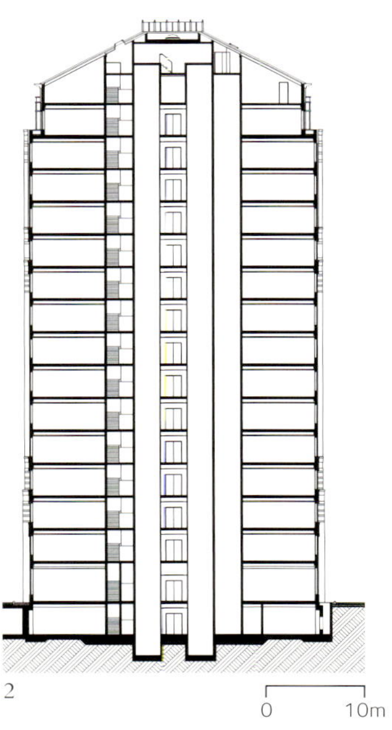

2

0   10m

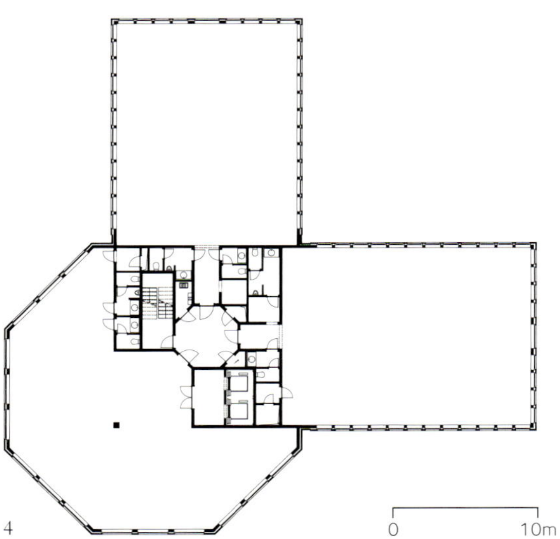

4

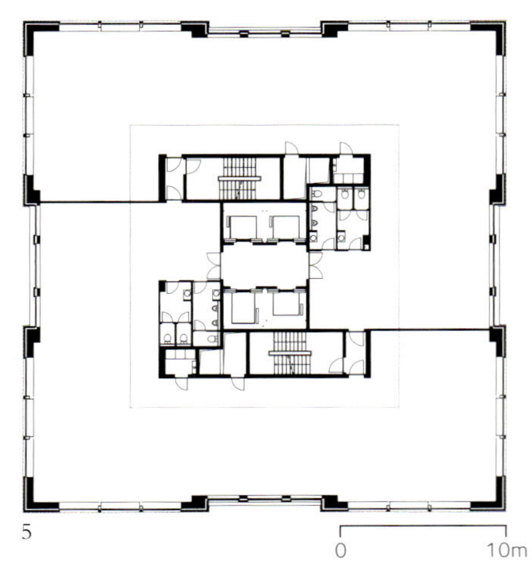

5

3 Mechelen Campus, gate buildings
4 Building A, typical floor plan
5 Tower, typical floor plan
6 Building C, typical floor plan
7 Aerial view, digital photomontage

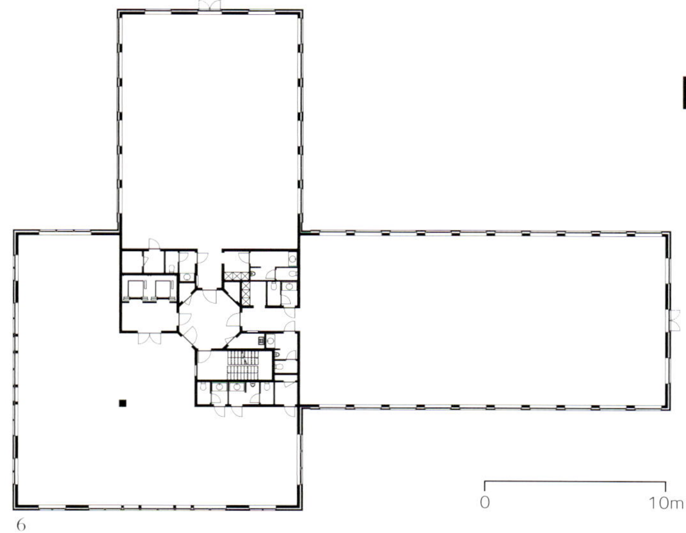

6

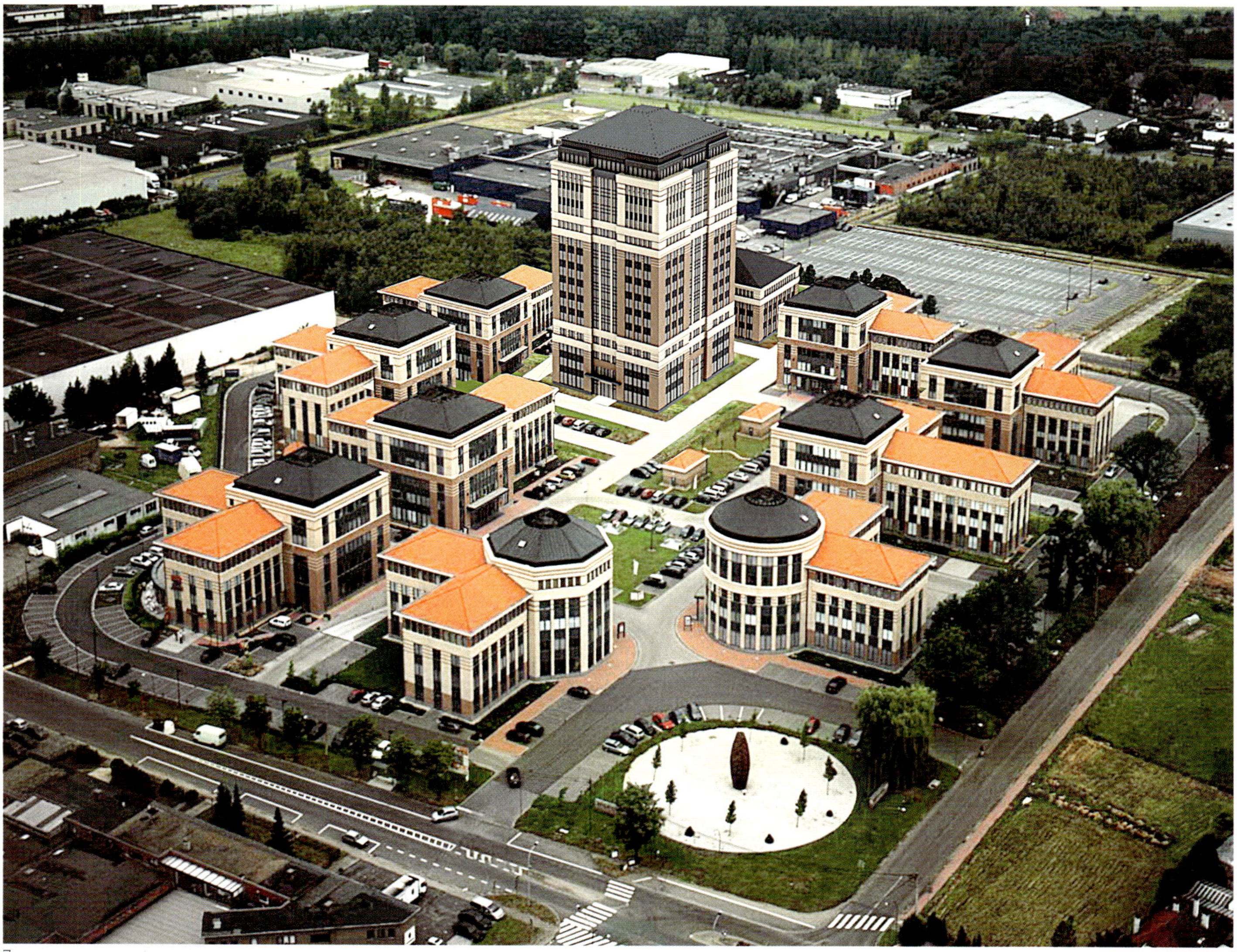

7

  The Walt Disney Company France Headquarters

The Walt Disney Company France Headquarters
Val d'Europe, Marne-la-Vallée, France

Client: Buelens – Almafin
Above ground area: 12,371 square metres
Completion: 2003

Developed by Buelens and Almafin, the six-storey, 12,371-square-metre Cassiopée building houses the The Walt Disney Company France headquarters. The project is located in the heart of Val d'Europe, in the immediate vicinity of the Disneyland Resort Paris. The success of Val d'Europe has turned the area into one of the most exciting new city developments in France in recent years.

Designed from the outset as a location in which people could both live and work, it is fulfilling its ambitions at a spectacular pace. The design for the new Disney France headquarters reflects this dual live–work aspect, and its classically inspired façades, featuring natural stone and plaster with aluminium window frames, add a sense of urbanity to this busy environment. Located in the rotunda on each level, the 'community centre' provides services such as copiers, fax machines and cafeteria facilities, and these centres have become important, informal meeting points within the company.

The Disney France headquarters is located at the major crossroad of Val d'Europe, situated at the doorstep of a RER express public transport station. In addition to an underground garage for 199 cars, at the rear of the building is a drive-through porte-cochère, which creates an impressive sense of arrival in addition to great convenience with its few short-term car spaces hidden in a landscaped courtyard. A remarkable aspect of this project is that this, the first office project completed at Val d'Europe, is the collaborative effort of a Belgian team of architects and developers.

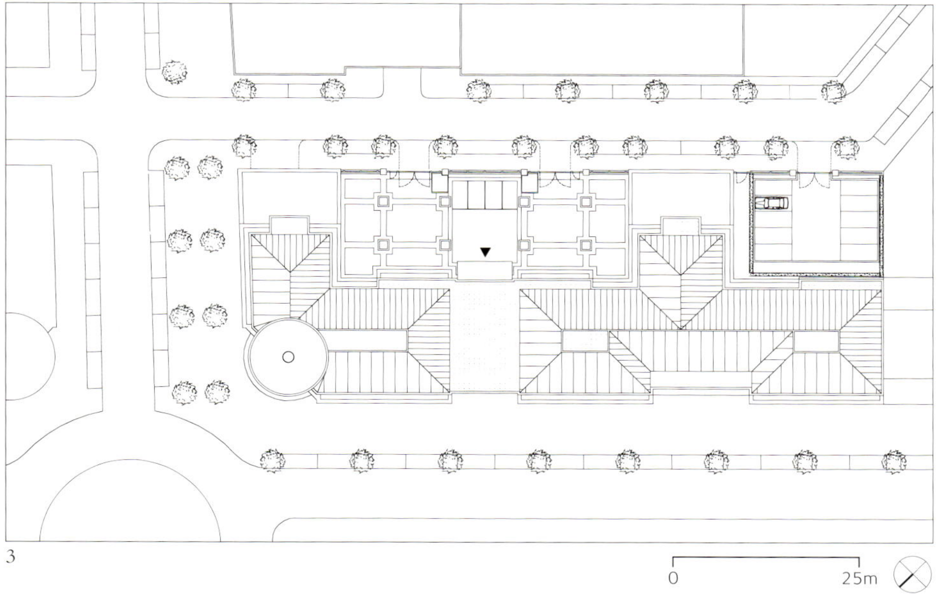

3

0   25m

1   General view along the main boulevard
2   Main entrance
3   Master plan
4   Main entrance, detail

4

Fortis Headquarters
Brussels, Belgium

Client: Fortis AG
Architect for the façades and the public lobby:
Michael Graves and Associates
Above ground area: 24,000 square metres
Completion: 2002
Award: Competition-winning project

Located in the historical city centre and replacing the previous headquarters building demolished in 1999, the Fortis Headquarters project aims to recreate the rhythm of the typical Brussels urban fabric.

The eight-storey project, completed in 2002, is the result of a long process. At the request of the client, VIZZION Architects studied several proposed design solutions: renovating the interiors of the existing building, rebuilding the interiors while preserving the 1950s façades and constructing a newly designed building. The third solution, a new building, was eventually decided upon given the increased value of the project as a long-term investment. VIZZION Architects was then requested to submit organisational plans for the project, which was expected to be taken into account a certain amount of flexibility pertaining to the headquarters' proposed 30-year life-span.

At that stage, at the end of 1997, the Belgo-Dutch financial corporation decided to organise a limited international competition. After reviewing nine proposals, Fortis selected the design submitted by American architect Michael Graves. VIZZION Architects, having already conceived the organisational plans for the headquarters project, was then entrusted by Fortis to oversee the construction of the headquarters according to both these plans and Michael Graves's winning façade designs. Eventually, VIZZION Architects was also asked by Fortis to design the new façade of the now renovated next-door nine-storey Jacqmain 83 building, originally completed in 1976.

2

3

1 Jacqmain 83 building and Fortis Headquarters, general view
2 Fortis Headquarters, general view
3 Fortis Headquarters, main lobby

Headquarters and administrative centres: new constructions
Swiss Life (Belgium) Headquarters at South Center and South Express
Brussels, Belgium

Client: Fonsny Midi; South Express
Above ground area:
  19,696 square metres, South Center
  20,758 square metres, South Express
Completion: 2004–2008

The Swiss Life Headquarters at South Center in Brussels is part of a larger urban project facing the Gare du Midi, a major railway station from which both Thalys and Eurostar rapid trains depart to Paris and London. The first phase, developed by Fonsny Midi and owned by Swiss Life, and which is partly used by Swiss Life as their Belgian headquarters and partly let, comprises 19,696 square metres of office space and 120 underground parking spaces.

The 11-storey project is designed in such a way as to create a plaza opposite the station's main entrance, and the architect was also directly commissioned by Swiss Life to design the company's interiors on the four upper levels. Respectful of the urban typology, the architecture features stone façades on the lower levels and metal spandrels from the seventh floor to the spires – arrows that give symbolic strength in an area dedicated to communication. In addition to those elements reminiscent of the New York City great skyscrapers era, the 'active' double-skin façades and the cool ceiling radiant HVAC technology contribute to better energy management by directly lowering energy consumption.

After the completion of South Center, construction continued with the 20,758-square-metre South Express project developed next-door, both projects forming a major urban renewal ensemble in what was formerly a derelict area facing Brussels' main railway station. The arches atop South Express that face the railway station are reminiscent of the vaulted roofs of major 19th- and 20th-century railway stations.

2

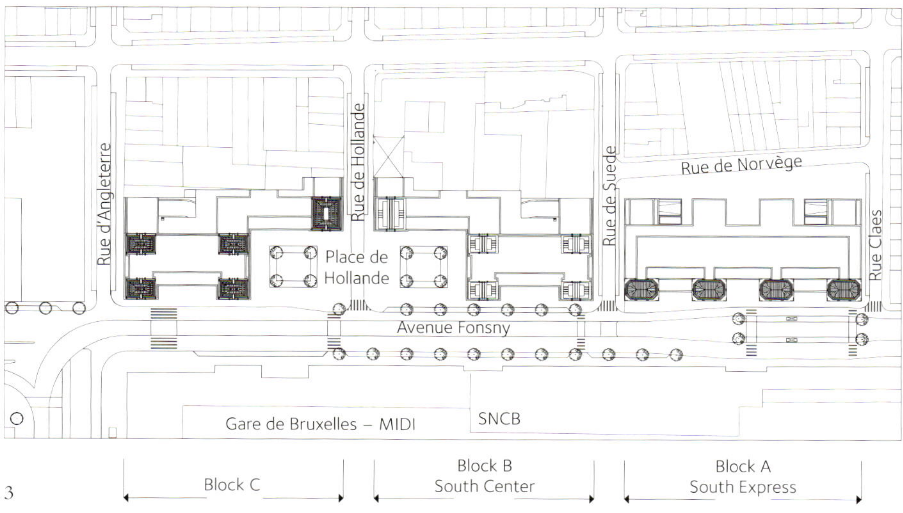

3

5

 Swiss Life (Belgium) Headquarters at South Center and South Express

6

0   10m

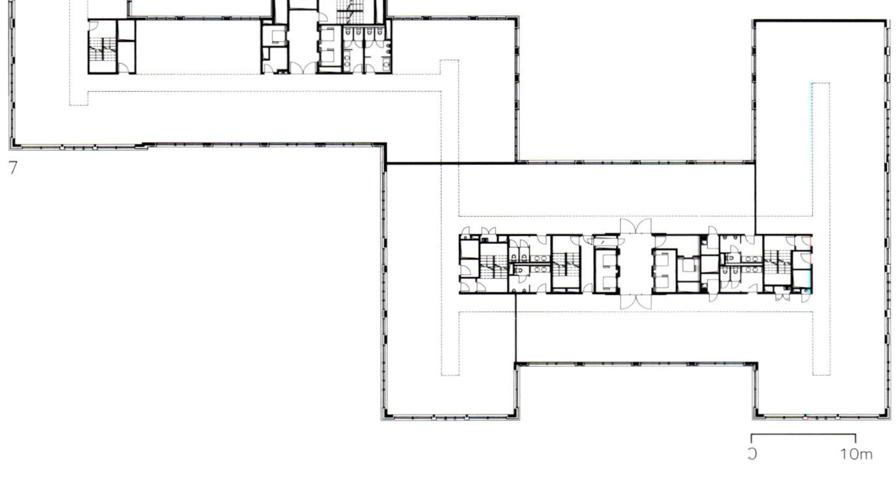

7

0   10m

Previous pages:
    Swiss Life (Belgium) Headquarters at South Center
5   *South Center, rendering study showing the newly created public square*
6   *South Center, elevation*
7   *South Center, typical floor plan*
8   *South Express, rendering*
Following pages:
    South Express and South Center (right to left)

8

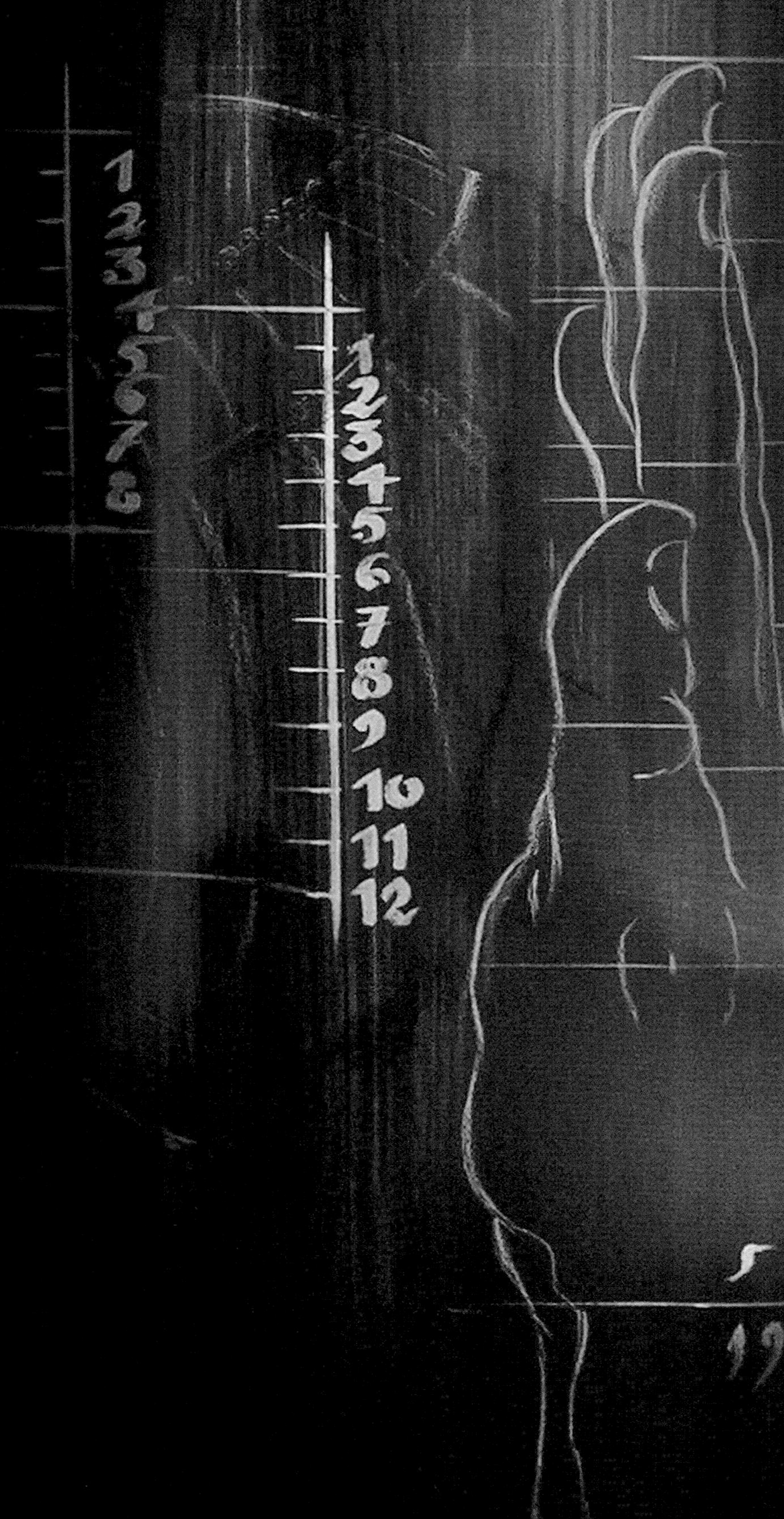

Housing
Joli Bois
Brussels, Belgium

Client: Fortis Real Estate
Above ground area:
5600 square metres, Joli Bois –
Clos des Lipizzans,
12,700 square metres, Joli Bois –
Résidences Alezan, Balzan and Tobiano
Completion: 2005/2007

Joli Bois comprises two projects: Clos des Lipizzans, featuring 39 apartments; and the Résidences Alezan, Balzan and Tobiano, featuring 87 apartments. Both projects form their own landscaped environment, and being located next to each other they have created a larger, two-full-block urban experience with a suburban flavour.

Clos des Lipizzans comprises two five-storey apartment buildings located around a triangular landscaped square, forming a whole with 17 townhouses developed by the same client but designed by another firm. On an even grander scale, the six-storey Résidences Alezan, Balzan and Tobiano, situated on the adjacent plot, are located on three edges of the rectangular site. The arrangement of these three buildings allows for the creation of a vast landscaped garden equipped with a lagoon, a cascading fountain and an elevated terrace. This luxurious environment is private in terms of access and use, but the open vistas in several directions allow the neighbourhood to enjoy the delightful environment as well. The lagoon also acts a storm basin, providing ample storage volume for excess stormwater flows.

Finely detailed façades, large terraces and pergolas and a luxurious green environment give the project a resort-like atmosphere in total symbiosis with its surroundings. Joli Bois combines quietness and a green environment with benefits from an ideal suburban location, with direct access to local retail shops, numerous local schools, sport and cultural centres as well as a subway line connecting the housing ensemble directly with the city centre.

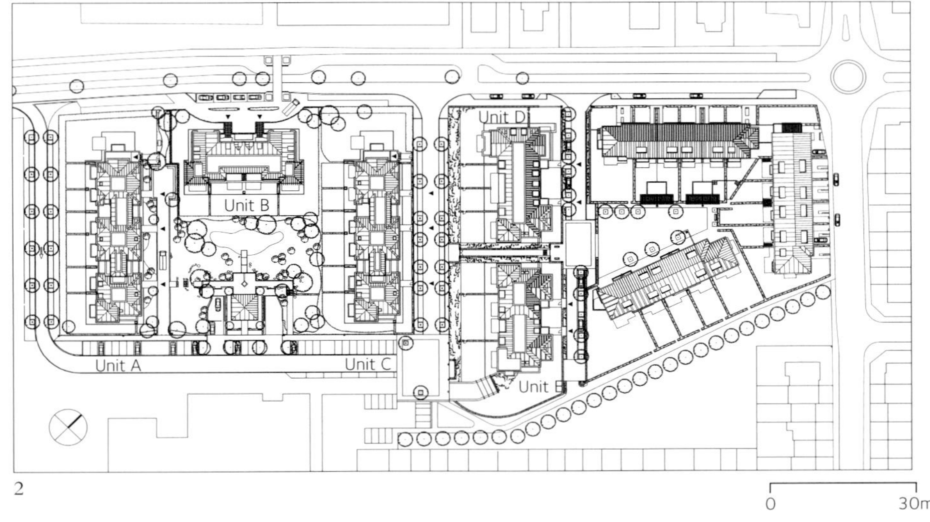

Opposite   Residence Tobiano (Unit C)
2   Master plan

3

3   *General aerial view*

4 *Unit D, typical floor plan*
5 *Façades on the common garden*
6 *Units A, B, C, section*
Opposite *Clos des Lipizzans (Unit E),*
terraces detail

4

5

Unit A
Unit B
Unit C
0   10m

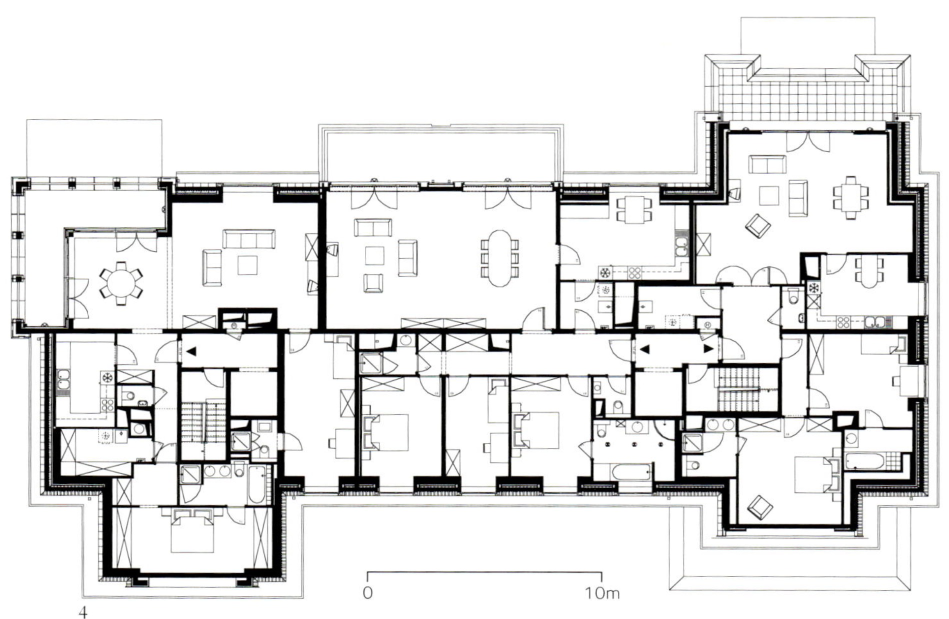

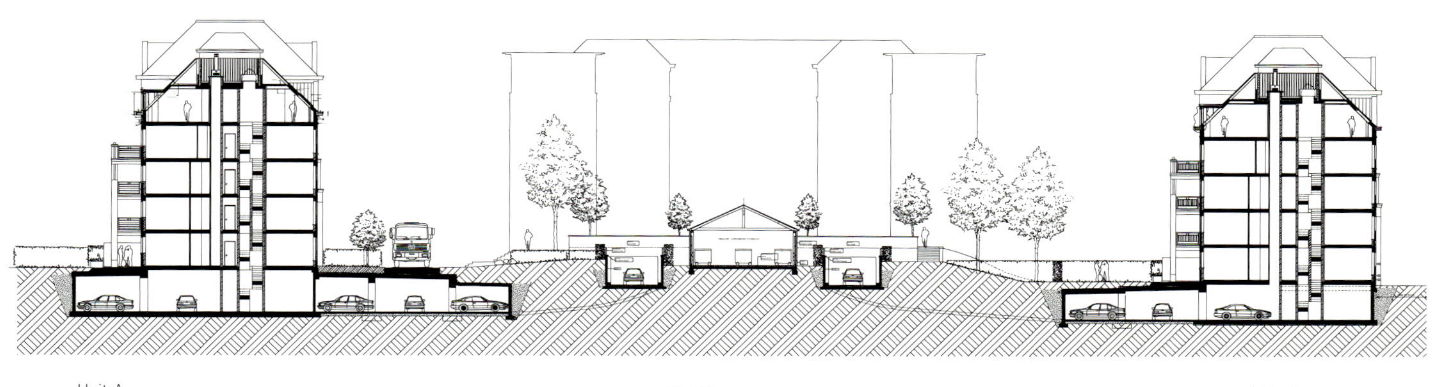

6

Le Jardin des Fonderies
Brussels, Belgium

Client: SDRB
Above ground: 4220 square metres
Completion: 1998
Awards: 1998 Prix Européen Philippe Rotthier de la Reconstruction de la Ville, mention; MIPIM Awards 1998, winner in the residential developments category.

Le Jardin des Fonderies is Brussels's largest example of a building conversion from an industrial structure to a housing estate. The aim behind the development was to attract inhabitants back to this working-class area, where economic activity had disappeared following the abolition of customs within the European Union. The former Nestor Martin factory, built in 1887, closed its doors in the late 1970s. Today, it has transformed into 39 housing units, including large, south-facing terraces with views onto an inner garden.

The architectural intention was to provide housing that offers all modern comforts while also retaining and accentuating the industrial character of the façades located in the area and along the nearby Brussels canal. The project was also to be a catalyst in leading other developers to renovate and transform other derelict buildings in the area.

2

Opposite   Elevation seen from the garden
2   Existing industrial building before renovation
3&4   Details

3

4

5

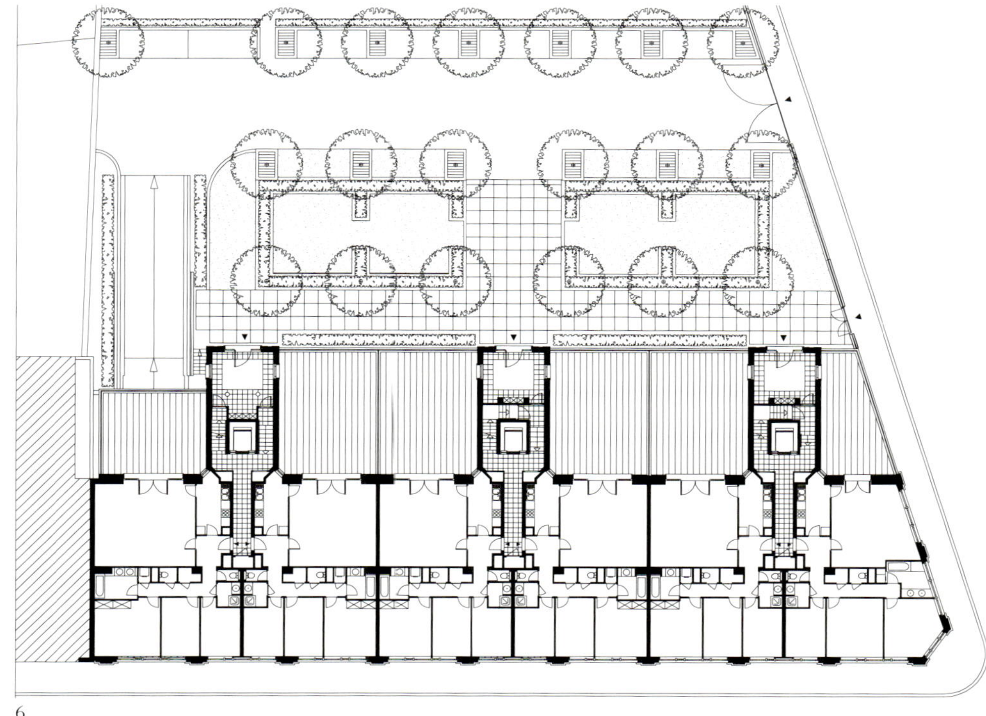

6

7

5   The renovated building seen from the street
    corner
6   Ground floor plan
7   General view from the garden
8   Main elevation, rendering

8

Housing

Housing
La Belle Chanson and Les Trois Mâts
Brussels, Belgium

Client: VIZZION Europe
Above ground area:
  6581 square metres, La Belle Chanson
  7015 square metres, Les Trois Mâts
Completion: 2008

La Belle Chanson and Les Trois Mâts are both located in a highly sought-after residential area in the heart of the Commune of Woluwé-Saint-Lambert in Southern Brussels – a green and quiet neighbourhood close to the Boulevard de la Woluwe, in between the city centre and the Soignes Forest.

La Belle Chanson is designed in the spirit of the Belle Epoque, with its distinctive rhythm created by the bow windows, the turrets and the pergolas. Les Trois Mâts, on the other hand, is characterised by cascading terraces and pierced sun-protectors and pergolas, and features a 461-square-metre crèche.

Both projects have been designed and developed by VIZZION according to their High Environmental Value principle based on exclusive use of recyclable materials and optimal management of natural resources. Each project benefits from an array of sustainable features combined for the first time in a Brussels apartment building.

The building construction involves highly effective techniques and solutions, which produce significant energy savings and add an exclusive character to the two residential projects. A specific HEV feature is a heat-exchanger system using the dual flux method which makes optimal use of heat loss – part of the extracted heat is recuperated and pre-heats solar energy panels, thus producing hot water; another important HEV aspect is the use of water tanks which utilize rainwater for the maintenance of gardens and public spaces, management of run-offs and the watering of grounds.

Broad, cleverly oriented terraces allow residents to enjoy a pleasant view of a neatly organised environment punctuated by private gardens.

2

3

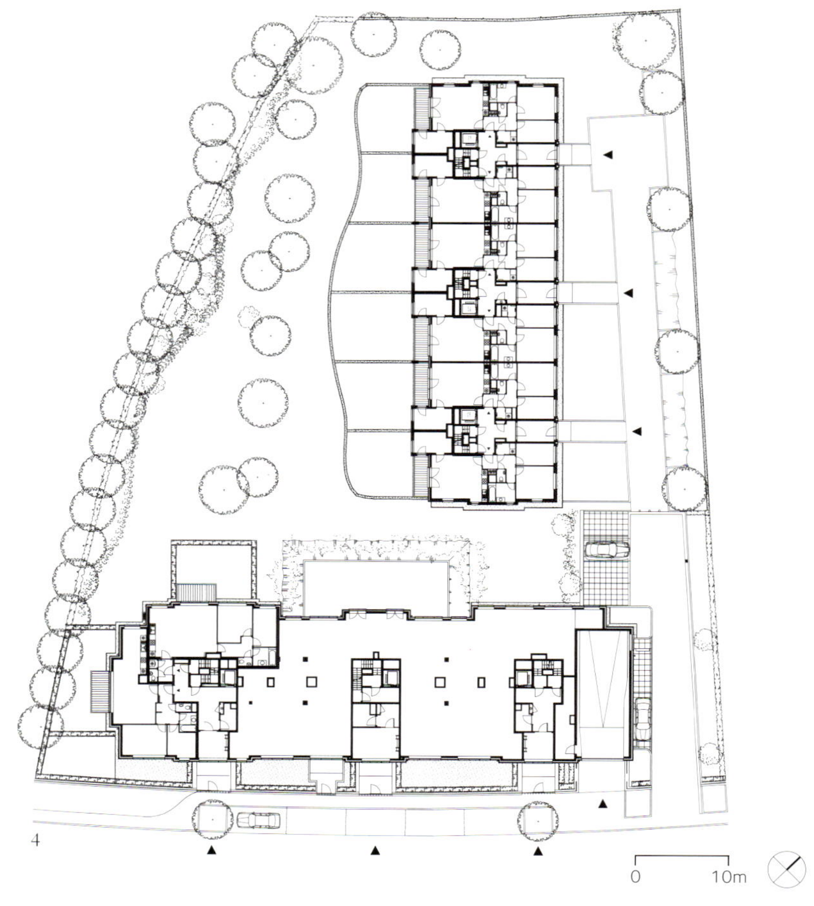

4

5

4 *Les Trois Mâts, ground floor plan*
5 *Les Trois Mâts, view from the street, digital rendering*
6 *La Belle Chanson, ground floor plan*
7 *La Belle Chanson, view from the garden, digital rendering*

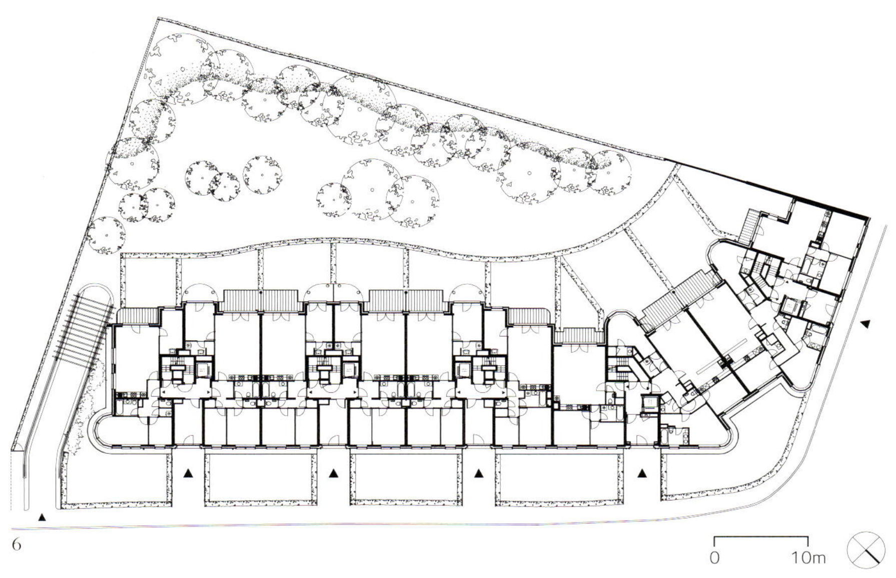

6

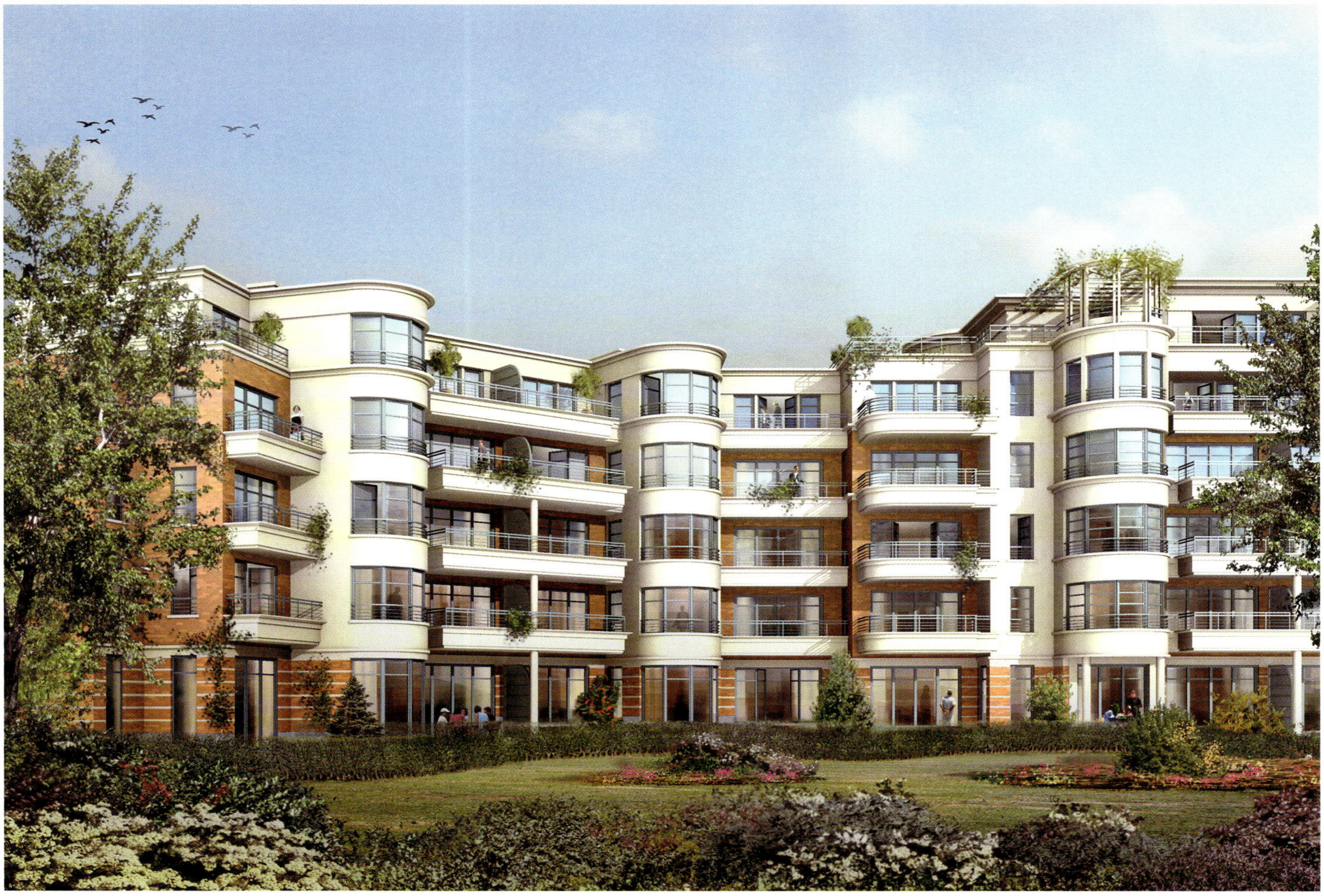

7

Euro Village
Brussels, Belgium

Client: Skyline Projects
Above ground area: 25,554 square metres
Completion: 2006

Euro Village comprises four buildings located along the European Parliament esplanade covering a commuter railroad station. The buildings feature a total of 274 one- to three-bedroom apartments, and an underground garage is located in the three basement levels.

Together with the adjacent 149-room Radisson SAS Brussels EU hotel – designed by the same architect – the Euro Village ensemble creates an urban link between the administrative building units of the European Parliament and the existing urban fabric. While the European Parliament looks inwards towards its own concrete plaza, Euro Village forms a transition with the nearby residential area both in terms of its volumes – the higher volumes facing the Parliament and lower facing the existing urban fabric – and the façade details and materials used.

2

Opposite Rotunda, detail
*   2   Façade*
*   3   General view, rendering study*

3

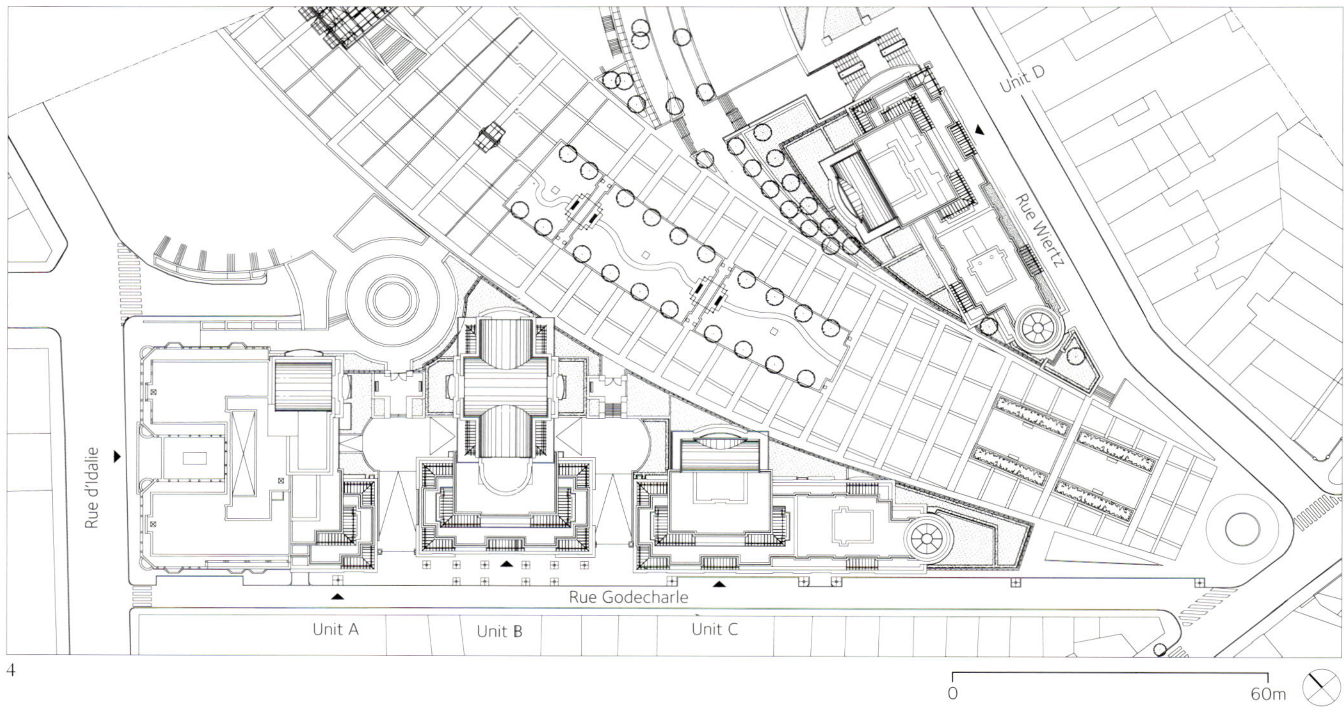

4 Masterplan
5 *Also designed by the architect, the next-
   door 149-room Radisson SAS EU
   Hotel Brussels is part of the Euro
   Village ensemble*
6 *General view, model*
Opposite *Esplanade, detail*

8

10

8 *General view seen from the landscaped pedestrian esplanade*
9 *Elevation*
10 *General view*

Housing
Villa Bozkaya
Ankara, Turkey

Client: Bozkaya Family
Above ground area: 600 square metres
Completion: 2000

Located in the suburbs of Ankara, in the Bilkent area, the Villa Bozkaya is part of a university estate. The proximity of the university and the residential units allows the academic community and the surrounding society to share service facilities such as sports and leisure centres.

The project's architectural spirit is inspired by art produced by the nomadic Seljuk people of Central Asia from the 9th to 13th centuries, who adopted elements of Persian art, for example pure geometric forms and ceramics. This influence is fully integrated into the architecture of this project and not merely applied to façades. Villa Bozkaya has been developed around two transverse, central service axes with four distinctive geometrical volumes. The project's main volume, which can be seen from the street, houses the master bedroom and the living room. The two-level glassed-wall revealing the main central staircase provides an overall lightness to the project, and a traditional coating comprised of marble and natural stone powder has been applied to the Villa Bozkaya's façade.

While all the living areas are located at ground levels, the master bedroom, two rooms for the children and a guest room are situated on the first floor. In addition, there is also a small office on the first floor, and another office is housed in the roof. The 400-square-metre basement accommodates three cars and provides storage for mechanical equipment; also located on the basement level are a fitness centre, a room for the maid, and a piano room, all of which face an inner courtyard in order to benefit from ample daylight.

In accordance with the client's admiration for Frank Lloyd Wright's architecture, exotic Afzelia wood has been used throughout the house, while the wooden window frames are made of Afromozia wood in lighter tones.

4

5

1

2

Housing
Ömerli
Istanbul, Turkey

Client: VIZZION Europe
Above ground area: 23,105 square metres
Completion: 2008-2010

This housing project is located in Ömerli, in the suburbs of Istanbul, one of the few districts in the city that is surrounded by forests. On the Asian side of Istanbul, and set within an exceptional landscape, an entirely private district comprising 81 villas is being built on a vast site of approximately 100,000 square metres.

The project comprises three- and five-room villas nestled in a secured landscaped zone. There are five different villa types ranging from 235 to 350 square metres. The villas are designed according to three different architectural styles, but each villa will have its own character. At Ömerli, a contemporary reinterpretation of Art Nouveau, Art Deco and Frank Lloyd Wright's architecture meets with traditional Turkish architecture.

Ömerli will feature an array of amenities and services available to residents, including a club house equipped with a restaurant, gaming room and fitness centre. Within the landscaped area, lined by a river and punctuated by promenade paths, the residents will enjoy outdoor facilities including a large open-air swimming pool, tennis courts and playgrounds for children.

1   *Villa, type E*
2   *General elevation*

3

4

5

1

2

   The Boat at the Quai des Princes

3

1 General view, rendering study
2 Master plan
3 Aerial view
4 Typical apartment layout

Housing
Quai des Princes
Cap d'Ail, French Riviera, France

Client: VIZZION Europe
Above ground area: 20,246 square metres
Completion: 2010

4

1 General view, rendering study
2 Master plan
3 Aerial view
4 Typical apartment layout

Quai des Princes is located next to the well-known Fontvieille area, a relatively newly built district of Monaco, partly erected on reclaimed land. The exceptional 5550-square-metre site, situated in between the hills and the sea, at the door of Monaco, at the Quai des Princes, faces a charming marina.

Featuring 109 serviced apartments, the project is designed with the flavour of a luxury ocean liner and comes equipped with an array of services including a restaurant, lounge/bar and fitness centre. However, it is undoubtedly the rooftop lagoon, with its numerous pools and landscaped gardens, that will make the three-level ensemble, surmounted with its penthouse leisure rooftop, one of the new trend-setters on the French Riviera.

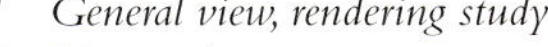

1

2

Domaine du Parc
Lorentzweiler (Bofferdange), Luxembourg

Client: VIZZION Europe
Above ground area: 21,355 square metres
Completion: 2009, apartments
2010, villas

Located in Bofferdange, 10 kilometres from the city centre of Luxembourg, the Domaine du Parc is a high-end residential ensemble designed according to the sustainability principles residing at the heart of each project developed by VIZZION Europe in recent years. The 21,355-square-metre project includes eight buildings, each comprising three to four levels, as well as twenty-seven 200- to 300-square-metre villas to be built in a second phase. All 105 apartments feature unusually large terraces, adding a special touch to the Domaine du Parc project that is already nestled in a quiet landscaped park.

The Domaine du Parc project has been designed to harmoniously integrate with its surroundings, and its architecture combines both beauty and functionality. The project's underlying ambition is to express a qualitative architecture with High Environmental Value by using ecologically sound materials and integrating technical solutions that enable better energy management. Examples of these technical solutions include reinforced insulation, centralised hot water production through shared condensation boilers, use of solar panels, individual double-flux ventilation and rainwater recycling. Specific attention has been paid to the design and landscaping of gardens and parks aimed at optimising the surroundings' sense of hospitality.

3

4

1&2   Apartment building, digital rendering
3   Master plan
4   Villa, digital rendering

Le Domaine de Montévrain, Le Parc d'Evrini and Le Clos du Mail

Montévrain, Marne-la-Vallée, France

Le Domaine de Montévrain
Client: Ile de France (Promogim)
Above ground area: 6909 square metres
Completion: 2006

Le Parc d'Evrini
Client: Citalis (Cogedim)
Above ground area: 6660 square metres
Completion: 2006

Le Clos du Mail
Client: Les Exclusives de Montévrain
Above ground area: 6459 square metres
Completion: 2006

The Etablissement Public d'Aménagement de la Ville Nouvelle de Marne-la-Vallée (EPAMARNE) - a public body in charge of urban planning - organised an invitation design competition for three projects located in the same area. The selected group of architects were also asked to propose a contemporary concept for the Cité-jardin, acknowledging the urban guidelines for the area. The strategically located plot allocated to VIZZION Architects was the first to be developed, thus the firm was responsible for both the urban planning and the development of architectural concepts.

The Domaine de Montévrain comprises 99 apartments arranged around a common garden, with the design inspired by the 1930s architecture found in Brussels and Paris. The fluid horizontal streamlines, the curved lines and the asymmetric composition have created a strong, readily identifiable project. The Parc d'Evrini (59 apartments) comprises three buildings that have the same typology, with each symmetrical project incorporating curved lines in order to add fluidity to the overall composition. Finally, the Clos du Mail (61 apartments) is elaborated according to the interconnections of voids and volumes, and the repetition of specific volumetric elements gives the project a clear identity within its surrounds.

Visually, all three projects are anchored via a plinth made of natural stone. Although each project has been designed with a different key aesthetic, when viewed together the overall effect is one of unity and coherence for this vast housing ensemble.

2

3

Opposite, 2, 3   Le Domaine de Montévrain: façades, details

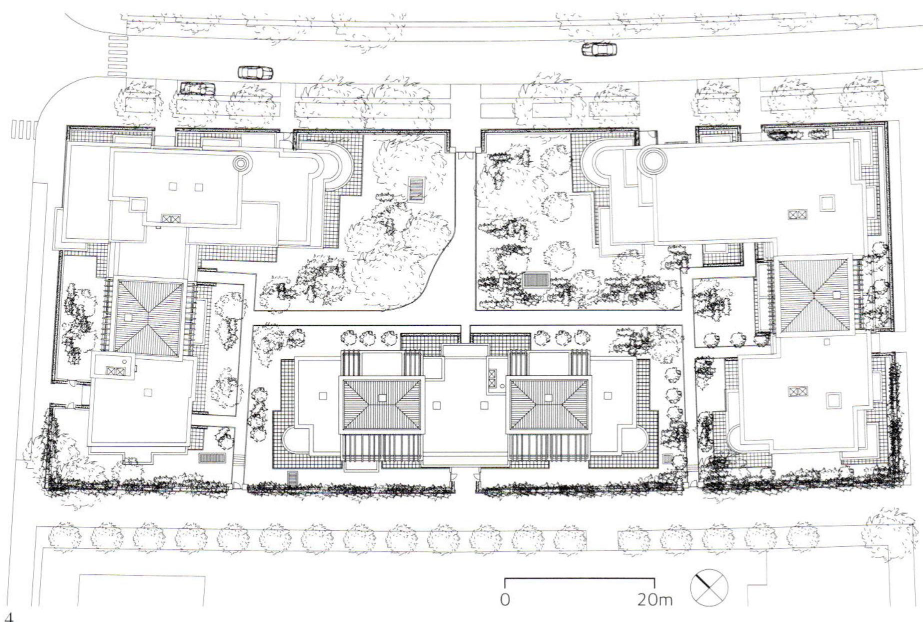

4

4   *Le Domaine de Montévrain, ground floor plan*
5   *Le Domaine de Montévrain, view from the gardens*
6   *Le Domaine de Montévrain, typical floor plan*

5

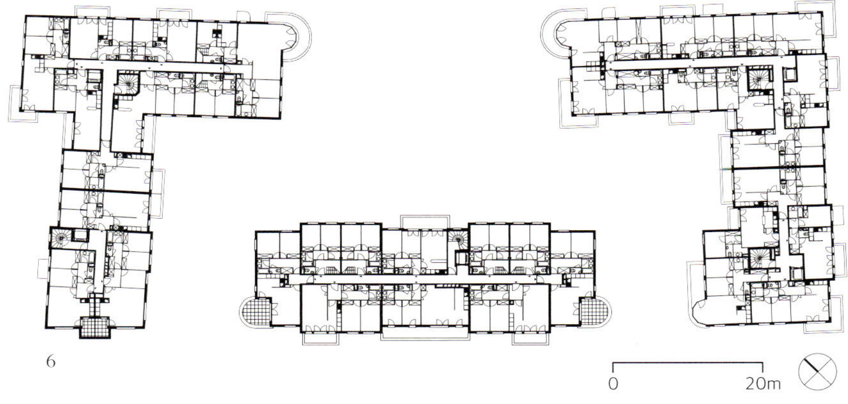

6

7 *Le Parc d'Evrini, ground floor plan*
8 *Le Parc d'Evrini, typical floor plan*
9 *Le Parc d'Evrini, façade, detail*

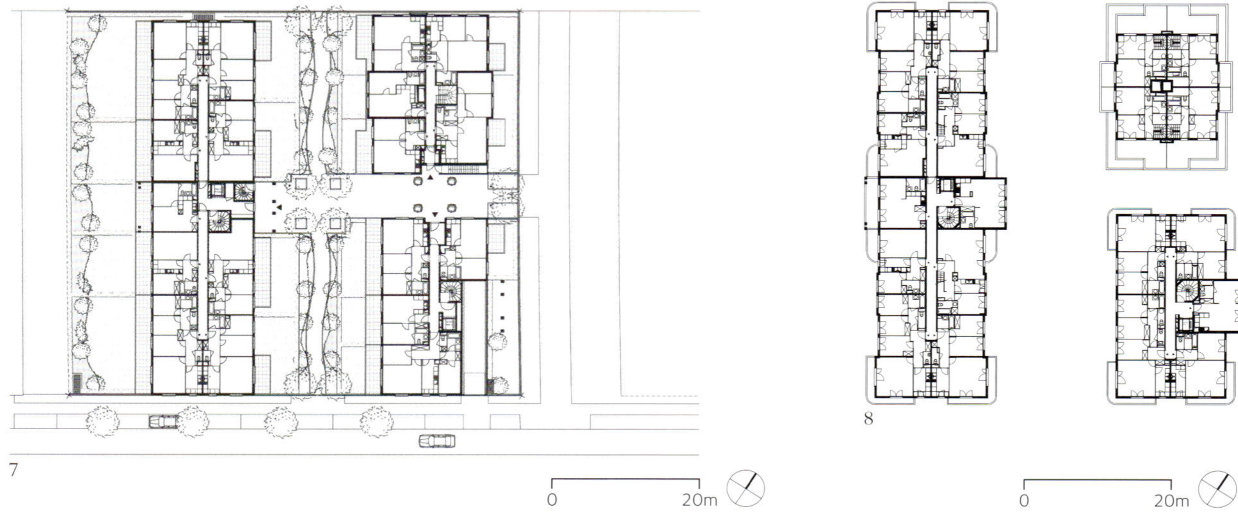

7

8

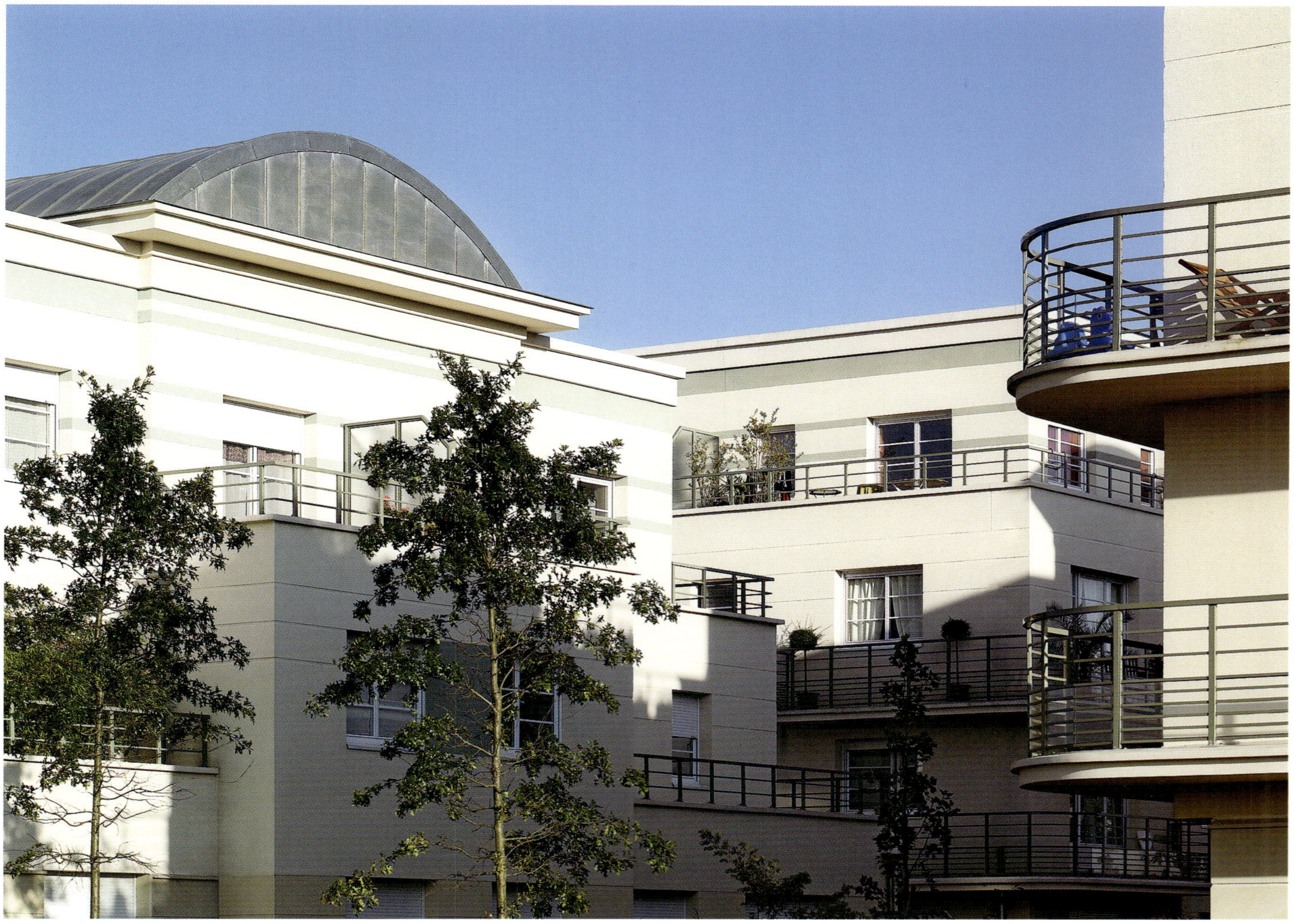

9

10 *Le Clos du Mail, ground floor plan*
11 *Le Clos du Mail, typical floor plan*
12 *Le Clos du Mail, façade, detail*

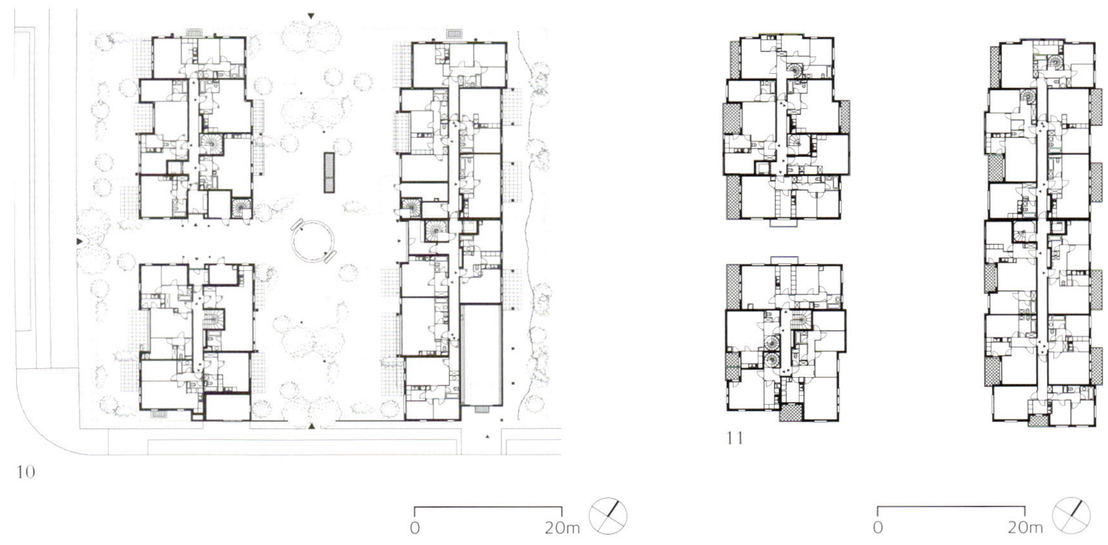

10

11

12

Les Jardins Victoriens
Val d'Europe, Marne-la-Vallée, France

Client: Marignan Habitat
Above ground area: 11,513 square metres
Completion: 2003

Les Jardins Victoriens, developed by Marignan Habitat, is composed of two residential buildings comprising 86 apartment units and landscaped gardens. The residential ensemble is located in the Val d'Europe, in Marne-la-Vallée, a newly created urban community in the immediate vicinity of Disneyland Resort Paris in France.

Located in the Quartier du Parc, which is intended to be the urban centre of the Val d'Europe, the project follows the urban guidelines drawn by Disneyland Resort Paris. These guidelines, which also related to the nearby The Walt Disney Company headquarters, require adherence to the design of a timeless architecture and the maintenance of homogeneity or a pre-set typological vocabulary in relation to gardens, balconies and loggias, cornices, proportions and alignments. In line with these guidlines, the façades are plaster-clad and the roof is made of zinc.

Although the streetscape of this newly built town creates back and front building sides, the rear façades of Les Jardins Victoriens are as elegantly detailed as those at the front, adding a prestigious touch to such moderately priced-apartments buildings.

2

Opposite   Porch, detail
2   Elevation
3   Main elevation

3

0   20m

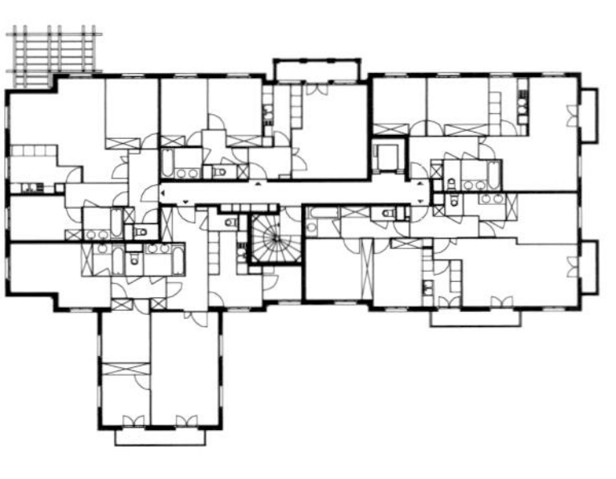

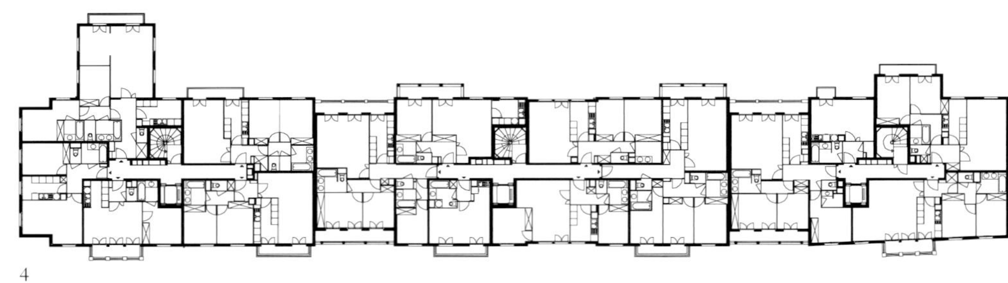

4

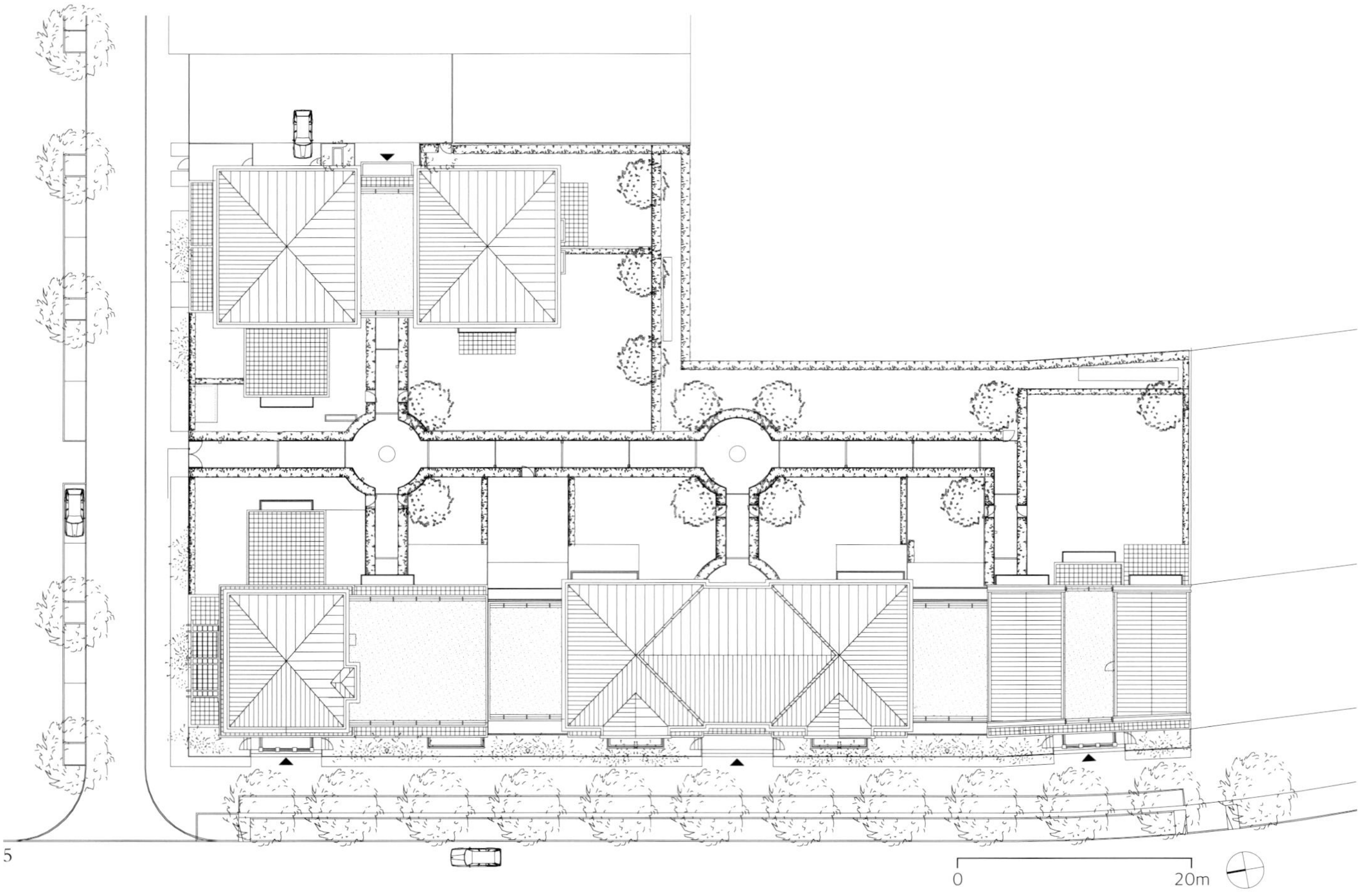

5

4   *Typical floor plan*
5   *Ground floor plan*
Opposite Rear views seen from the garden

7

7   *General view*

Shopping malls and mixed-use projects

City2
Shopping Mall

Shopping malls and mixed-use projects
City Center and City 2 Shopping Mall
Brussels, Belgium

Client: Fortis Real Estate
Gross building area: 98,370 square metres
Completion: 1999/2003

Completed in 1928, the former Bon Marché department store in central Brussels is part of the city's urban memory and has now been rebuilt and transformed into the mixed-use City Center, which includes the City 2 Shopping Mall. Originally designed as a full block along the boulevard, the 1928 department store was never completed as envisioned. The corner of the block remained an odd place for 75 years, while the 1978 City 2 Shopping Mall quickly became obsolete due to its Brutalist architecture.

At the request of the Monuments and Sites Commission, the Bon Marché's characteristic Art Deco façade has been restored and preserved. The client wanted the spirit of the original Bon Marché façade to be reflected in the new façade of the building above the City 2 Shopping Mall entrance, giving the appearance of a large building with a homogeneous appearance on the boulevard.

City Center comprises 30,938 square metres of offices organised around two glass-roofed atriums, retail shops at ground level as well as 450 parking spaces, which benefit from natural ventilation. The two seven-storey atriums, which can be used for social events, have detailed inner façades featuring natural stone and powder-coated aluminium that complement the building's façade.

Together with the renovated 27,000-square-metre City 2 Shopping Mall, which also comprises two glassed-roofs atriums, City Center is quite likely the largest mixed-used ensemble built in more than 30 years in the centre of Brussels. A five-storey housing building has been included at the rear of the project, and this, together with the urban treatment of the entire façade, has completed the urban renewal at this strategic city centre location and has returned to the neighbourhood a more respectful aesthetic relationship to the rest of the city.

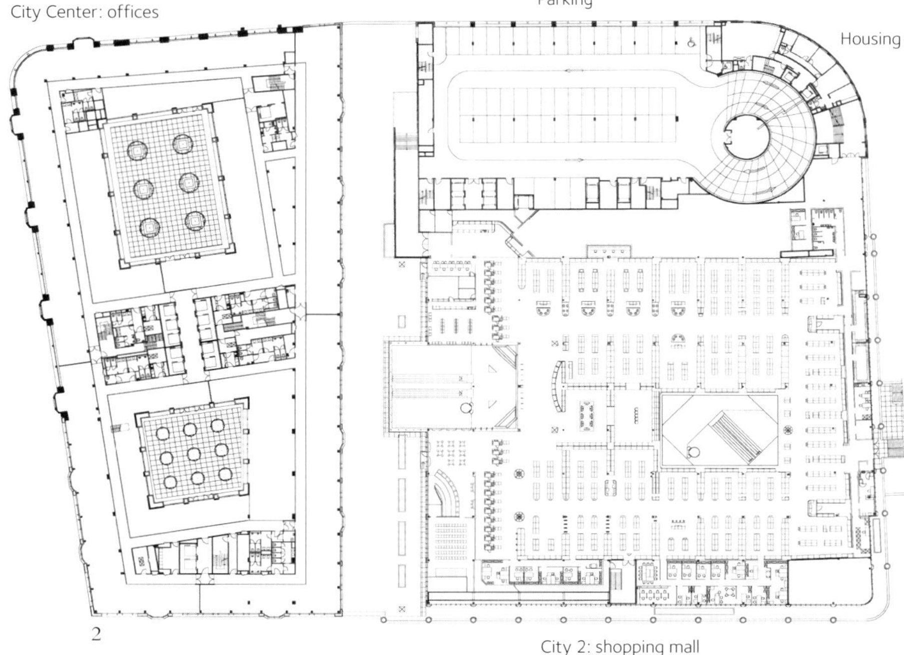

2

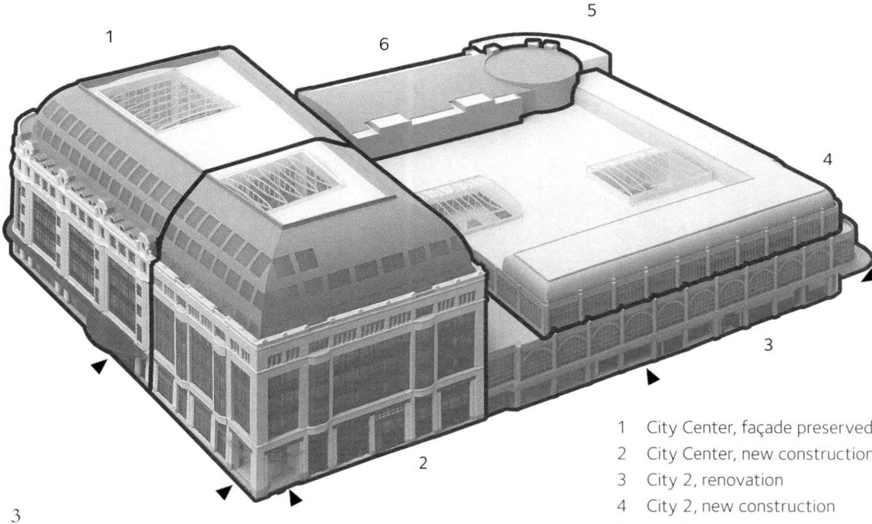

1   City Center, façade preserved
2   City Center, new construction
3   City 2, renovation
4   City 2, new construction
5   Housing, new construction
6   Parking, new construction

4, 5, 6 City 2 Shopping Mall, details

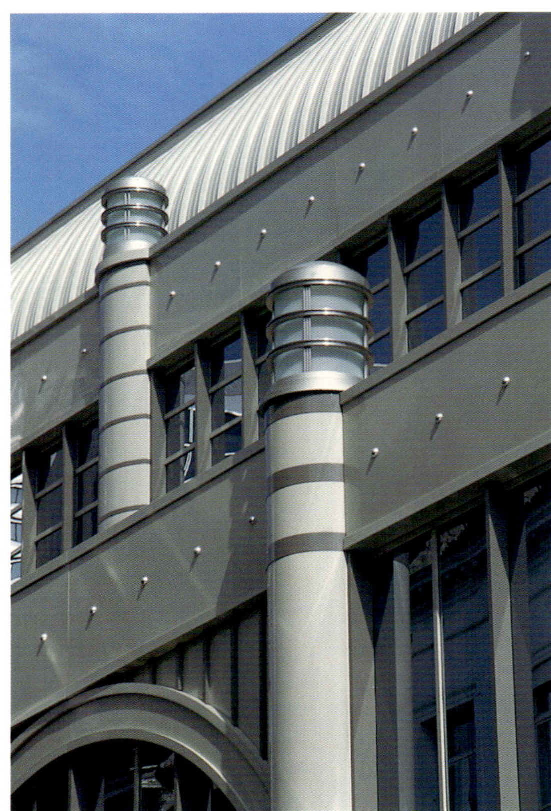

4

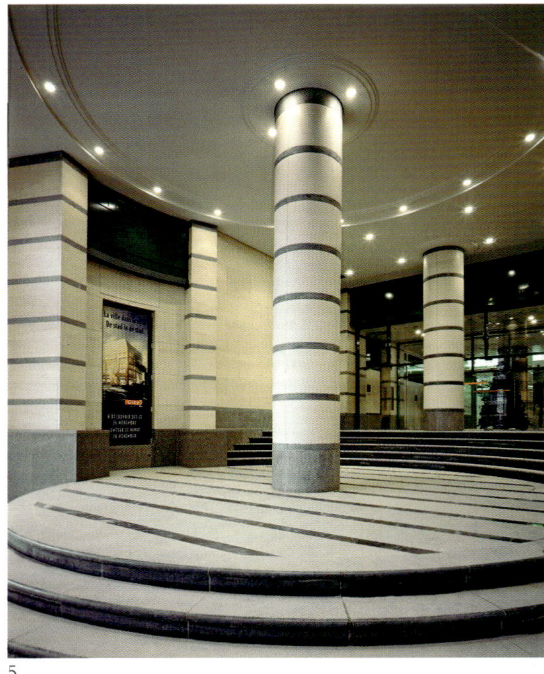

5

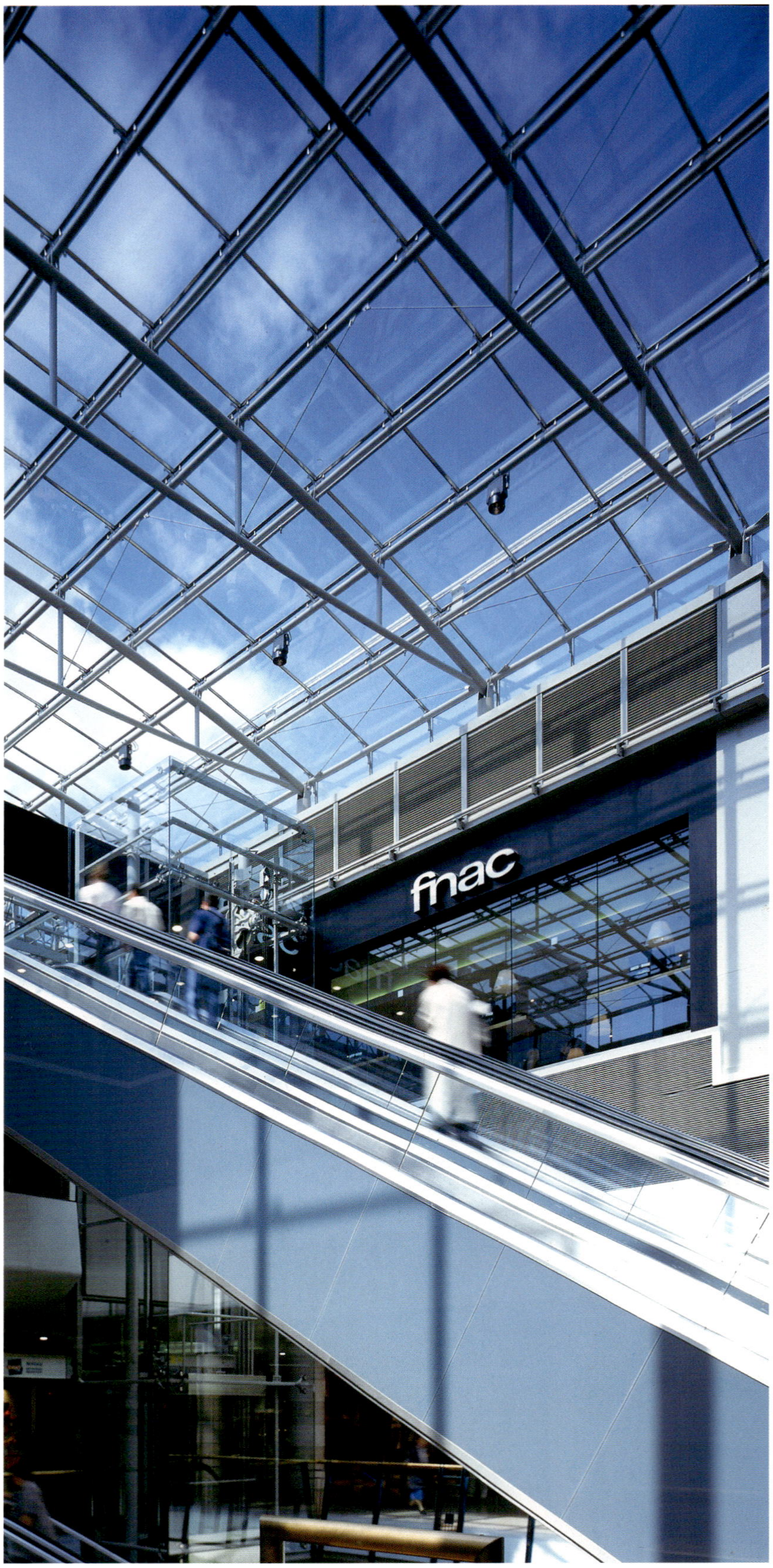

6

7

8

9

Shopping malls and mixed-use projects
Les Grands Prés
Mons, Belgium

Client: Foruminvest
Above ground area: 46,754 square metres
Completion: 2003
Award: ICSC (International Council of Shopping Centers) 2005 European Awards, large new centres category, commendation

On September 25, 2003, Les Grands Prés became one of the largest shopping malls completed in Belgium in many years. The construction time was less than 12 months and the shopping centre is part of the development of a vast 60-hectare ensemble west of the Mons city centre. The project is situated in the vicinity of the historical centre, 600 metres away from the main station, and next to the Imagix 14-movie theatre multiplex and the Initialis Scientific Park.

The 46,754-square-metre ensemble, equipped with a 2800-space carpark, comprises 75 retail units located under glass-enclosed shopping galleries and one Carrefour hypermarket, Belgium's largest and most ambitious supermarket chain.

Opposite   Atrium and food court
2   Ground floor plan

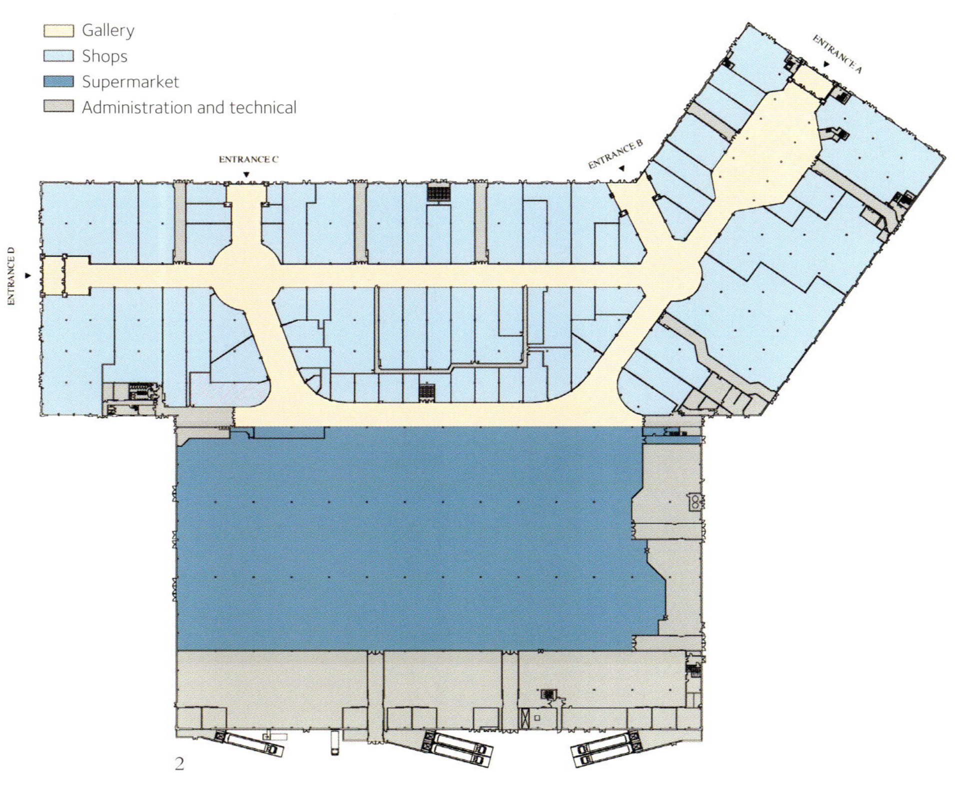

2

3

The façades are composed of a series of arcades and pilasters, crowned by 76 light boxes that at night create constant animation. The structure comprises a mix of natural stone, steel and glass, and four monumental porticos form main entrances of the Grands Prés.

According to their own architectural credo, the architects' designs were inspired by the local urban fabric. Elements reminiscent of well-known and established Mons city projects, such as the 19th-century buildings Casemates or la Machine à Eau, can be found in the series of pilasters and arcades on one side, with the buildings' entrances on the other.

The galleries' interior decoration is comprised of high-end materials including natural stone and glass-roofed skylights. The food court skylight is nestled above those of the other galleries, while the main glass-roofed atrium of the Grands Prés is 13 metres high. There circulation of the centre has been designed so that there are no dead-ends in the galleries, and the average area of each retail space is exceptionally large.

4

mowo
Groupe

Mowo Center
Bereldange, Luxembourg

Client: VIZZION Europe
Above ground area: 5817 square metres
Completion: 2006

The location of the building, set back as it is from the road, has led to an architecture that stands out for its strong, vertical, portal-type volumes, rhythmically integrated into a façade that favours horizontal lines.

The recessed façades at the upper level lend a certain lightness of volume that harmoniously and naturally fits in with the lentil-shaped façade of the Mowo section and the access portal to the fitness section. The detailing of the façade, the rhythm of the small columns to the upper level and the wide modulated windows of the ground floor guarantee shadows in perpetual movement, which further underlines the dynamic character of the building's architectural expression.

The light colour of the plasterwork and stone, along with the light-grey tone of the aluminium cladding, enable access to the three shops to be personalised through signage, with the use of bright colours enhancing the dynamic character of the commercial activities.

Opposite Façade detail
2 Ground floor plan

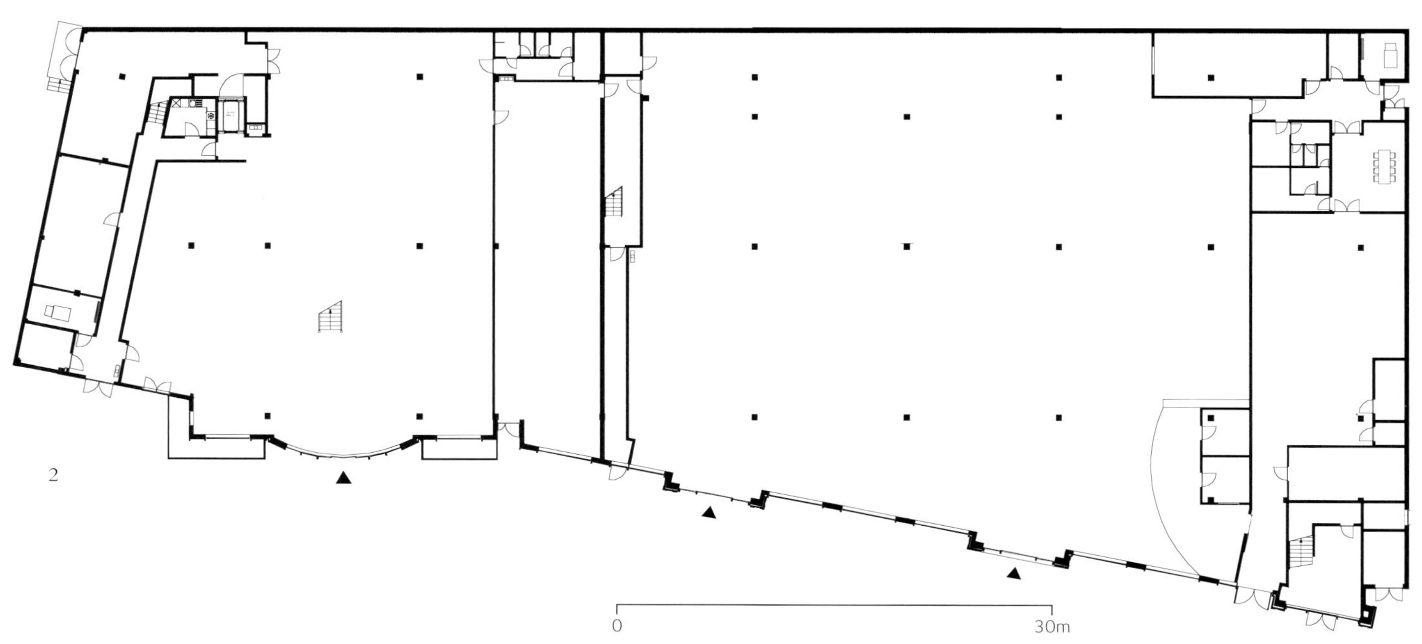

2

0　　　　　　　　　　30m

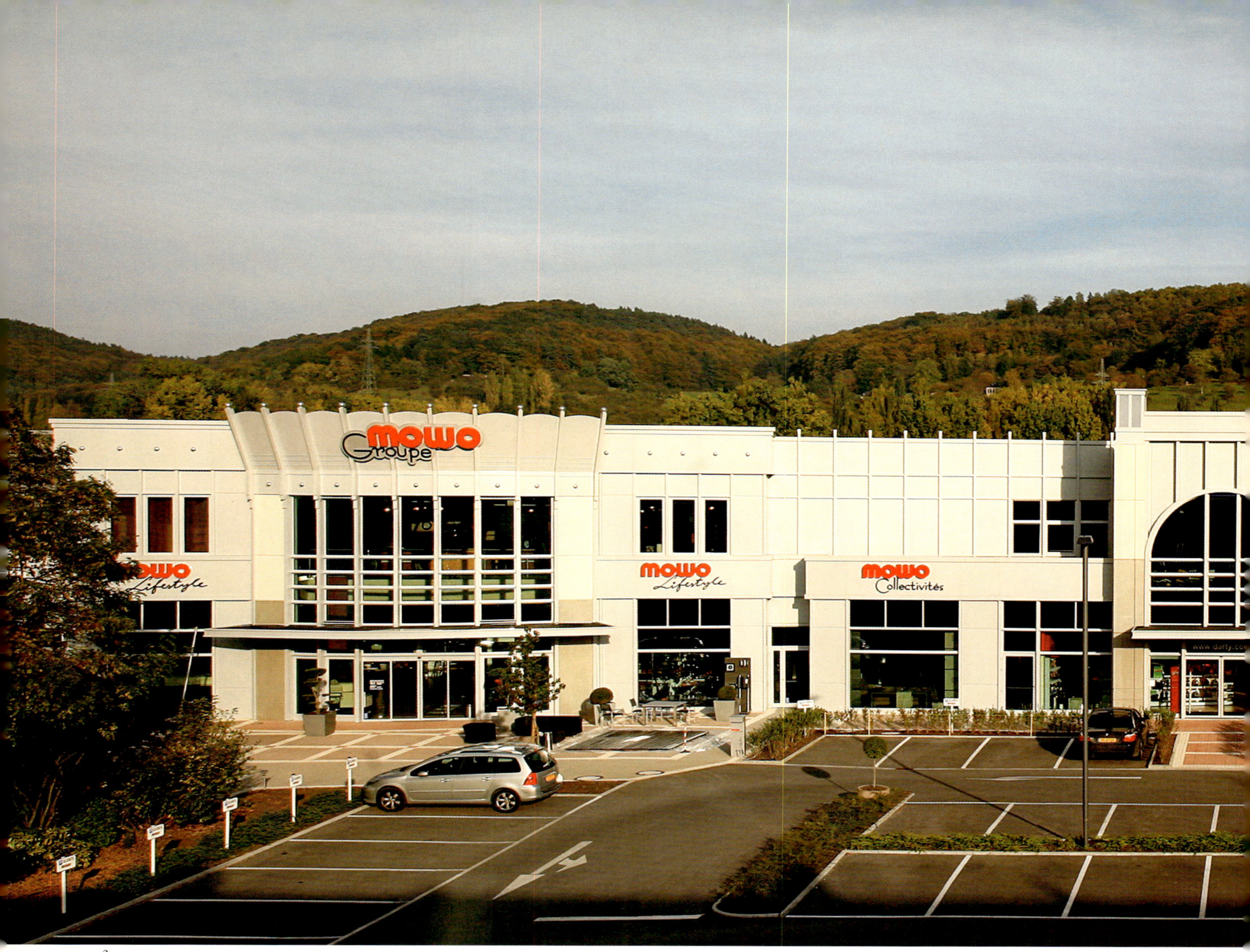

3

4

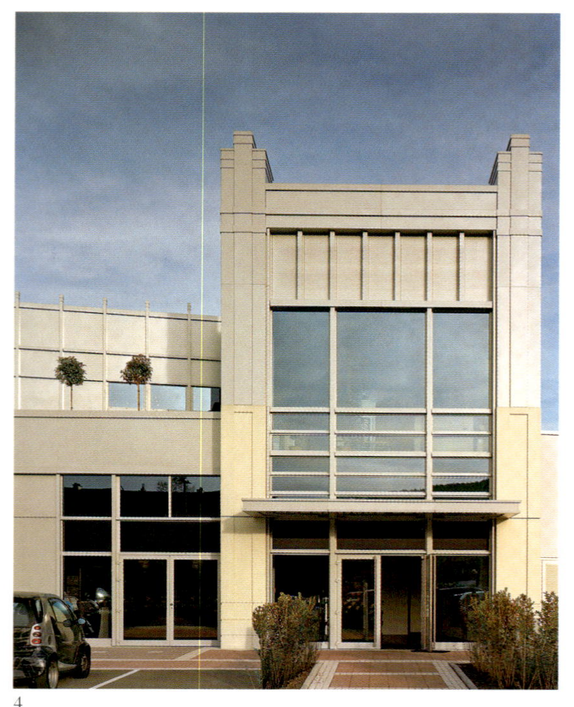

3 *General view*
4&5 *Entrance elevation*

mowo
Groupe
mowo
Lifestyle
mowo
Collections

Shopping malls and mixed-use projects
Media Square
Brussels, Belgium

Client: Benvenuta
Above ground area:
  4266 square metres, office
  1962 square metres, housing
Completion: 2003
Award: Les Règles de l'Urbanisme 2004, finalist in the newly built ensembles harmoniously integrated within the urban fabric category

Media Square faces the huge box-like headquarters of two Belgian national public television and radio networks studios and is located in between two urban blocks of different scales. The project is a mixed-use ensemble comprising three building units of different scale intended to unify this previously disorganised urban zone.

At the rear of the site, facing the garden, the three-level, semi-circular, 4266-square-metre office building and its landscaped garden provide a background for the residents of the two housing units by hiding from view semi-industrial barracks located in a nearby site.

The two housing units – one townhouse and a seven-storey building – are themselves hiding previous existing blank walls, thus creating a harmonious transition between the street's low- and the mid-rise sections at this particular location. The project's architecture combines a varied mix of materials, such as stone and bricks for the residential units and metal and glass for the office unit.

2

3

Shopping malls and mixed-use projects
Nile City
Cairo, Egypt

Client: Nile City Investments
Above ground area: 196,647 square metres
Completion: 2003, office towers and mall;
    2008, hotel

Nile City comprises a shopping mall, two 143-metre, 35-storey towers and the 100-metre, 26-storey, V-shaped Fairmont hotel tower located in the heart of the Egyptian capital, opposite the island of Zamalek. Upon their completion, the office towers became the most sought after business addresses in town.

Nile City's architecture shows links with traditional Levantine architecture. The variety of masses and details allows for clear views of the various buildings, their functions and their entrances. Decorative pillars and monumental porticos at ground level, and pergolas and golden cupolas at the top of the towers, along with pilasters, cornices, banding, balconies and coloured stone, give Nile City its particular character.

The twin towers feature strong vertical divisions and large, glazed panels. The towers' elevation is balanced by cornices, while the setbacks of the upper levels accentuate the visual effect of the gold cupolas crowning the buildings. The architect's aim was to create a set of towers that added interest to the urban composition of this mixed-ensemble, and careful analysis and design ensured that these buildings need not stand directly opposite each other. This placement creates a compatible relationship with the surrounding area, while also providing maximum views towards the pyramids, which can be glimpsed on the horizon.

The structure is made of reinforced concrete, while the façade's cladding is glass-reinforced concrete. There are five floors of luxury residential apartments with panoramic views of Cairo's horizon located on the uppermost levels of the South Tower. The apartments are totally independent from the business and commercial complex and have their own entrances and elevators.

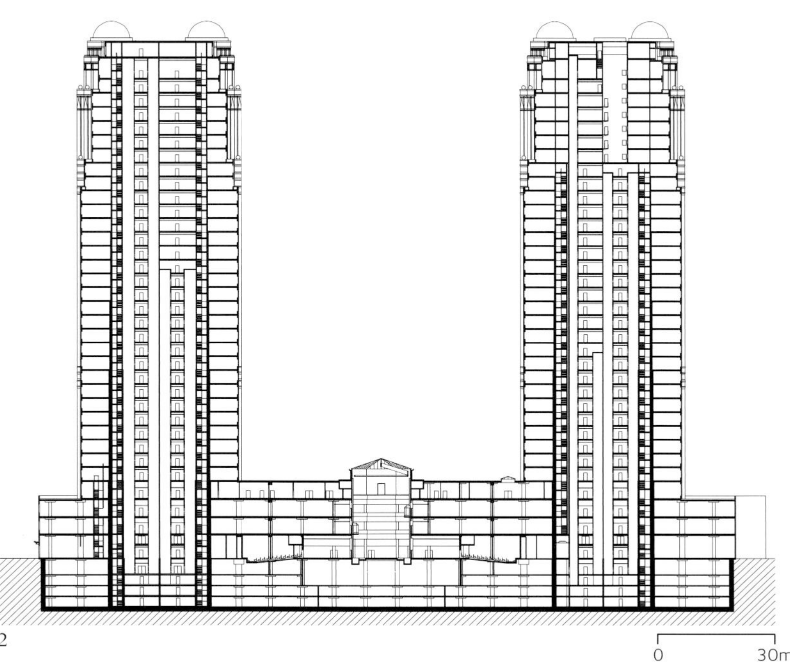

2

0   30m

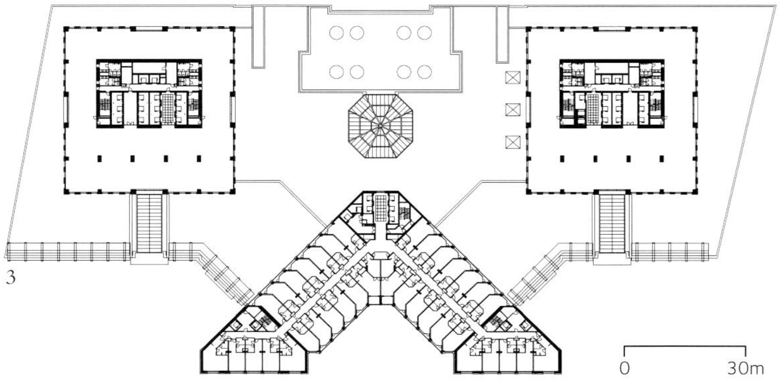

3

0   30m

4

The central podium, topped by a skylight, rises from the ground level to the third floor and joins the towers. Upon entering, guests are greeted by bright, naturally lit, spacious atria in the middle of which emanate decorative fountains. From the Nile Corniche, the Nile City Mall is accessible through two entrances at street level, one at each end of the pedestrian gallery. A third entrance is incorporated in the north façade of the podium. In front of the Nile Corniche entrance there are two vehicle drop-off areas. In addition to shops and restaurants, the mall includes eight movie theatres, and movement inside the podium is provided by two glass-enclosed elevators and two pairs of escalators.

6

7

4   *Shopping mall, glass-enclosed elevator*
5   *Shopping mall*
6   *Office tower, mezzanine*
7   *Office tower, entrance lobby*
8   *Office tower, main entrance*
Following pages:
9   *Shopping mall entrance, detail*
10   *Detail of the top of the tower*

5

8

1   *General view from the main boulevard, digital rendering*

Green Square
Brussels, Belgium

Client: VIZZION Invest
Above ground area: 30,676 square metres
Completion: 2011

Green Square is a major project that initiates and symbolises on a grand scale the environmental approach of VIZZION Architects for sustainable urban living. The aim of the Green Square serviced apartments and residences project is to create a multi-use ensemble taking advantage of the latest energy-conscious and environmentally friendly techniques, not only for the construction itself, but also for the long-term life of the building and even for its potential demolition.

Located at a major crossroads along the Brussels inner ring road, Green Square serviced apartments and residences enjoy a high level of visibility and will stand as an urban landmark. The project comprises two main units. The serviced apartments face the main boulevard while the residences are located at the back, facing both the side streets and the large, inner, landscaped garden. The two sections are separated by a newly built landscaped street, while a new retail complex and one of the housing buildings will conceal the blank wall of a neighbouring supermarket. This multi-use concept integrates several building types in an overall environment that is itself home to a variety of activities.

Incorporated into the site, the listed 51.62-metre-long Glacière building – an old ice factory – is one of very few such monuments in Brussels to be preserved in its original state, following the renovations undertaken by the neighbouring VUB University.

Located not far from a major subway station, this derelict block, which was left vacant for years, will soon accommodate a mixed-use ensemble of where all elements will be built in a single phase. The architectural language allegorically refers to nature, using smooth curves and evocative shades of colours. Specific attention has been paid to the global concept

2

of greenery: green façades, a private interior garden, green roofs and large amounts of vegetation around the buildings.

VIZZION's High Environmental Value approach to the Green Square project is demonstrated through expressive urban language and forms inspired from nature. The building provides high performance levels in areas such as thermic, acoustic and visual comfort, and energy and water management. Wind turbines on the roof further contribute to the HEV approach for this project. Through this mixed-use development, VIZZION Architects displays its commitment to the development of sustainable urban architecture.

2 Rear building elevation seen from the garden
3 Typical floor plan
4 Section plan
5 Rear building with the semi-private street,
  digital rendering
Following pages:
  Front façade detail at sunset, digital rendering

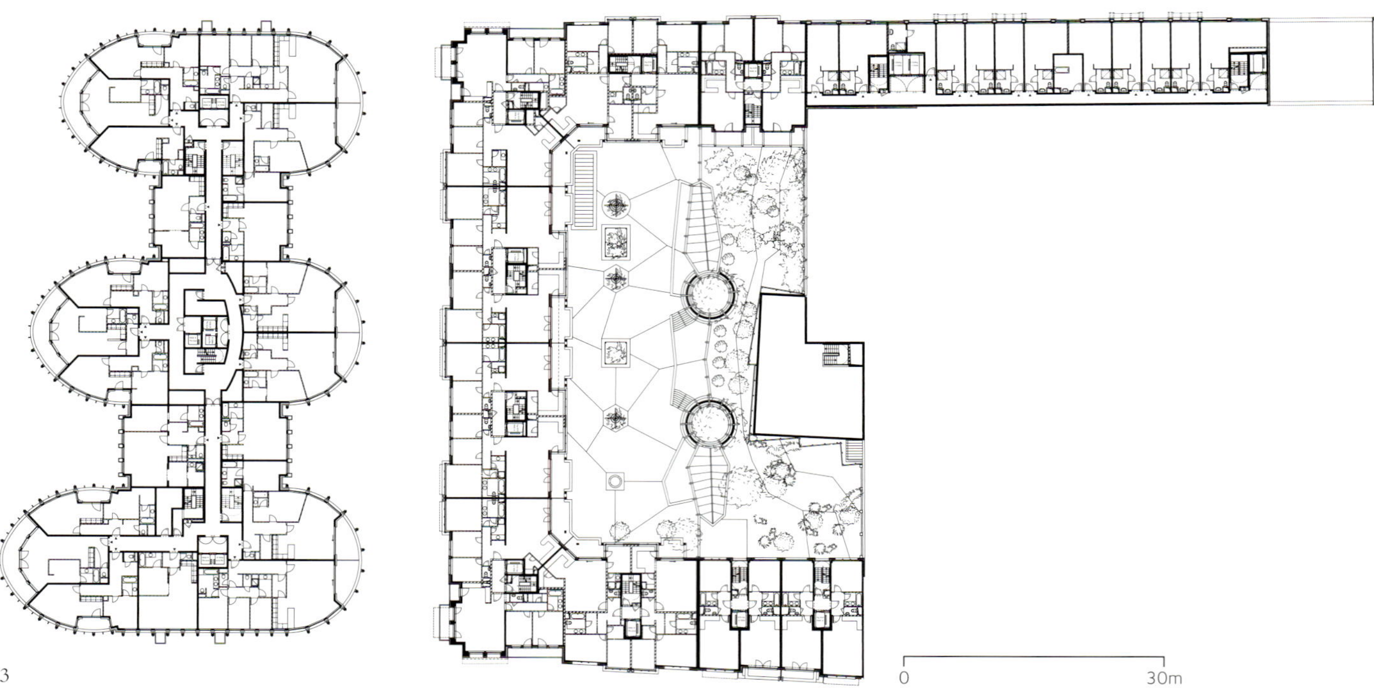

3

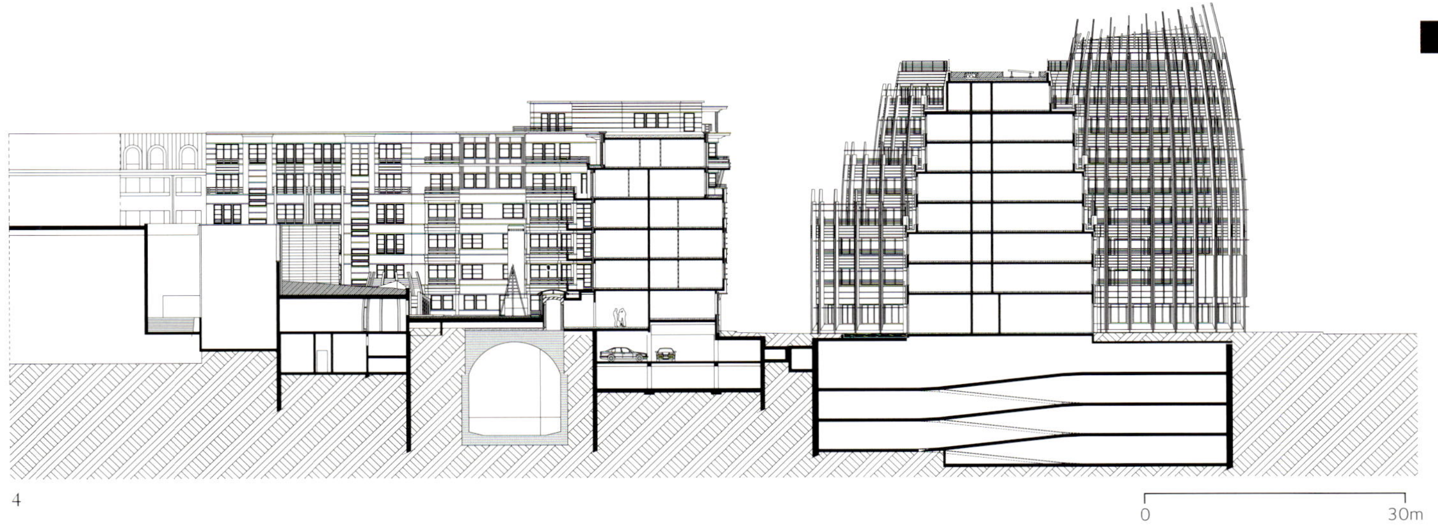

4

5

Studies and projects under progress

1

2

Hoek van Holland
Hoek van Holland, The Netherlands

Client: BAM Vastgoed
Use: Housing
Above ground area: 25,166 square metres
Competition study: 2003

Located to the west Rotterdam, of which Hoek van Holland is a part, the project location faces the North Sea and is surrounded by the beauty of a dune-filled natural landscape. With its clear façades and the streamlined detailing of both the large, horizontal building units and the curved, pyramidal, 11-storey tower, it is evident that inspiration was taken from the forms of the nearby large cruising boats. There are sharp contrasts between the different building shapes, but at the same time the strong and unified architecture style creates a peaceful and relaxing ambiance suitable for a seaside resort, located not too far from a busy city centre.

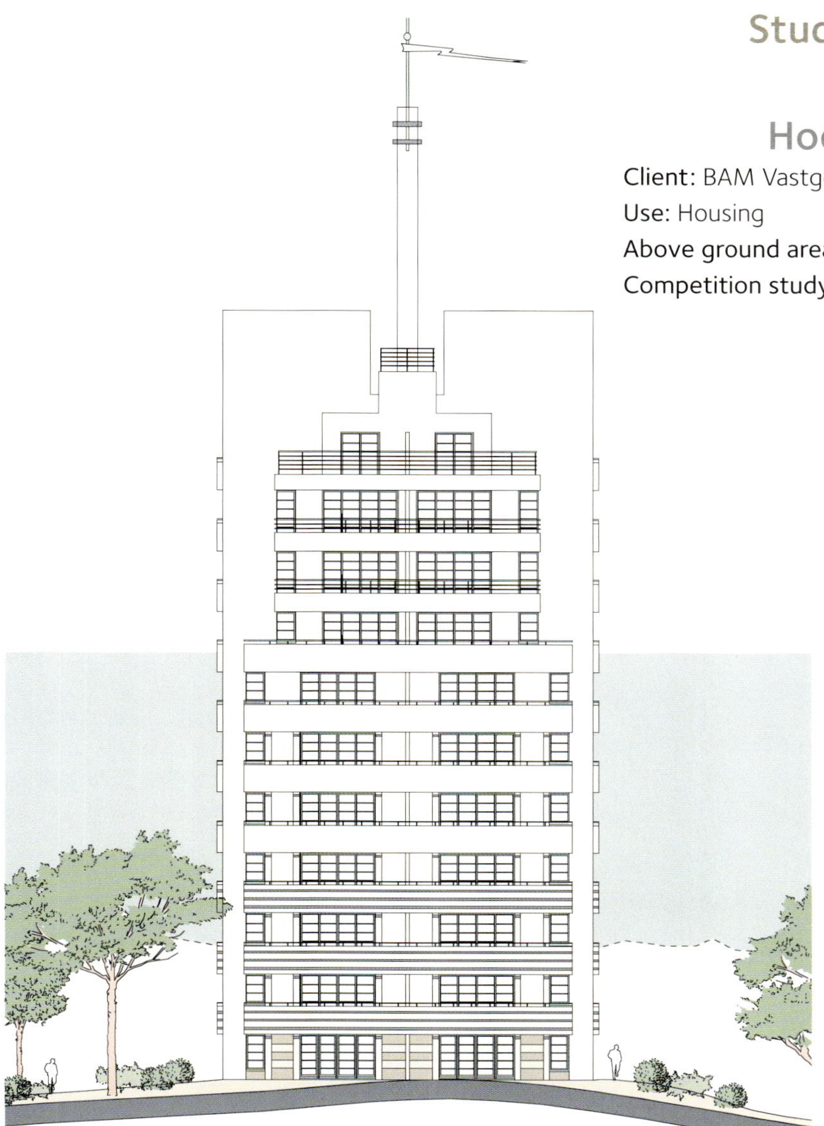

3

Studies and projects under progress
Heron Plaza
Brussels, Belgium

Client: Heron Group
Use: Mixed-use ensemble
Above ground area: 38,865 square metres
Study: 2001–2006

Located at the edge of a residential zone, the area was once one of the most fashionable shopping districts in Brussels; over the years, the high-end shops relocated on the other side of the boulevard. Heron Plaza has been designed to recreate a coherent, mixed-use urban ensemble for the once-lively area. The building's stone façade is designed to contribute a timeless character, which in turn produces a similar sense of grandeur found in the Haussmann buildings in Paris.

In the building facing the main boulevard, retail shops are found on three levels (ground level, first floor and basement) and a luxury hotel occupies the upper levels. A newly designed street created at the back of the hotel allows easy vehicular access to the hotel, and a new residential building is situated on the other side of this new street. The housing project is complemented by a suspended garden and some existing housing are marked for renovation. Suspended gardens are to be implemented on the first level of the hotel for the visual enjoyment of both the hotel guests and the residents of the housing projects.

The whole block is to be opened through the creation of the new open-air passage, which is a rare phenomenon in the city, and the new street will allow the residents of the housing ensemble to walk out of their housing quarter via a quiet street while they are actually 50 metres away from a major busy city boulevard. In total, Heron Plaza comprises a new hotel, 50 new and 11 renovated apartments, retail shops, a life and fitness centre and an underground garage. The present study is two-fold: one includes a major international hotel located in the front building, while the other one includes apartments instead of the hotel.

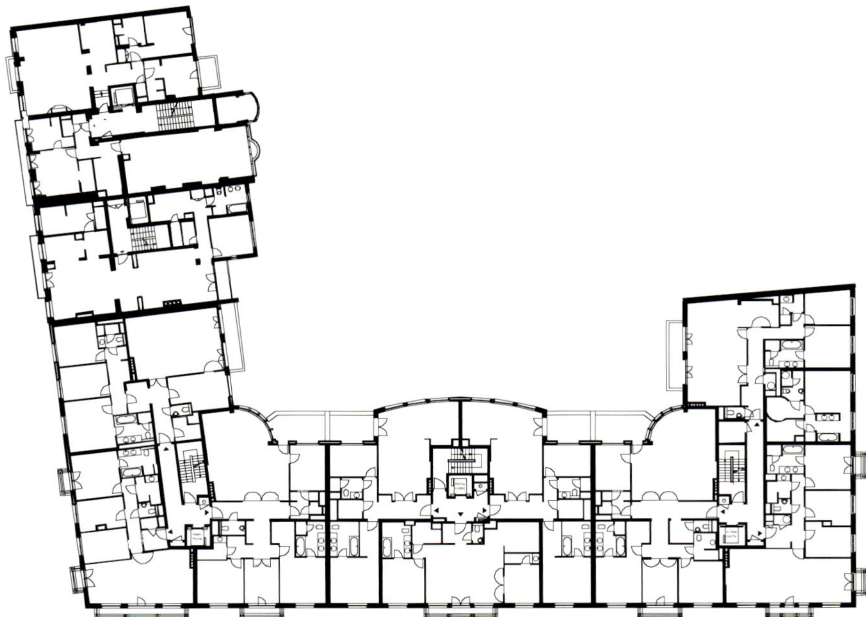

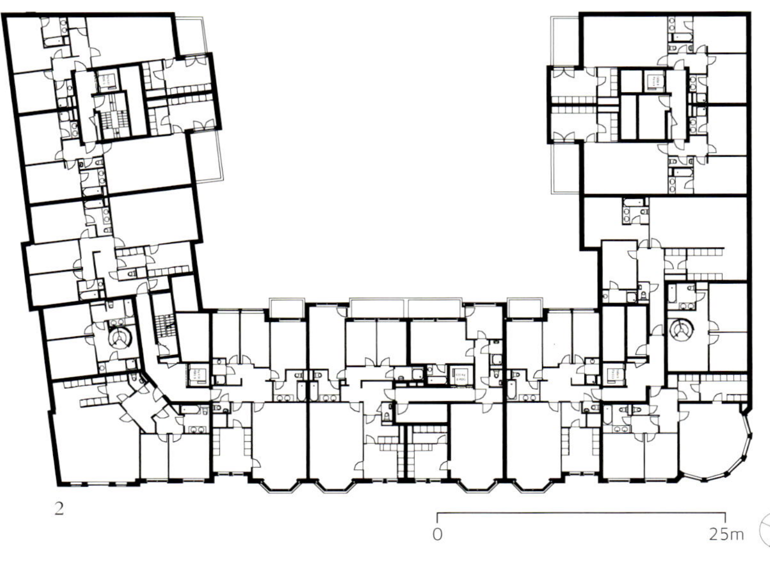

2

0   25m

3

4

3   General view at night, digital rendering
4   Side elevation
5   Main elevation

5

0   25m

Crédit Mutuel du Nord and shopping arcade
Brussels, Belgium

Client: BKCP Crédit Professionnel
Client's representative: Nexity
Uses: Office and retail
Above ground area: 8556 square metres
Study: 2000–2005

The Crédit Mutuel du Nord project is located in Brussels's most exclusive area, which features Chanel, Louis Vuitton and Versace retail stores as well as the Hilton Brussels hotel. The project is aimed at studying the renovation and transformation of a Brutalist office building originally built in 1961, which was inserted in between typical Brussels townhouses. The proposed renovation aimed to realign the recessed 1960s building along the street's historic alignment to create an open and inviting ground-level retail arcade. The proposed development connects the structure to adjoining arcades, and the building façades were designed to create the effect of a majestic Parisian-style building reinterpreted in a contemporary way.

While the building's volume was to be reduced in keeping with the height of the adjoining townhouses, the bow windows and the rhythm of the newly designed main façade was to bring back character to the derelict area on this part of this major boulevard. A similar approach has also been carried out by VIZZION Architects for the Heron Plaza project, located on the opposite side of the boulevard.

2

3

4

Opposite   Elevation detail study, digital rendering
2   Existing 1961 building
3   Street elevation showing the 1961 existing building with its bulky volume
4   Elevation showing the proposed project with lower volume blending in with the next-door townhouses

Parfumerie

SHOPS

SHOPS

LA LIBRAIRIE

LAURENT FASHION

star fashion

Au fil de l'Eau
Verviers, Belgium

Client: Foruminvest
Use: Shopping mall
Above ground area: 51,589 square metres
Completion: 2011

Located in Verviers, in the south of Belgium, the Au fil de l'Eau project is designed to cater to both Belgian and German customers. The project aims at creating a link between the two banks of the Vesdre River, which runs through the City of Verviers, a city of about 90,000 inhabitants.

The project features 113 mid- to large-size retail units spread over three aboveground levels, while the three basement levels accommodate 1412 parking spaces. The mall has three main accesses: via Place du Martyr, Rue du Brou and Rue Spintay. Au fil de l'Eau evolves around a vast central atrium conceived as a window over the river.

The project creates a link between two neighbourhoods in the form of a 'bridge' connecting the two banks of the city. By building this bridge, the project acts as a regeneration catalyst, yet preserves almost all of the existing and derelict on-site urban fabric. The project also contributes to the rejuvenation of the Rue Spintay, one of the city's main commercial roads, and the typical regional architecture of the buildings found along this busy street. The Au fil de l'Eau project also includes 10,000 square metres of housing developments.

Opposite   *Main entrance, digital rendering (top);*
Atrium, digital rendering (bottom)
2   *Master plan, model view*

2

1&2   General views at night, renderings

Anka Hill
Ankara, Turkey

Client: VIZZION Europe
Use: Mixed-use ensemble
Gross building area: 652,936 square metres
Study: 2006

Anka Hill is a vast mixed-use ensemble located in Ankara, Turkey. Situated on a 14-hectare site, a podium will accommodate a three-level shopping mall complemented by an entertainment and health centre on one side and a congress centre and multi-purpose convention hall on the other.

Rising above the multi-level podium, two high-rise buildings reaching 150 metres and 230 metres will feature housing and a hotel with unmatched views over the city. At the other end of the site, two buildings will provide housing for the municipality. The twin curved buildings are designed to rise gradually at opposite ends up to a height of 133 metres, in such a way as to not block each other's views and at the same time to increase the architectural drama. From the base up to the tip of the towers, the design is reminiscent of the famous Cappaddoce's landscapes.

1

2

Kayseri
Kayseri, Turkey

Client: VIZZION Europe
Use: Mixed-use ensemble
Above ground area: 150,600 square metres
Study: 2007

The Kayseri project involved studying the transformation of the Kayseri stadium into a meeting point for social interaction. The site brings together a shopping and leisure mall, a luxury hotel and two residential buildings.

The shopping mall occupies six levels. A supermarket and large retail spaces are located on the basement level, while the shops are located from the ground floor level to second-floor levels. The two upper floors are dedicated to leisure activities, movie theatres and food courts. From the upper level, visitors have access to the rooftop gardens.

The 250-room, 82-metre hotel comprises an array of bars and restaurants, a wellness centre and a congress centre allowing the organisation of seminars, shows and private events. The housing units, located within two residential buildings covering a total of 30,000 square metres, include high-end apartments, some of which have access to hotel services. Five thousand underground parking spaces are provided for the new facilities: 4500 for the shopping mall and 500 for the hotel and residences.

Kayseri is nestled in a landscaped park and all parks and gardens will be open to the general public. Together, the master plan and the overall architectural concept aim at creating a new social centre for the city. The buildings' aesthetics represents a lyrical interpretation of the traditional Selcukide architecture, combined with the fantastic forms of the Cappaddoce landscape. The visual force of this project and the quality of the proposed facilities are meant to give rise to a central landmark, testament to the dynamism of the city's contemporary development.

*1&2 General views,
       digital renderings*
3 Master plan

1

1 *Master plan*
2 *Aerial view, rendering*

2

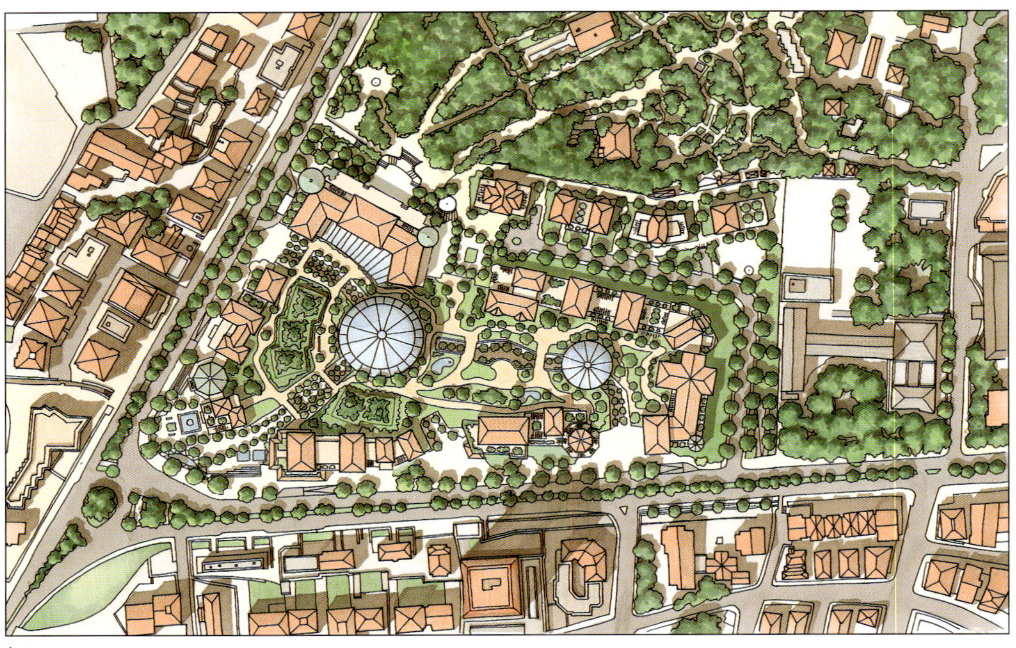

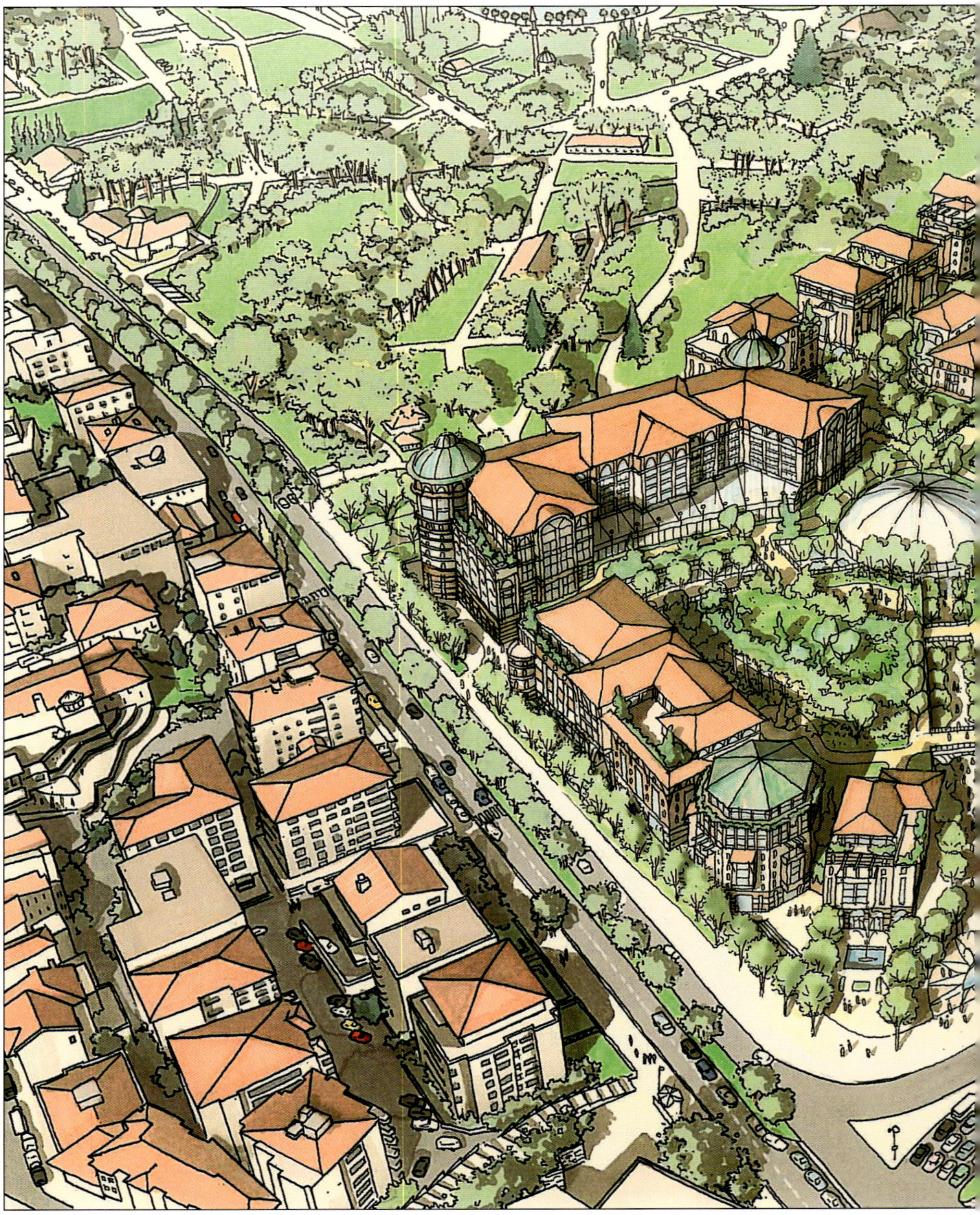

Bursa shopping mall
Bursa, Turkey

Client: VIZZION Europe
Use: Mixed-use ensemble
Above ground building area:
172,997 square metres
Study: 2007

The Bursa shopping mall project is located on the site of the Bursa stadium and is intended to become a genuine urban district of its own. The Bursa stadium is to be demolished and rebuilt at the periphery of the city. The project includes all the functions usually found in a city and ensures a suitable connection between the existing urban fabric and the park. The 137,828-square-metre shopping mall is the project's main function, while surrounding buildings will provide for 51,482 square metres of housing, 14,644 square metres of office space, a 15,150-square-metre hotel, and retail options.

The prevailing size and character of the buildings located along the boulevard are inspired from Bursa's traditional architecture. The architecture of the mall itself is designed to be innovative and is a lyrical interpretation of Ottoman architecture. The hotel and residential building units act as a volumetric and functional transition between the mall and the park. The public square located at the boulevard's crossroads is designed as a plaza and grants access to the mall's main entrance.

Eventually, Bursa shopping mall will become a catalyst for the future development of Bursa. The new Bursa sport centre to be rebuilt at the periphery of the city will feature a 35,000-seat football and athletics stadium, a 2,000-seat secondary football field and a 7000-seat sports hall for sports such as mini-foot, basketball and tennis.

1   Aerial view, rendering study

1

Şancity
Istanbul, Turkey

Client: VIZZION Europe
Use: Mixed-use ensemble
Gross building area: 162,079 square metres
Study: 2007

Located in the Taksim area, the heart of Istanbul, Şancity is a new shopping mall oriented towards leisure and culture. It is being developed on the site of the famous San Theatre, which burned down three decades ago. The current site includes an open-air parking lot that will be demolished to allow Şancity to transform the vast block into a prominent urban development. Şancity architecture is largely inspired by Ottoman aesthetics, revised by the Art Deco style from the early 20th century.

Şancity evolves along a main curved axis and is articulated around two ovoid-shaped five- and eight-storey-high atriums that form the main focal points and open towards a large, landscaped area comprising gardens and terraces. Natural light enters via three glass skylights. Erected on a 14,760-square-metre area, Şancity will comprise a 58,384-square-metre shopping mall, a 6978-square-metre theatre, cultural and conference centre, 10,623 square metres of office space and a 3016-square-metre retirement home. The theatre is located at the highest point of the project and contributes to the project's status as one of the Dolap Dere district's most important urban landmarks.

In using material such as glass and integrating vegetation within the lyrical architecture of Şancity, the architect demonstrates commitment to implementing High Environmental Value features throughout the project. This new concept of a shopping environment has been designed to become the prime location for the future of the Taksim area.

1

Istanbul seaside
North of Istanbul, Turkey

Client: VIZZION Europe
Use: New city
Gross building area:
   4,001,109 square metres
Study: 2007

The Istanbul seaside project is a new city encompassing all the typical urban functions such as housing and retail developments, office buildings, hotels, sports and education facilities, cultural and administrative centres, hospitals and wellness services and a large congress centre.

The city is to be built along the banks of the Black Sea on a vast 1320-hectare site, creating a harmonious urban ensemble which will stand in contrast to the chaotic development of Istanbul. The project favours functions such as housing, retail and services taking advantage of the exceptional natural settings ideal for leisure activities.

A business-oriented unit will be part of the development through the construction of a large convention and congress centre as well as a new university. The multi-function city is self-contained and social and business functions are designed according to a harmonious urban continuum. In accordance to its development credo, VIZZION Europe is designing the new city according to the latest High Environmental Value standards.

1   Master plan

1

2

1   *Master plan*
2   *General view, digital rendering*
3   *Marina, digital rendering*
4   *381-metre tower at sunset, digital rendering*

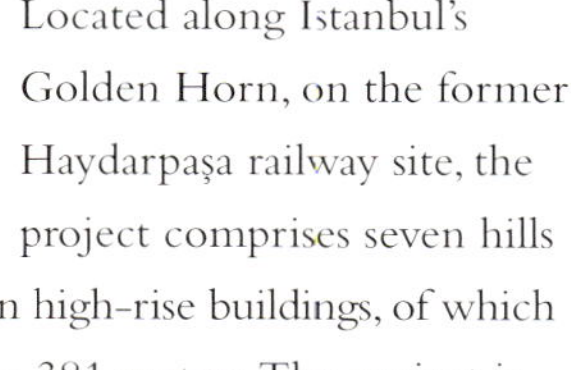

Studies and projects under progress
Istanbul 'da Haydarpaşa
Istanbul, Turkey

Client: Çalık Holding A.Ş.
Use: Mixed–use ensemble
Gross building area:
   2,218,664 square metres
Study: 2005

Located along Istanbul's Golden Horn, on the former Haydarpaşa railway site, the project comprises seven hills crowned by seven high-rise buildings, of which the tallest reaches 381 metres. The project is nestled in a landscaped urban environment recreated according to typical, local seacoast districts. The seven 39- to 74-storey-tall buildings, with their slender, organic shape and multiple detachments, are intended to become a metaphor recalling Istanbul's cypress silhouette. The use of oxidized green copper will reinforce the organic expression of the steel-structured towers.

The programming will ensure coherence between the various functions such as residential accommodation (583,000 square metres), hospitality projects (149,000 square metres), hospitals and housing for seniors (35,000 square metres), offices (280,000 square metres), together with retail shops (197,000 square metres), malls (196,000 square metres) and other functions such as fairs (134,000 square metres), convention centres (99,000 square metres), sports facilities (14,500 square metres), yacht clubs (9000 square metres), museums (6000 square metres), themed parks and other socio-cultural activities including theatres and cinemas.

An important aspect of the project is to take into account the ramifications for traffic in terms of extending both the existing road network and public transport system. The larger facilities developed on the site are concealed and integrated into the landscape in a qualitative manner through the use of the seven man-made hills laid out as landscaped parks. Smaller buildings, housing a rich array of diverse activities, will be located on the peripheral roads. The Istanbul 'da Haydarpaşa project, together with the development of the surrounding districts, aims at creating a new hub for Istanbul as well as a major landmark along the Bosphorus.

4

3

1

Istanbul – Levent IV
Istanbul, Turkey

Client: VIZZION Europe
Use: Office
Above ground area: 24,617 to 39,388
  square metres
Study: 2007

Over the years, the Levent area has become the most sought-after business districts of Istanbul.

Strategically located at the crossroads of major subway and bus lines, and nearby to freeways, Istanbul – Levent is intended to become a major high-rise landmark in Levent area, which is the location for several existing high-rise office towers.

The pure and dynamic elliptical forms of Istanbul – Levent will allow the project to be the focal point of a series of vistas and perspectives converging at the project's site. The building's double skin, in conjunction with its energy-efficient values, will allow the creation of a vertical garden integrated within the façade skin.

In addition to the office tower, the base of the building will feature one level devoted to a state-of-the art congress centre, while three levels will accommodate a themed shopping mall, enriching the variety of retail shops already available in the area.

Depending of the floor area ratio (FAR) implemented, the project's above ground area would comprise 24,617 square metres (FAR: 2.5), 29,541 square metres (FAR: 3) or 39,388 square metres (FAR: 4).

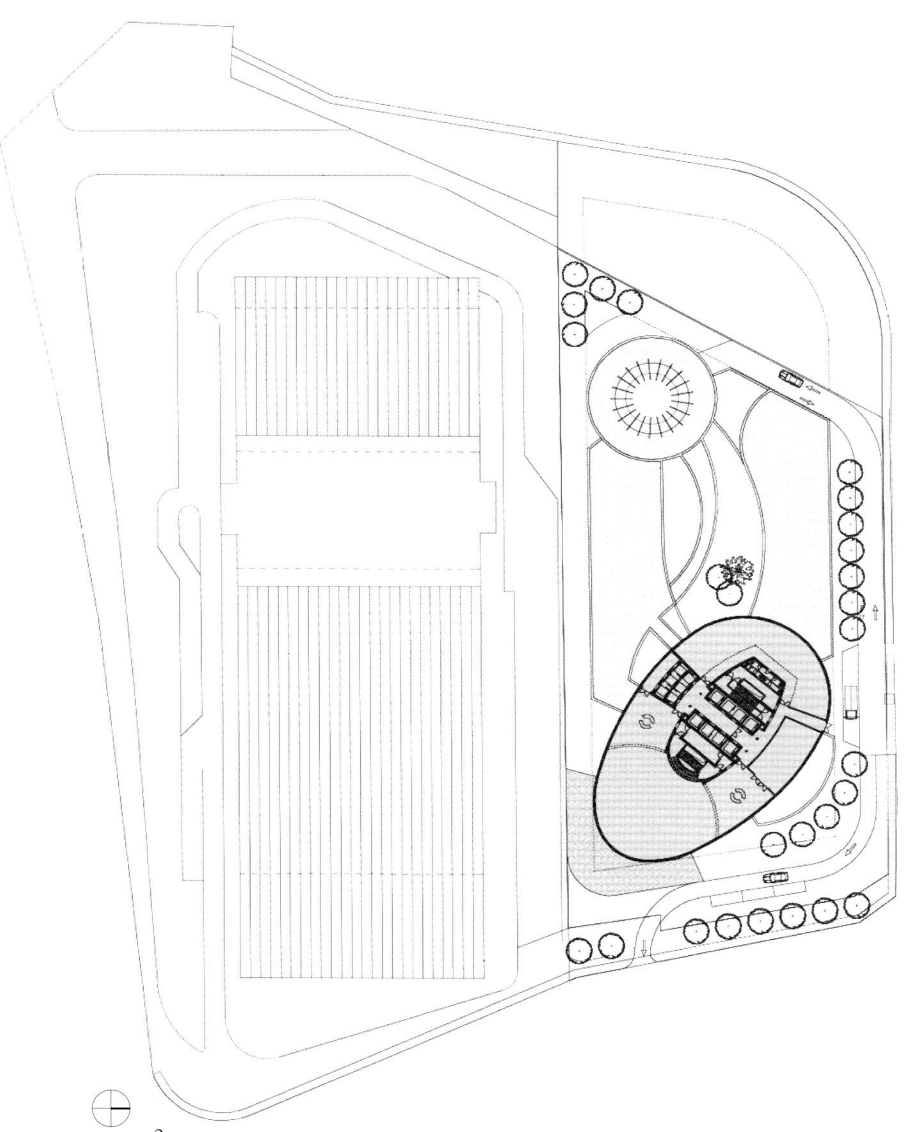

2

1 *General view at night, rendering*

Oyak Towers
Istanbul, Turkey

Client: VIZZION Europe
Use: Office
Above ground area: 29,400 to 49,000
     square metres
Study: 2007

Oyak Towers are located along the European shore of Istanbul in Levent, a booming business district. The Büyükdere Avenue development is characterised by the construction of a series of tall office buildings. Major financial companies have decided to establish their headquarters in this area, and the area also benefits from exceptional transportation facilities and plentiful retail and entertainment venues. Büyükdere Avenue is directly linked to Istanbul's highway network, which includes the TEM and E5 highways. The site is also served by an underground subway station (Taksim/4 Levent) and is located near two major shopping malls, Metrocity and Kanyon.

On the 9800-square-metre site, two projects are being studied; depending of the floor area ratio (FAR) implemented, the project's above ground area would be 29,400 square metres (FAR: 3) or 49,000 square metres (FAR: 5). Taking into account that above ground built areas are not limited in height, the scheme allows the design of a high-rise building with a height of between 16 and 37 storeys. Oyak Towers are designed to comprise office, congress and fitness centres as well as a department store above a 400- to 600-space underground garage space.

Altunizade
Istanbul, Turkey

Client: VIZZION Europe
Use: Mixed-use ensemble
Gross building area:
280,309 square metres
Study: 2007

Altunizade is a mixed-use project located in the Altunizade area – administratively part of Uskudar – on the Asian side of Istanbul, facing the historic peninsula near the Bosphorus.

The project includes five 21- to 30-storey residential towers to be erected on a four-level commercial podium and a five-level underground garage. The residences take advantage of their own fitness centre, spa and swimming pool as well as their own restaurant and cafés. The residents will enjoy these services surrounded by a rooftop garden with an open-air swimming pool.

2

1   *Aerial view, rendering study*
2   *Master plan*

Resneli Niyazi Bey
Istanbul, Turkey

Client: VIZZION Europe
Use: Mixed–use ensemble
Gross building area: 40,531 square metres
Study: 2007

Located on the European side of Istanbul, Resneli Niyazi Bey is a project situated on a 4,200-square-metre site currently occupied by a college of the same name.

The mixed-use project aims at building a new 4-storey college equipped with housing units for the teachers in exchange for the right to build a mixed-use ensemble comprising 2503 square metres of retail shops and a 13,200-square-metre residential tower featuring 88 apartments on the same location. The 22-storey-tall building is surrounded by a generous 1000-square-metre landscaped garden.

Opposite   Aerial view, rendering study
2   Master plan

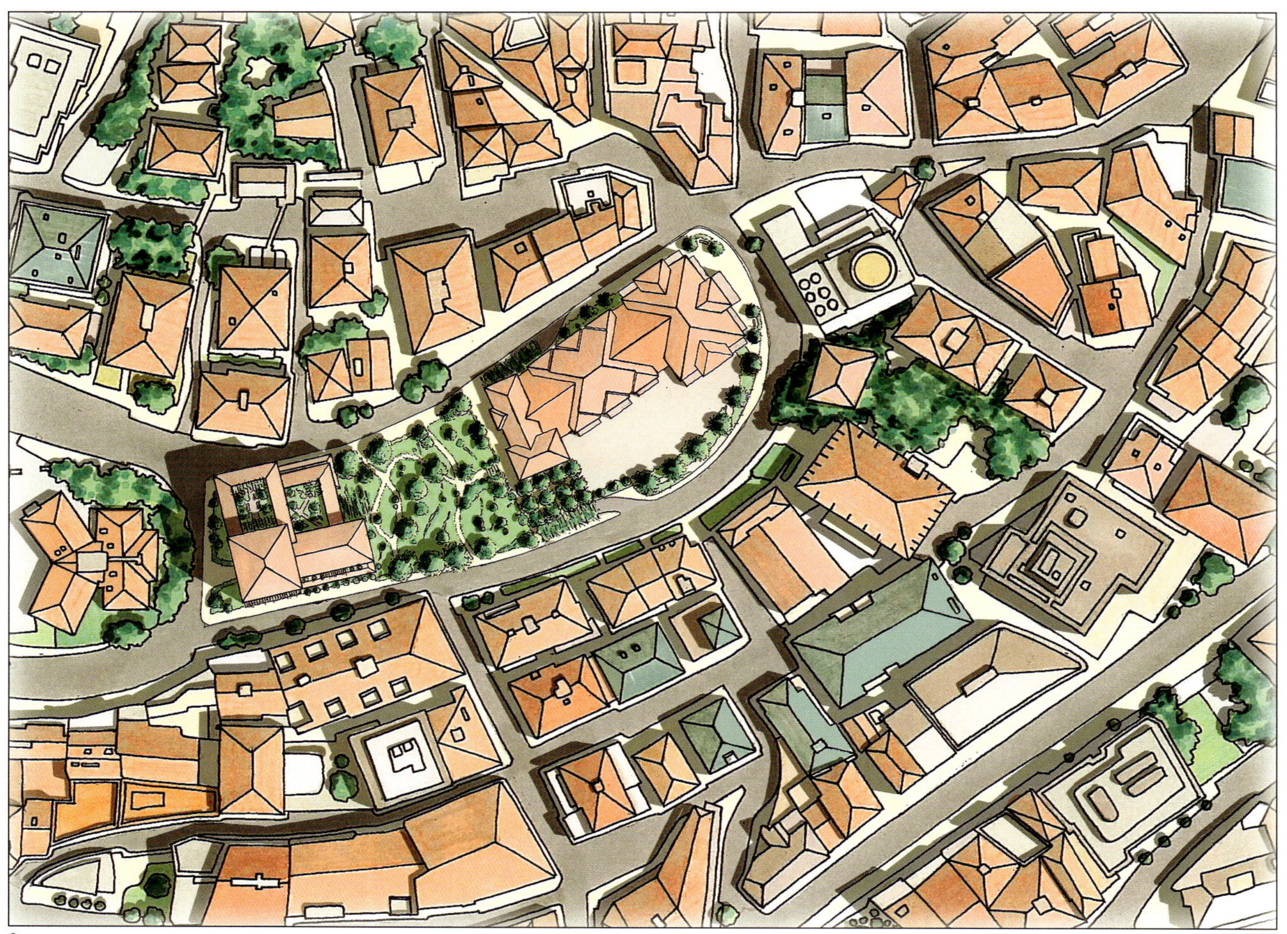

2

West Bay Tower
Doha, Qatar

Client: VIZZION Europe
Use: Mixed-use tower
Above ground area: 58,154 square metres
Study: 2008

The 310-metre West Bay Tower is conceived as a timeless landmark for Doha's diplomatic district. The tower architecture is made up of clearly defined volumes and light-catching bold relief. The project is a contemporary reinterpretation of Art Deco architectural components and lyrically integrates features of traditional Arabic architecture. The slender 58-storey tower will be surmounted by a four-level mechanical penthouse, which together with a series of spires will create a distinctive giant arrow on the Doha skyline reminiscent of the great skyscrapers of New York.

West Bay Tower is a truly mixed-use ensemble integrating retail units, a 274-room hotel equipped with bars, lounges, restaurants, and a conference centre in the lower zone, 112 high-end apartments in the middle zone and 15,599 square metres of luxury office suites in the upper zone.

All occupants will have their own individual entrance lobby centrally located on each side of the tower, while the ground-level corners will be used as retail spaces. This layout allows for each occupant to feel as if they are the building's main occupant, while a series of transfer levels provides ease of interaction between people and businesses.

Hotel services and amenities will be available to both residents and occupants of the office suites, thus creating a sense of community throughout the West Bay Tower. All 627 parking spaces are located in the seven basements, allowing for the creation of a landscaped park covering about 40 percent of the site.

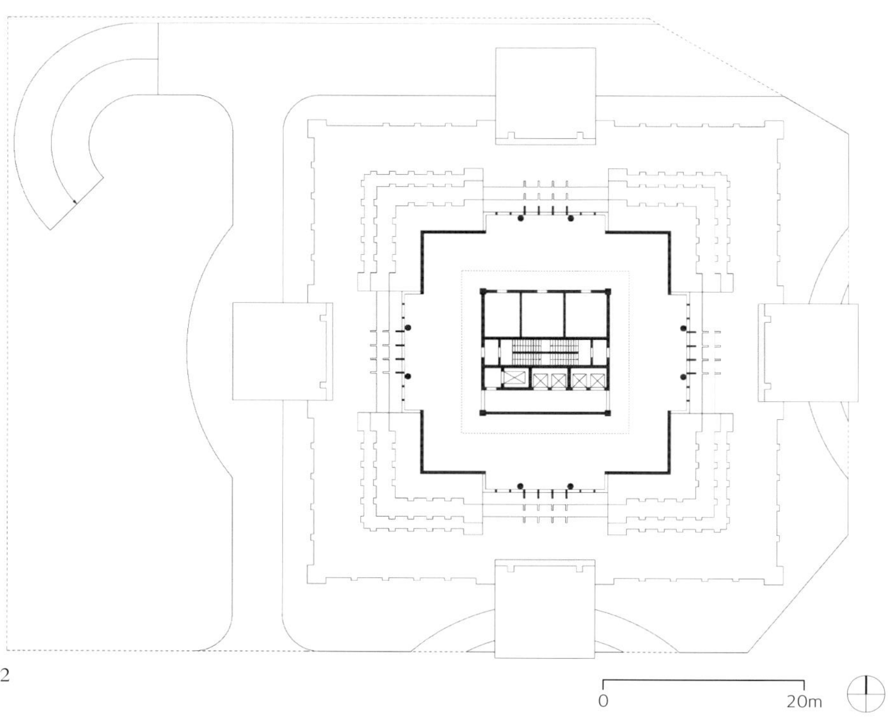

2

Opposite   Upper level detail at night, rendering
2   Typical office floor plan, levels 36 to 43

TRANSFER LEVEL
TRANSFER LEVEL
TRANSFER LEVEL
TRANSFER LEVEL
MAIN LOBBY

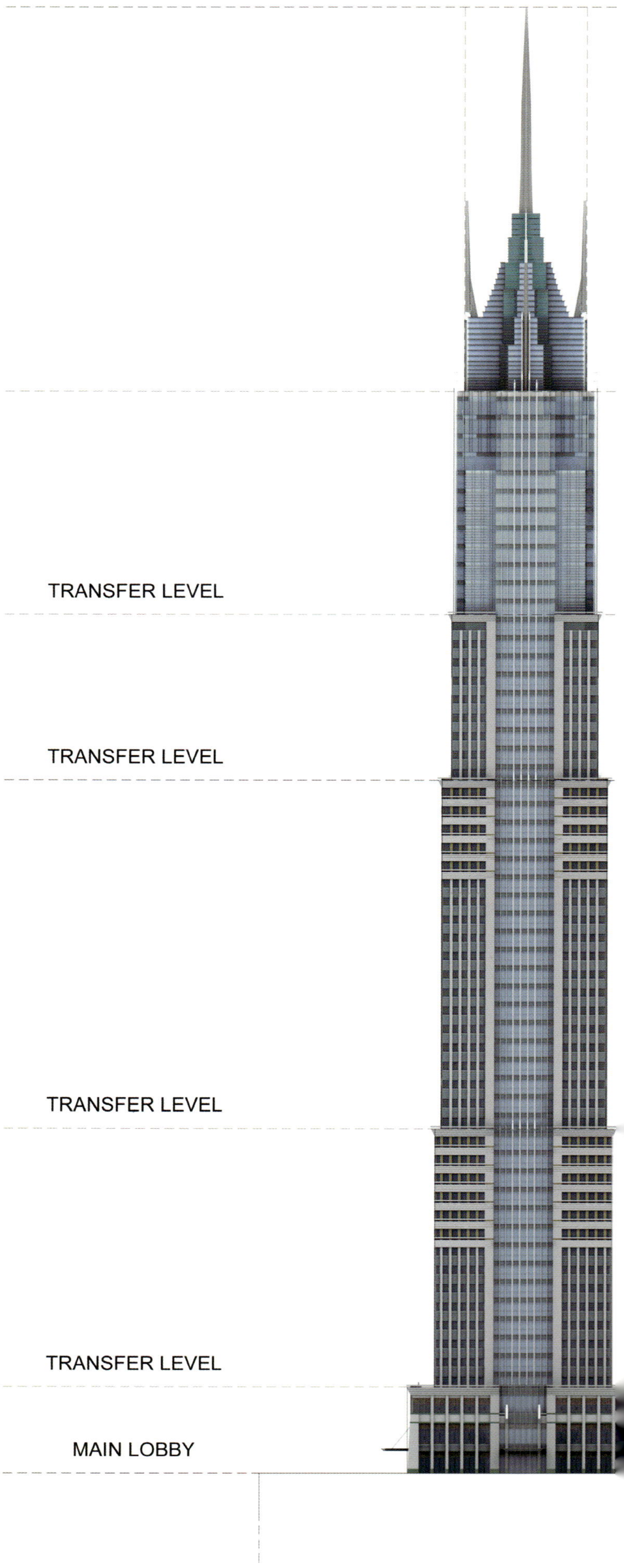

3

0 METRES
MECHANICAL
0 METRES
OFFICE
6 METRES
0 METRES
APARTMENTS
HOTEL
METRES
METRE
PARKING
4
5

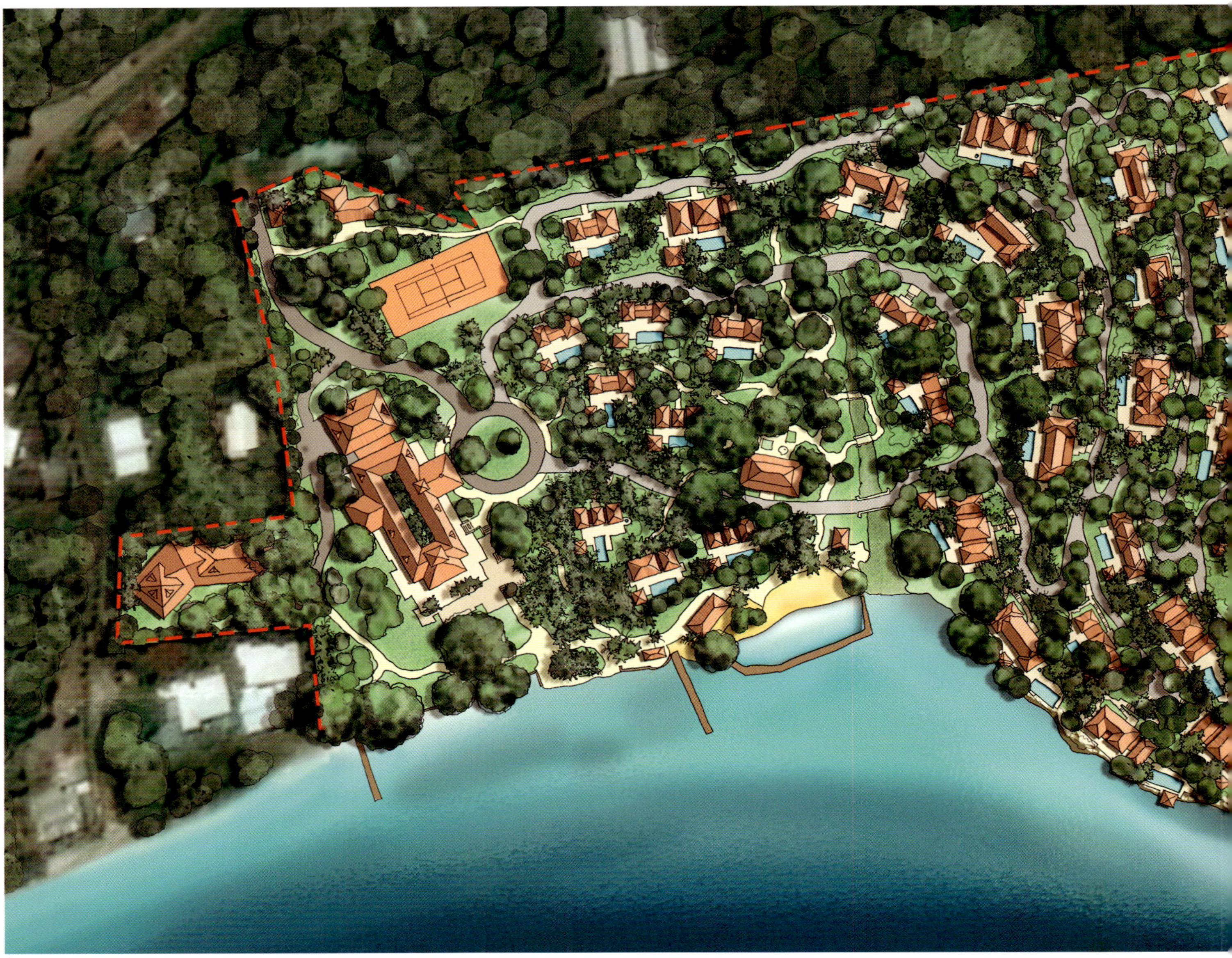

1

2

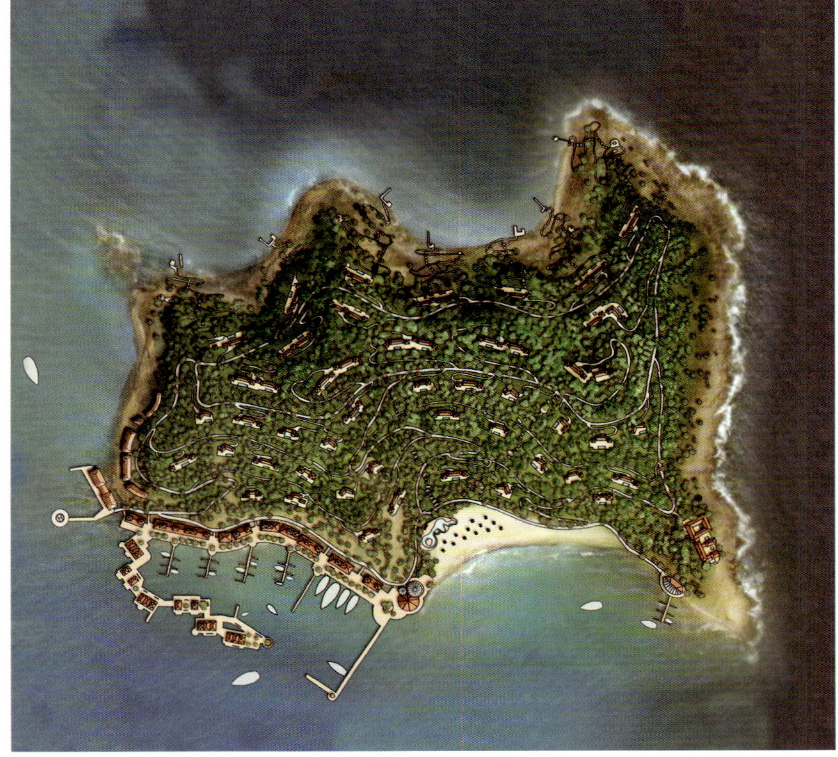

1 *Bequia, master plan*
2 *Petit Mustique, master plan*
3 *Eden Resort, master plan*

Selected master plans

Bequia
Location: Bequia, St. Vincent and the Grenadines
Client: VIZZION Europe
Use: Resort
Above ground area: 8839 square metres
Study: 2007

Petit Mustique
Location: Petit Mustique, St. Vincent and the Grenadines
Client: VIZZION Europe
Use: Resort
Above ground area: 39,469 square metres
Study: 2007

Eden Resort
Location: Police Bay, Seychelles
Client: IRET (The Robelco Group)
Use: Resort
Above ground area: 27,000 square metres
Study: 2006

As a conclusion to the current chapter that presents a variety of building types showing the expertise of the firm in designing small- or large-scale projects, sometimes encompassing several million square metres of built areas, such as in the case of the Istanbul seaside project in Turkey, this double-page focuses on more remote locations such as St. Vincent, the Grenadines and the Seychelles. These examples demonstrate VIZZION Architect's interest in designing projects that blend with their natural surroundings in a similar manner to those projects designed during the past three decades that integrate seamlessly into urban environments.

Şefik Birkiye

Şefik Birkiye was born in 1954 in Ankara, Turkey, and after a well-travelled youth (his father worked for NATO), he went on to graduate from La Cambre School of Architecture (ENSAAV) in Brussels in 1978 and took his Masters in Town Planning from the Catholic University of Louvain (UCL) in 1981.

In the beginning

It was in 1979 that Şefik Birkiye founded VIZZION Architects, previously known as Atelier d'Art Urbain, a firm of architects and urban planners fully committed to the improvement of the urban environment.

He was later joined by his partners, Dominique Delbrouck, Christian Sibilde and Grégoire de Jerphanion. Together with his 100-strong team, Şefik Birkiye has built a worldwide reputation for excellence.

In 2006, Şefik Birkiye split from his partners, eager to give a new impetus and direction to his company. This move allowed him to directly manage the entire development process of his projects.

Since the firm's establishment, Şefik Birkiye has personally contributed to the design of each project. He believes that every building has its own cultural identity inspired by its location and the history of its surroundings. His creative approach takes into account elements of the past and today's expectations.

How it developed

The first projects of VIZZION Architects were located primarily in Brussels and have contributed in a positive way to change the urban landscape. VIZZION Architects has taken part in major urban redevelopment projects such as the revitalisation of the formerly industrial district bordering the Brussels canal and the renovation of City 2, the largest shopping mall in central Brussels.

VIZZION Architects has also built and renovated corporate headquarters for financial institutions such as the KBC, Dexia and Fortis banks as well as Zurich Insurance and Swiss Life Insurance.

The growing international reputation of Şefik Birkiye has led to commissions in France, Luxembourg, The Netherlands, Turkey, Egypt and the Virgin Islands. A track record of more than eight million square meters already built or projected has helped VIZZION Architects to become one of the leading architectural firms in Europe.

In 1998 and again in 2000, VIZZION Architects won the prestigious MIPIM Award for Le Jardin des Fonderies apartment

building and the Green Island office complex. More recently, the Monte-Carlo Bay Hotel & Resort, the only five-star resort in Monaco, was nominated for a MIPIM Award.

What the future holds

In 1997, Şefik Birkiye founded VIZZION Europe in order to create a more global approach to architecture and to extend his direct involvement in the development stage of any given project. The objective of the group is to develop High Environmental Value in mixed-use projects, to ensure competitive prices and the highest possible standards. The firm has worked out an innovative system of administration and financing; described as vertical integration, it is responsible for every phase of the project, from the search and selection of the ideal building site through to any eventual sale. It thus offers complete assurance that, from start to finish, no detail will be overlooked.

As registered architect in Belgium, Luxembourg, France from time to time and Turkey, Şefik Birkiye has lectured widely on various aspects of his profession, and for more than 15 years has served as Board President of the Archives d'Architecture Moderne in Brussels. Internationally admired not only for his 30-year career as an architect and urban developer, Şefik Birkiye is respected for his qualities of leadership and as a man of rare vision.

Michel Andre – Principal

Michel Andre was born in Brussels in 1962 and earned his degree in architecture from the La Cambre School in Brussels in 1987.

In 1994, he joined VIZZION Architects as a project officer. Michel Andre has built and renovated many important buildings in Belgium, France and Luxembourg, including the Jardin des Fonderies, which received the prestigious MIPIM Award in 1998. In 2000 he was appointed Associate Partner, and in 2006, with 18 years' experience as an architect and manager of complex major projects, he took over the direction of VIZZION Architects in 2006.

As adviser and former secretary of the Central Society of Architecture of Belgium, he has organised lectures on architecture with, in particular, Sir Rogers, Santiago Calatrava, Michel Macary and the engineering firm Ove Arup.

Michel Andre is a member of the Belgian contemporary art selection committee and of the Pierre Paul Hamesse Foundation, 2005-2006.

He was also a reader of theses at the Horta School of Architecture in 1998.

Michel Andre was guest architect in the studios of La Cambre School in 1998 and has been a member of numerous architectural committees at that institution.

In 2004, he founded the 'Atelier AM Architecte', which has carried out numerous projects and interiors in Belgium.

Jose Patxot Vera – Principal

Jose Patxot Vera was born in Coin, Spain in 1949. He earned his degree in architecture from the Saint-Luc Institute in Brussels.

He joined VIZZION Architects in 2008 to head the coordination of execution department after working as a consultant, and as Construction Project Manager for Fortis Real Estate Development from 1999 to 2008.

In the 1990s, Jose Patxot Vera worked in Barcelona together with the Taller d'Arquitectura Ricardo Bofill, where he was in charge of the technical development teams and projects in Europe such as the National Theatre of Catalonia and the Convention Centre in Madrid.

In the 1980s, he was the representative of the Architects Polak and Stapels in the Ivory Coast, where he was in charge of the International Trade Centre of Abidjan. He then headed the Brussels office from 1983 to 1987.

Jean-François Dumoulin – Principal

Jean-François Dumoulin was born in Brussels in 1956. He earned his degree in architecture from the La Cambre School in 1980.

Jean-François Dumoulin joined VIZZION Architects in 1989 as Design Manager. He was appointed Partner of VIZZION Architects in 2000 and became Head of the Planning and Design Department in 2006.

Between 1985 and 1997, he created numerous theatre designs for different theatres such as the Théâtre National, the Nouveau Théâtre de Belgique, the Tréteaux de Bruxelles, the Spa Festival and others. The quality of his work has been featured and lauded in numerous articles. In 1985 he founded the Atelier 17, which has carried out numerous major renovations.

As a Design officer, he worked with the firm Paul Becker from 1983 to 1987 and the GROEP Planning from 1981 to 1983, on projects such as the Concert Noble, the committees of the European Parliament, BACOB headquarters in Brussels and various other projects.

Jean-François Dumoulin is respected not only for a career in architecture spanning 28 years, but also for his qualities as town planner, designer and team leader.

Michel Larose – Principal

Michel Larose was born in Brussels en 1962.

After obtaining a qualification in joinery and a qualification in technical and architectural drawing for construction, he earned a degree in architecture from the Saint-Luc Institute in Brussels and won the 'Willy van Hove' first prize in architecture.

Michel Larose joined VIZZION Architects in 1997 as Project Leader, was appointed Associate Partner in 2000, and became Head of Technical Development for Projects. In 2006, he became Head of the Planning and Design department of VIZZION Architects.

Between 1987 and 1991, he worked as a project officer for the firm BEAI.

In 1989, he founded the Bureau Grade (graphics, architecture, design), today known as ML architecture, a firm specialising in renovation, furniture design, and the arrangement of commercial premises.

From 1991 to 1993 he was a lecturer at the Saint-Luc Institute in Brussels for courses leading to the technical diploma in architecture (construction, materials technology, research and composition), and from 1993 to 1996 he worked as project officer for the firm Atelier de Bruxelles.

Thanks to his education, training and experience, he is recognised as a well-rounded architect, advocating architectural quality through his technical and planning skills and aesthetic vision.

Stéphane Bousse – Principal

Stéphane Bousse was born in Brussels in 1970.

He graduated from Saint-Luc Institute in Brussels in 1994 with a degree in architecture and joined VIZZION Architects in 1997.

His architectural work at the outset focused particular attention on the aesthetic aspect, programming building projects and the supervision, in all stages, of large-scale office buildings, hotel resorts and residential buildings.

In 2004, he honed his professional skills further by attending the Executive Programme in Real Estate of the Solvay Business School.

Stéphane Bousse became Head of the Research and Development Department in 2005 and is now responsible for the development and programming of new projects in European countries as well as in other parts of the world.

From 1994 to 1997, he worked with the office of Archi-Buro, where he designed and built numerous villas and residential buildings, and worked on the full renovation of the five-star Palace Hotel in Brussels.

Yves Grauls – Finance & Administration Director

Yves Grauls was born in Brussels in 1958. A graduate in nautical sciences, he served as a merchant marine officer on oil tankers and large container vessels from 1980. Six years and several times round the world later, he decided to cast anchor and focus on finance. He worked for four years as a financial analyst at Ericsson, then from 1990 to 1994 as assistant to the financial manager at Texas Instruments.

He also focused on completing his training in this field, and in 1993 earned a Special Degree in Financial Management from the Saint-Louis Business School in Brussels.

In 1994, he was appointed Finance and Administration Director of the multinational corporation Nederlandse Post/TNT Group. Yves Grauls completed his training and earned an MBA and then a doctorate in business administration from the University of Newport in California, with a dissertation on chaos theory, fractals and non-linear dynamics on financial markets.

Yves Grauls joined VIZZION Architects in 2004 as Finance and Administration Director and in 2006 extended this post to other service firms of the VIZZION group.

He is now also in charge of the management of human resources, IT and insurance for this group. Appreciated for his great human qualities, his capacity to solve complex problems, his open mind and availability, Yves Grauls is also, after a 28-year multi-disciplinary career, a respected leader and financier.

Gaëtan Le Clercq - Senior Partner

Gaëtan Le Clercq was born in Brussels in 1963.

He earned his degree in architecture in 1988 from the Saint-Luc Institute in Brussels, while simultaneously finishing his painting course at the Uccle Academy of Fine Arts Brussels.

Gaëtan Le Clercq joined VIZZION Architects in 1998 as a project officer, later becoming Design Manager. He was appointed Senior Partner at VIZZION Architects in 2006 and assumed the coordination of planning and design.

Between 1988 and 1989, he was cited during an architecture competition for the arrangement of the Lion Mount of Waterloo, selected for the Young Belgian Painting prize and also worked as a designer with the architect E. de T'Serclaes.

From 1989 to 1996, he participated, within the Atelier Espace Léopold, in the building of the European Parliament in Brussels, and then worked together with the firm Lahon & Partners until 1998.

Since 1995, he has been director of Dyninvest SA, a holding company active in the construction industry.

In 1997, he founded the firm Language & Architecture, which specialises in the renovation and construction of single-family houses and office buildings.

Through these diversified experiences he has acquired a global knowledge of the trade, he is also recognised for his design and planning qualities as well as for the architectural design of large-scale projects.

Gabriel-Nicolas Banice - Senior Partner

Gabriel-Nicolas Banice was born in Constanza, Romania in 1949. He earned an architecture degree in 1974 from the Institute of Architecture and Town Planning in Bucharest.

He joined VIZZION Architects in 2001 as Architect-in-charge of projects in the Grand Duchy of Luxembourg. He became Senior Partner at VIZZION Architects in 2006 and manages projects in Luxembourg.

In 1999, Gabriel-Nicolas Banice founded the architectural firm AR'PASS International, which has been responsible for numerous studies and the development and monitoring of projects, especially those abroad; the Public Area of the Carlton Hotel in Bratislava can be cited by way of example of a major project.

Between 1990 and 1999, he undertook many projects as partner architect of the Bureau Marijnissen for various office buildings, such as blocks 9 to 11 on the Avenue Marcel Thiry, the headquarters of the World Customs Organisation, the offices of Price Waterhouse Woludalle II and many blocks of flats in Brussels.

From 1975 to 1989, as project manager at IPJ Constanta, he carried out many important projects, including several hotels on the Black Sea Coast, such as the Lido, Ambassadeur, Savoy, and Admiral. He was awarded the prize of the Order of Rumanian Architects in 1985 for the Lido-Savoy Complex.

His professional qualities have been confirmed by numerous articles published in technical reviews and publications. He is appreciated and respected not only for his experience and achievements as an architect, but also for his communication skills and as a project manager and team leader.

Bernard Colin - Senior Partner

Bernard Colin was born in Jemappes in 1954 and earned his architecture degree in 1981.

After ten years of working with the firm Samyn & Partners and nine years in his own capacity, he joined VIZZION Architects in 2000. In 2006, he was appointed Senior Partner of VIZZION Architects.

His basic training and personal experience as architect, alongside with his technical expertise and consulting assignments for property management, have made him a specialist in invitations to tender and in the execution and supervision of worksites, both for renovation and restoration works and for new constructions.

Olivier Minguet - Senior Partner

Olivier Minguet was born in Bastogne in 1962. He earned his architecture degree in 1985 from the Saint-Luc Institute, participated in the International Laboratory of Architecture and Urban Design in Siena, Italy in 1983, and obtained a degree in town planning in 2006 from the Institute of Town Planning and Urban Renovation.

He joined VIZZION Architects in 1997 as a project officer, and in this capacity headed numerous projects for hotels, offices, housing and the renovation of listed historic buildings. In 1999, he took charge of the vast and prestigious Nile City project in Cairo, Egypt, and carried out numerous hotel development missions in four continents. In 2001, he took part in the investigative committee for the completion of the Berlaymont building (EU) commissioned by the Belgian State.

With more than 20 years of experience, during which he has conducted many vast projects in international multidisciplinary teams, he now heads major architecture and town planning projects for VIZZION Architects, chiefly in Turkey and the Middle East.

He is also a member of the Chamber of Town Planners of Belgium.

Diane Busselen - Partner

Diane Busselen was born in Brussels in 1959. She earned a degree in architecture from the Brussels Academy of Fine Arts in 1984.

In 1998, she joined VIZZION Architects, where she deals chiefly with the coordination of invitations to tender, technical, planning and housing studies, as well as buyer management. She was made partner of VIZZION Architects in 2006.

In 1996, Diane Busselen joined Sicabel, a facility and project management firm, and in 1992 she worked with Tatoo, a packaging company, on packaging for L'Oreal, Unilever, Beiersdorf, and President.

Between 1984 and 1992, she worked with the architectural firms ARCHI+I, Montois and Atelier de Genval.

Frédéric Doerflinger - Partner

Frédéric Doerflinger was born in Uccle in 1974. He earned his degree in architecture from the Saint-Luc Institute in Brussels.

He joined VIZZION Architects in 2000 and took part in the training session for private and judicial expertise organised by the National Board of Expert Architects of Belgium.

He coordinates building permits, invitation to tender, and the supervision of office and hotel complexes, for example the Kempinski Hotel Duke's Palace in Bruges, the Glacis Business Center in Luxembourg and the Regency Office - Merode Hotel on the Place Poelaert in Brussels.

Frédéric Doerflinger was appointed Partner in 2006 and Architect-in-charge of the management of the firm's internal procedures.

In 2007, he became Department Head for the Publication of Architectural Projects in synergy with VIZZION Europe.

His organisational mind and rigorous approach are much appreciated within the structure of VIZZION.

Sevgi Beyhan Sağlam - Partner

Sevgi Beyhan Sağlam was born in Ankara, Turkey in 1975. She earned a degree in architecture as an honour student in 1996 from the Middle East Technical University in Ankara.

Sevgi Beyhan Sağlam joined VIZZION Architects in 2003, and in 2006 she was made Partner and put in charge of various international projects.

Between 1998 and 2003, she worked at Artu Mimarlik in Ankara and between 1996 and 1998 she worked at Mesa Housing Industry in Ankara.

During these years, she was in charge of various housing, hotel and office projects, from the preliminary draft to the supervision of the execution plans.

In 1993, she attended the engraving course at the Falmouth School of Art and Design in England.

Her keen interest in classical music and dance, and a penchant for writing essays and novels, complete her sensitive approach to architecture.

Olivier De Meulemeester - Partner

Olivier De Meulemeester was born in Brussels in 1975. He earned his degree in architecture from the Saint-Luc Institute in Brussels in 2001. In 2003, he obtained a health and safety coordinator's diploma and underwent judicial expertise training in 2004 from the Order of Expert Architects of Brussels.

He joined VIZZION Architects in 2002 as an assistant in the unit working on architectural projects in Luxembourg. He was made Partner of VIZZION Architects in 2006 and also deals with the internal procedures and IT support of the firm.

In 1999, Olivier De Meulemeester founded AVPV, a firm specialising in real estate valuation.

In 2001, he joined the Cefety Group as a court and insurance expert and in 2007 he founded the firm ODM Architecture et Développement.

He is appreciated for his architectural skills, which have been further honed by his organisational aptitude and expertise through the expertise of the valuation work he performs.

Cem Kırbaş - Partner

Cem Kırbaş was born in Samsun, Turkey in 1972.

He earned a degree in architecture in 1993 from the Istanbul Technical University, and one month after graduating he joined VIZZION Architects. Since then, he has taken an active part in numerous projects in architecture and town planning, from the drawing to implementation phase. He was appointed Partner of VIZZION Architects in 2006 and currently performs important duties in the design department.

Cem Kırbaş obtained a certificate in Property Management from the Inter-University Centre for Continuing Education (known by the French acronym CIFOP) in 2001.

In 2000, he earned a third-cycle diploma in Urban Architecture from the Catholic University of Louvain-la-Neuve.

In addition to his passion for architecture, he followed his keen interest in nature and attended a nature guide programme in 2007, organised by the Circle of Naturalists of Belgium.

Haki Yıldırım - Partner

Born in 1972 in Boussu, Belgium, Haki Yıldırım earned his diploma in architecture in 1997 from the Tournai Institute of Architecture.

While pursuing his studies, he won a first prize twice, one awarded by Catalan architect Ferrater and the other by the Association of Belgo-Luxembourgish Architects.

In 1999, he joined VIZZION Architects, where he dealt with projects in all phases of studies in Belgium and abroad (Egypt, British Virgin Islands – Tortola, France and the Netherlands).

Today, Haki Yıldırım is responsible for the design of projects as well as IT management and the implementation of IT methodologies and procedures.

He is also in charge of IT coordination for the international section.

VIZZION Architects

Raphaël Abraham

Sinan Akay
IT Manager

Marcos Alvarez
Architect

Michel Andre
Principal

Cezary Apiecionek
Architect

Kiki Athanassopoulos

Gabriel-Nicolas Banice
Senior Partner

Coraline Barbieri

Bertrand Barthelemy

Catherine Bauwens
Architect

Florence Bellis

Şefik Birkiye
Founding Architect

François Blain

Jean-Jacques Boccard

Stéphane Bousse
Principal

Philippe Bradfer
Architect

Sylvie Bratic
Architect

Diane Busselen
Partner

Adrienne Clairembourg
Head of Graphic Design

Candice Colas

Jean-Christophe Colin

Bernard Colin
Senior Partner

Gérard Colin
Architect

Cyril Collin
Architect

Christel Commeau-Montasse
Architect

Josiane de Klerk
Architect

Laurent de Loecker

Olivier De Meulemeester
Partner

François Dekoster
Architect

Frédéric Doerflinger
Partner

Johanna Dréan

Jean-François Dumoulin
Principal

Johan Ergo

Laurence Fontaine
Head of Image Design

Frédéric Francuck
Architect

Nathalie Garrebeek

Sabine Gaudissart

Philippe Genon
Architect

Marianne Goffin

Jonathan Gomez

Yves Grauls

Jean-François Gustin

Denis Haesen

George Harpau

Anne-Sophie Hombert

Cem Kırbaş

Şaziye Kızıl

Muriel-Laurence Lambot

Michel Larose

Gaëtan Le Clercq

Bettina Lemoine

Thierry Majoie

Sandrine Malchair

Stefan Mattern

Vincent Mercier

Olivier Minguet

Costa Mitracos

Rodrigo Montecino Figueroa

Nadine Neuckens

Nathalie Noël

Frédéric Oveicy

Galia Patxot

Jose Patxot Vera

Wei Yin Peng

Florence Perlberger

Hery Rémi Richard

Benoit Riche

Sevgi Beyhan Sağlam

David Schalenbourg

Laurent Tielemans

Aziz Ünal

Antony Van Vaerenbergh

Elodie Vuagnoux

Sonia Waterschoot

Valérie Wouters

Haki Yıldırım

Aslıhan Yılmaz

VIZZION Istanbul

Ayşin Aker

İhsan Alperen

Pınar Aydın

Mayda Baygan

Tarık Binbaşı

Betül Bölük

Akgüncem Bozkulak

Özkan Bulgan

Ayşegül Çakıcı

Gülperi Çalgav

İlker Canvarol

Cem Çetin

Merve Çetindemir

Banu Dalaman

Selim Dalaman
Managing Director

Songül Duran

Kartal Eryaman

Mehmet Eser Tuna

Tuğçe Evren

Ece Gezer

Gülabi Günay

Övgü Hançerlioğlu

Rüya İdil

Songül Kalkavan

Timur Karasu

Tuğba Kaygusuz

Esra Keskin

Evran Kığılı

Aslan Kılıç

Yusef Metin Sarıgül

Ümit Mutluay

Üklü Özcan

Tuget Özkaya

Alp Şahin

Bora Soykut

Efran Taboğlu

Sibel Temiz

Nüvit Tolongüç

Galip Ünal

Selçuk Uzer

Taner Vaizoğlu

Ümıt Yıldırım

THE PARTNERSHIP BETWEEN 1979 AND SEPTEMBER 2006

VIZZION Architects, originally known as Atelier d'Art Urbain, was founded in 1979 by Şefik Birkiye, who was
later joined by Dominique Delbrouck in 1980, Christian Sibilde in 1981, Muriel-Laurence Lambot in 1982,
by Grégoire de Jerphanion in 1984 and Brigitte Bruyninckx in 1989.

Şefik Birkiye
Architect

Founding and Design Partner since 1979

Dominique Delbrouck
Architect

Partner from 1989 to 2006
In charge of Design

Christian Sibilde
Architect

Partner from 1989 to 2006
In charge of Design and Execution

Grégoire de Jerphanion
Architect

Partner from 1989 to 2006
In charge of Design and Execution

Brigitte Bruyninckx
Economist

Partner from 1994 to 2006
In charge of Finance and Administration

Muriel-Laurence Lambot
Architect

Partner from 1989 to 2006
In charge of Presentation Coordination

THE TEAM BETWEEN 1979 AND SEPTEMBER 2006

FOUNDING ARCHITECT
Şefik Birkiye

PARTNERS
Dominique Delbrouck (1989–2006)
Christian Sibilde (1989–2006)
Grégoire de Jerphanion (1989–2006)
Brigitte Bruyninckx (1994–2006)
Muriel-Laurence Lambot (1989–2006)

ASSOCIATES
Jean-François Dumoulin
Jean-Pierre Vassalli
Catherine Verdood
Olivier Callebaut
Michel Andre
Michel Larose

COLLABORATORS
Raphaël Abraham
Annick Adriaensens
Sinan Akay
Olivier Alexandre
Cezary Apiecionek
Sigrid Ardoullie
Sophie Arnold
Kiki Athanassopoulos
Gabriel-Nicolas Banice
Marc Barbier
Catherine Bardiau
Carole Baudin Dubrulle
Mohamet Bayna
Luigi Bellello
Sara Bernar
Muriel Bettonville
Benoît Beyens
Dirk Bigaré
Jean-Jacques Boccard
Jacques Boton
Geoffrey Bottequin
Mohammed Boucham
Olivier Bougelet
Stéphane Bousse
Martine Brancart
Catherine Brixy
Brigitte Bruyninckx
Gilbert Busieau
Diane Busselen
Raphaëlle Cabouret
Sarah Camu
Vincent Carbonnelle
David Carion
Baudouin Carlier
Sylvia Cascione
Fernando Casij Pena
Florence Chaidron
Vincent Chapelier
Nasser Chemais
Frédéric Chevalier
Charlotte Christiaens
Arnaud Christiane
Giacomo Ciani
Erdem Çınar
Eve-Marie Clabots
Valérie Claes
Adrienne Clairembourg
Christian Clairembourg
Filip Cleynen
David Cloetens
Bernard Colin
Gérard Colin
Bernard Coomans de Brachène
Isabelle Coppens
Gaëtan Cordi
Raphaël Cornelis
Isabelle Courtin
François Couvreur
Marc-Edouard Crassaerts
Daniel Culot
Annie Cuvelier
Charles Dasilva Ntanda
Murielle Dasnoy
Isabelle Dastot
Benedikte De Baets
Livia de Béthune
Virginie De Boeck
Olivier De Bruyn
Isabelle De Clerck
Sabine De Cuyper
Bob De Man
Olivier De Meulemeester
Guillaume de Ribaucourt
Anne-Julie De Wever
François Dekoster
Fabien Delalande
Marie Demiddeleer
Françoise Desprechins
Raphaël Devroey
Dirk D'Herde
Juan Diaz
Frédéric Doerflinger
Esin Dorsan
Hervé Dossin
Patricia Doyen
Eric Draper
David Droesbeke
Marius Dudziuk
Michel Dugeny
Vincent Dupont
François Durt
Levna Engelhardt
Jacques Engelhardt
Tufan Ersin
Claudia Falcinelli
Christian Farber
Marc Favresse
Jean-Paul Ferbach
Anne Filosof
Laurence Fontaine
Jean-Jacques Foulon
Michel Franck
Frédéric Francuck
Marc Frankard
Bruno Gabaret
Jean-Pierre Gallez
Firmin Garcia Maestu
Nathalie Garrebeek
Philip Gaube
Cécile Gaudissart
Sabine Gaudissart
Didier Gaveriaux
Philippe Genon
Valérie Georges
Alix Gewelt
Massoud Gharabaghi
Ann Gilson
Françoise Govaerts
Joana Grauls
Yves Grauls
Jean Grenez
Véronique Greuse
Chloé Grumeau
Tévie Hac
Hinda Haïk
Isabelle Hamburger
Marlyse Hanssens
Olivier Hasquin
Semih Hatipoğlu
Marc Heene
Laurent Hemelaers
Benoît Hemmeryckx
Eric Hennico
Véronique Henry
Françoise Herman
Pierre-André Hermans
Michel Hernalsteen
Sandrine Horinka
Erdinç Horzum
Erica Houtreille
Frédéric Huwaert
Raphaël Ibarrondo
Claudio Iodice
Samuel Jager
Lambert Jannes
Daria Jezierska
Dilek Kadıoğlu
Aidin Khoei Ebrahimzadeh
Patrick Kinsoen
Cem Kırbaş
Bernard Kirsch
Andras Koppany
Bruno Lacombe
David Lambert
Bénédicte Lampin
Sophie Langlet
Géraldine Laurent
Perrine Lauweryns
Richard Le Biannic
Gaëtan Le Clercq
Hughes Leblois
Christine Lebrun
Christophe-A. Leemans
Ariane Lefébure
Julien Legros
Michel Leloup
Geoffroy Lemaigre
Christine Lemasson
Dao Li-Nhu
Bulle Leroy
Karel Lindemans
Frédéric Lischetti
Philippe Logie
Ardeshir Mahmoudian
Gabriel Mambu
Etienne Marion
Patrick Mascaux
Stefan Mattern
Erwin Mayne
Michel Mein
Martine Mercier
Sergiu Mija
Olivier Minguet
Rodrigo Montecino Figueroa
Monica Montes Diaz
Jacques Morlion
Benoît Morsa
Corine Mortier
Monique Moyson
Sevda Musellim
Anne-Catherine Namèche
Michel Neusy
Bernard Nève de Mévergnies
Vincent Newman
Fariba Nikzad
Nathalie Noël
Juan Ochogavia
Frédéric Oerlemans
Adam Okzuz
Jonathan Ortegat
Véronique Otten
Frédéric Oveicy
Caroline Pabis
Marie Palmblad
Silvia Passoni
Jose Patxot Vera
Galia Patxot
Catherine Paulissen
Paolo Pecci Boriani
Florence Perlberger
Geneviève Petre
Kyriakos Photiadis
Michel Picavet
Hervé Pierart
Véréna Pitz
Esther Plantinga
Marleen Poelmans
Rita Portugal Fortes
Aleksander Prifti
Olivier Provoost
Jean-François Puissant Baeyens
Nuria Quiroga
Carine Quoidbach
Anne Rambo
Loïc Rateau
Christelle Reculez
Michel Renchon
Valérie Rigaux
Nuno Rocha Pinto
Sabine Roland
Henri Rollier
Jeanine Rösler
Jonathan Mike Rothé
Yves Rouillon
Aurore Rousseau
Thomas Royal
Sevgi Beyhan Sağlam
Şule Salihoğlu
Carine Santelé
David Schalenbourg
Catherine Scheid
Brigitte Schiemsky
Régis Scrève
Ugur Seker
Isabelle Sobotka
Hélène Soldai
Martine Somerhausen
Michel Sougné
Luc Sulon
Minh To Tu
Anne Trebitsch
Sevgi Ülker
Isabelle Van Asbroeck
Vanessa Van Belle
Mathieu Van Den Bergh
Christine Van Elewyck
Sébastien Van Esch
Frédéric Van Hoof
Anne Van Lishout
Claire Van Mosuinck
Valérie Van Reepinghen
Antony Van Vaerenbergh
Anne Vandenhaute
Joke Vander Mijnsbrugge
Inès Vanderhoeven
Françoise Vanhomwegen
Geert Vansteelant
Véronique Verhulst
Cécile Verougstraete
Stefan Vervaecke
Jean-Jacques Vervoort
Maxime Verwilghen
Donatienne Vierset
Nadia Vrancken
Luc Vujasin
Lionel Wargnier
Thomas Wéry
Kenneth Wettlin Papalli
Haki Yıldırım
Ekila Zanga

THE COLLABORATORS WHO WORKED WITH VIZZION ARCHITECTS BETWEEN OCTOBER 2006 AND APRIL 2008
Luigi Bellello
Salvatore Biondo
Melier Cortes
François Couvreur
Mélina Dugue
Caroline Janssen
Isabelle Kahn
Alexandre Kontossis
Richard Le Biannic
Olivier Petit
Hervé Pierart
François Rausch
Emmanuelle Reusens
Perrine Sanna
Ugur Seker
Seden Senemek
Isabelle Stanson
Mathieu Van Den Bergh

THE COLLABORATORS WHO WORKED WITH VIZZION ISTANBUL BETWEEN 2006 AND MARCH 2008
Şefika Akpınar
Fırat Alagöz
R. Erkut Alperen
Ayşegül Bulut
Ümit Coşar
Esra Deveci
Mehmet Karakaş
Zeynep Küçük
Mehmet Ülgez
Buğra Yüksekkaya

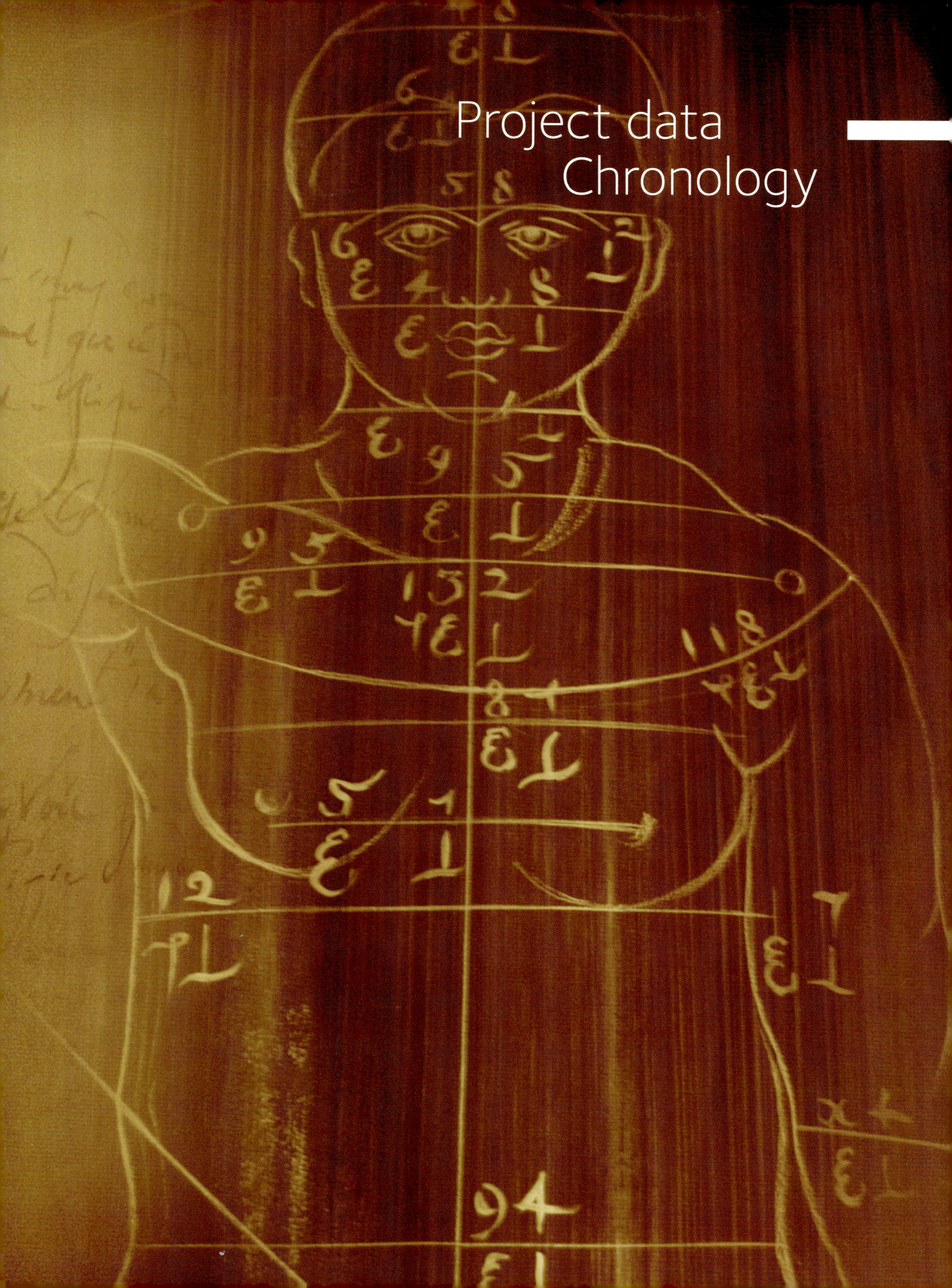

Project data
Chronology

Hotel and resorts

Monte-Carlo Bay Hotel & Resort
Location: 40, Avenue Princesse Grace, MC-98000
   Monaco, Principality of Monaco
Client: Société des Bains de Mer
Client's representative: Sogetel
Architect: VIZZION Architects
Execution architect: Iori & Giraldi
Interior design: Pierre-Yves Rochon
General contractor: Built under separated lots
Use: 334-room hotel, 4 restaurants, meeting rooms,
   casino, swimming pool
Above ground area: 42,000 square metres
Below ground area: 26,400 square metres
Number of levels: 3 B + GF + 11
Garage: 252
Site area: 4 hectares
Structure: Concrete
Materials: Painted concrete, prefabricated concrete,
   natural stone, ceramic, metal and tile roof
Completion: October 2005
Awards: Competition-winning project; MIPIM
   Awards 2006, finalist in the hotels and tourism
   resorts category

Klassis Resort Hotel
Location: 34930 Silivri (Istanbul), Turkey
Client: Klassis Turizm
Architect: VIZZION Architects
Interior design: VIZZION Architects
Landscape architect: VIZZION Architects
Use: 308-room resort hotel, casino, convention
   centre, sports centre
Room type details: 202 standard rooms, 22
   executive rooms, 11 suites, 5 king suite, 47 garden
   standard rooms, 2 garden executive rooms, 14
   pool villas and 5 garden villas
Gross building area: 40,000 square metres
Structure: Concrete
Materials: Stone
Completion: 1984–January 1989
Award: Competition-winning project

Radisson SAS Royal Hotel
(formerly SAS Royal Hotel)
Location: Rue Fossé-aux-Loups 47, B-1000
   Brussels, Belgium
Client: SAS International Hotels
Architect: Bureau d'Architecture M. Jaspers &
   Partners
Design and execution architect: VIZZION Architects
Structural engineer: TKB
ME consultant: Varendonck – Vincent; Studiebureel
   Heedfeld nv
Acoustical consultant: Cauberg & Verbeemen
Public areas interiors: VIZZION Architects
Interior design: Christian Lundwall;
   Nicolas Lecompte
Lighting consultant: Lighting Design Partnership
Project consultant: Jones Lang Wootton
Hotel consultant: Kinfield
Quality control: Seco

General contractor: Beerts Bouwwerken – IGB
   Belgium j.v.
Use: 281-room hotel including 23 suites, restaurants,
   bar, meeting rooms, fitness centre
Above ground area: 23,500 square metres
Below ground area: 4500 square metres
Number of levels: 3 B + GF + 7 + mechanical
Garage: 89 spaces
Structure: Concrete
Materials: Limestone, granite, plaster, aluminium,
   powder-coated zinc roof
Completion: October 1987–January 1990

Novotel Brussels Centre Tour Noire
Location: Rue de la Vierge Noire 32, B-1000
   Brussels, Belgium
Client: Accor Hotels Belgium
Architect: VIZZION Architects
Interior design: Patrick Dumont and Annick
   Delvigne
Structural engineer: LM Chapeaux and Raoul
   Thomas jv
MEP engineer: RVR Van Reeth (HVAC/fluids),
   Botec (electricity)
Quality control: Seco
General contractor: Louis De Waele
Use: 217-room hotel, restaurant, bar, meeting rooms
Above ground area: 13,883 square metres
Below ground area: 1453 square metres
Number of levels: 1 B + GF + 7 + mechanical
Structure: Concrete
Materials: Red and white brick, pre-cast concrete
   elements, aluminium roof
Completion: October 1997–March 1999

Kempinski Hotel Dukes' Palace
Location: Prinsenhof 8, B-8000 Bruges, Belgium
Developer: Tractebel Engineering
   International/Louis De Waele j.v.
Investor: Royal Center (P&V)
Architect: VIZZION Architects in association with
   Antoine Dugardyn for the preserved parts
Execution architect: DDS & Partners Architects
Structural engineer: S.C.E.S.
MEP engineer: Tractebel Development Engineering
Acoustical engineer: Technum nv
Land surveyor: D&D Group
Quality control: Seco
Security co-ordinator: SEFMEP
Interior design: Inter Arts
General contractor: sm Interbuild/Louis De
   Waele/Tractebel Engineering International
Hotelier: Kempinski
Use: Hotel (80 rooms, 15 suites)
Above ground area: 10,027 square metres
Below ground area: 6393 square metres
Number of levels: 2 B+ GF + 5
Parking spaces: 130 (interior), 6 (exterior)
Structure: Concrete, masonry
Materials: Natural stone, wood, wooden window
   frames, zinc roof
Completion: September 2005–March 2008

Dream Castle Hotel at Disneyland Resort Paris
Location: 40, Avenue de la Fosse des Pressoirs, Val de
   France, Magny le Hongre, F-77703 Marne la
   Vallée, France
Client: UBX Development (PORR Group)
Architect: VIZZION Architects
Structural engineer: Structure IDF
MEP engineer: Barbanel
Acoustical engineer: Espace Acoustique
Landscape architect: D. Paysage
Kitchen engineer: Restauration conseil
Quality control: Veritas
General contractor: GTM/SUPAE/SNEF
Hotelier: Vienna International
Use: 400-room resort hotel, 3 restaurants, bar,
   meeting rooms, indoor swimming pool, fitness
   centre, outdoor terraces, landscaped gardens
Above ground area: 24,668 square metres
Below ground area: 2374 square metres
Landscaped gardens: 46,000 square metres
Number of levels: 1 B + GF + 4
Outdoor parking spaces: 300
Structure: Concrete
Materials: Tinted plaster, slate roof
Completion: December 2002–July 2004

The Fairmont Cairo at Nile City
Location: Corniche El Nil, 11221 Cairo, Egypt
Client: Nile City Investments
Architect: VIZZION Architects
Architect of record: Etienne Watelet-I.D.S Limited
   and Partners; Dar Al-Handasah Consultants
Structural engineers: BESIX Engineering
   Department; Hamza Associates
MEP engineer: Shaker Consultancy Group
General contractor: JVBO (BESIX – Orascom j.v.)
Use: 552-room hotel, rooftop swimming pool
Above ground area: 52,757 square metres
Below ground area: 408 square metres
Number of levels: 4 B + GF + mezzanine + 25 +
   mechanical levels between levels 18 and 19
Height: 100 metres
Structure: Concrete
Materials: Glass-reinforced concrete (GRC), glass,
   powder-coated aluminium
Completion: 2005–June 2008

Le Parc
Location: Rue du Col de la Croix, Villars-sur-Ollon,
   Switzerland
Client: Domaine du Parc Holding Development
   (VIZZION Europe)
Architect: VIZZION Architects
Land surveyor: Duchoud Haymoz Bühlmann sa
Use: 64 apartments, 32 chalets, 96-room hotel, 92
   serviced apartments, retail
Above ground area: 10,356 square metres,
   apartments; 9400 square metres, chalets; 6045
   square metres, serviced apartments; 17,462 square
   metres, hotel
Below ground area: 14,767 square metres,

Project data

apartments; 3250 square metres, chalets; 9766 square metres (serviced apartments and hotel)
Site area: 87,086 square metres
Site footprint: 10,151 square metres
FAR: 0.51
Structure: Concrete
Completion: 2012

Headquarters and administrative centres: renovations and transformations

Loi 62
Location: Rue de la Loi 62, B-1000 Brussels, Belgium
Client: Compagnie de Bruxelles 1821 sa (Fortis/Compagnie Immobilière de Belgique)
Client's representative: Essor-ILDWD am
Architect: VIZZION Architects
Structural engineer: Rensburg sa
MEP engineer: Air Consult Engineering sa
Acoustical engineer: Venac
Quality control: Seco
General contractor: Louis De Waele – Socatra
Use: Office
Above ground area: 6755 square metres
Below ground area: 3145 square metres
Number of levels: 3 B + GF + 7 + mechanical
Garage: 48 spaces
Structure: Concrete
Materials: Limestone, red brick facings and glass
Completion: 1965, original construction (architect A.& J. Polak)
Renovation: 1996–October 1997

The European Union at the Eudip Three building
Location: Rue de la Loi 80/Rue Joseph II 73-91, B-1040 Brussels, Belgium
Client: Eudip Three (Baninmo)
Architect: VIZZION Architects
Structural engineer: b Group
MEP engineer: Tractebel Engineering Development
Quantity surveyor: Monk Dunstone Associates
Acoustical engineer: Venac
Quality control: Seco
General contractor: CIT Blaton
Use: Office
Above ground area: 16,220 square metres
Below ground area: 9190 square metres
Number of levels: 3 B + GF + 7
Garage: 86 spaces
Structure: Concrete
Materials: Limestone, red granite, powder-coated aluminium
Completion: 1961, 1962, 1975, original construction (architect G.&R. Ide, Hugo Van Kuyck – Groupe A, R. Brunswyck – O. Wathelet)
Renovation: 1999–December 2001

The European Union at Park Avenue
Location: Rue de la Loi 76/Rue de Spa 3/Rue Jospeh II 67A-71, B-1040 Brussels, Belgium
Client: Robelco

Architect: VIZZION Architects
Structural engineer: Stedec nv
MEP engineer: Van Reeth
General contractor: CFE/ABEB
Use: Office
Above ground area: 12,094 square metres
Below ground area: 3146 square metres
Number of levels (Loi): 1 B + GF + 8
Number of levels (Joseph II): 2 B + GF + 6
Garage: 60 spaces
Structure: Concrete
Materials: Limestone, powder-coated aluminium, zinc roof
Completion: 1963, original construction (architect Robert Théry)
Renovation: August 2002–October 2003

The European Union at the Pavilion
Location: Rue de la Loi 72-74/Rue de Spa, B-1040 Brussels, Belgium
Client: Robelco
Architect: Archi 2000
Architect for the façades (concept and aesthetic advice): VIZZION Architects
Structural engineer: Stedec nv
MEP engineer: Van Reeth
Project manager: Borealis
General contractor: CFE/ABEB
Use: Office
Above ground area: 19,796 square metres
Below ground area: 6018 square metres
Number of levels: 2 B + GF + 8
Garage: 108
Structure: Concrete
Materials: Limestone, powder-coated aluminium
Completion: 1963, original construction (architect Robert Théry)
Renovation: 2004–March 2005

City Garden
Location: Rue Joseph II 59, B-1000 Brussels, Belgium
Client: Nexity Belgium
Architect: VIZZION Architects
Structural engineer: Stedec nv
MEP engineer: Tractebel Development Engineering
Quality control: Socotec Belgium
General contractor: Van Laere nv
Use: Office
Above ground area: 9625 square metres
Below ground area: 2449 square metres
Number of levels: 2 B + GF + 8 + mechanical
Garage: 44 spaces
Structure: Concrete
Materials: Powder-coated aluminium, granite
Completion: May 2004–February 2006, new construction

Lloyd George 7 (formerly Zurich Assurances Headquarters)
Location: Avenue Lloyd George 7, B-1000 Brussels, Belgium

Client: Zurich Assurances
Architect: VIZZION Architects
Project manager: ELD partnership
Structural engineer: Verdeyen & Moenaert
MEP engineer: Coget
Acoustical engineer: Venac
Contractor (carcass, HVAC): Herpain
Use: Office
Above ground area: 13,319 square metres
Below ground area: 10,181 square metres
Number of levels: 3 B + GF + 6 + mechanical
Garage: 286 spaces
Structure: Concrete
Materials: Limestone, green granite, powder-coated-aluminium, cast aluminium
Completion: 1975, original construction (architect Hugo Van Kuyck)
Renovation: 1996–October 1997

Dexia Bank at the Galilée Building
Location: Avenue Galilée 5, B-1210 Brussels, Belgium
Client: Dexia Bank
Architect: VIZZION Architects
Structural engineer: Verdeyen & Moenaert
MEP engineer: Marcq & Roba
Acoustical engineer: Venac
General contractor: Interbuild
Use: Office
Above ground area: 34,100 square metres
Below ground area: 17,670 square metres
Number of levels: 4 B + GF + 12 + mechanical
Garage: 371 spaces
Structure: Concrete, masonry
Materials: Limestone, glass curtain wall, powder-coated aluminium
Completion: 1971, original construction (architect Hugo Van Kuyck)
Asbestos removal: 1999
Renovation: February 2000–November 2001
Award: Competition-winning renovation project

Dexia Management Headquarters
Location: Square de Meeûs 1, B-1000 Brussels, Belgium
Client: Copropriété 1 Square de Meeûs/Dexia Bank
Architect: VIZZION Architects
Structural engineer: Bureau d'études CIT Blaton
MEP engineer: Bureau d'Etudes Coget sa
Acoustical engineer: Venac sprl
Quality control: Seco
General contractor: CIT Blaton sa
Use: Office
Above ground area: 5660 square metres
Below ground area: 2245 square metres
Number of levels: 3 B + GF + 7 + mechanical
Garage: 50 spaces
Structure: Concrete
Materials: Granite, powder-coated aluminium, stainless steel
Completion: 1966, original construction (architect Isia Isgour)
Renovation: 2000

Headquarters and administrative centres: new constructions

Canal Front

Award: RICS Awards 2005, finalist in the regeneration award category

Canal Front – KBC Bank Headquarters (formerly Kredietbank)

Location: Avenue du Port 2, B-1080 Brussels, Belgium
Client: Kredietbank
Architect: Michel Jaspers & VIZZION Architects
Design and execution: VIZZION Architects
Structural engineer: Constructor-Stabo
MEP engineer: Coppée-Courtoy
General contractor: Besix – Vanhout
Use: Office
Above ground area: 60,000 square metres
Below ground area: 40,000 square metres
Number of levels: 4 B + GF + 9
Garage: 738 spaces
Structure: Concrete, masonry stonework, brickwork
Materials: Limestone, red granite, powder-coated aluminium window frames, powder-coated zinc roof
Completion: 1992–December 1994
Award: Competition-winning project

Canal Front – Admiral Building (a.k.a. BIP)

Location: Avenue du Port 4-10, B-1080 Brussels, Belgium
Client: Betonimmo (Besix Group) – Investissements & Promotion (CFE Group)
Architect: VIZZION Architects and Michel Jaspers
Design and execution: VIZZION Architects
Structural engineer: Atenco sa
MEP engineer: Air Consult Engineering sa
Quality control: Seco
General contractor: Vanhout – CFE
Use: Office
Above ground area: 20,500 square metres
Below ground area: 12,000 square metres
Number of levels: 3 B + GF + 7 + mechanical
Garage: 273 spaces
Structure: Concrete, stone facing
Materials: Limestone, powder-coated aluminium window frames
Completion: 1999–December 2001

Canal Front – Green Island (phase 1)

Location: Avenue du Port 16, B-1080 Brussels, Belgium
Client: Brustar One sa (NCC Group)
Architect: VIZZION Architects & Michel Jaspers
Design and execution: VIZZION Architects
Structural engineer: TCA
MEP engineer: LEB-axro – Tractebel Development Engineering
Quality control: AVI
General contractor: Van Laere nv
Use: Office
Above ground area: 10,672 square metres
Below ground area: 5617 square metres
Number of levels: 2 B + GF + 6
Garage: 151 spaces
Structure: Concrete, precast panel walls
Materials: Limestone, powder-coated aluminium window frames
Completion: 1993–December 1995
Awards: MIPIM Awards 2000, winner in the business centres category; FIABCI 2001 Prix d'Excellence, special mention

Canal Front – Green Island (phase 2)

Location: Avenue du Port 12-14, B-1080 Brussels, Belgium
Client: Eurobalken (NCC Group)

Architect: VIZZION Architects & Michel Jaspers
Design and execution: VIZZION Architects
Structural engineer: TCA
Mechanical engineer: Solitech – Tractebel Development Engineering
Quality control: AVI
General contractor: Van Laere nv – Thiran
Use: Office
Above ground area: 25,320 square metres
Below ground area: 9700 square metres
Number of levels: 2 B + GF + 6
Garage: 154 spaces
Structure: Concrete, precast panel walls
Materials: Limestone, powder-coated aluminium window frames
Completion: 1996–December 1998
Awards: MIPIM Awards 2000, winner in the business centres category; FIABCI 2001 Prix d'Excellence, special mention

Canal Front – Lavallée

Location: Rue Adolphe Lavallée 1, B-1080 Brussels, Belgium
Client: Immomills-Louis De Waele/AllFin
Architect: VIZZION Architects
Structural engineer: Ingénieurs Associés
MEP engineer: Tractebel Development Engineering
Quality control: Seco
General contractor: Louis De Waele
Use: Office
Above ground area: 14,512 square metres
Below ground area: 7681 square metres
Number of levels: 3 B + GF + 6
Garage: 138 spaces
Structure: Concrete
Materials: Brickwork, granite, powder-coated aluminium, glass
Completion: February 2003–January 2005

Canal Front – Porte de Ninove

Location: Chaussée de Ninove 1/Square A. Smets 7, B-1080 Brussels, Belgium
Client: Watan sa
Architect: VIZZION Architects
Structural engineer: Solid
MEP engineer: Solitech
Use: Office
Above ground area: 19,781 square metres
Below ground area: 9755 square metres
Number of levels: 3 B + GF + 10
Garage: 198 spaces
Structure: Concrete
Materials: Natural stone, granite, powder-coated aluminium
Study: 2003

Canal Front – Nautea

Location: Chaussée de Ninove 1/Square A. Smets 7, B-1080 Brussels, Belgium
Client: Watan sa
Architect: VIZZION Architects
Execution architect: DDS & Partners Architects
Structural engineer: Ordigram
MEP engineer: GEI
Acoustical engineer: Venac
General contractor: BESIX
Use: Office
Above ground area: 20,484 square metres
Below ground area: 9903 square metres
Number of levels: 3 B + GF + 8
Garage: 198 spaces
Structure: Concrete
Materials: Brickwork, granite, powder-coated aluminium
Completion: 2010

Canal Front – Résidence Le Lorrain

Location: Rue Bouvier 14/Rue le Lorrain 4, B-1080 Brussels, Belgium
Client: Eurobalken (NCC Group)
Architect: VIZZION Architects & Michel Jaspers
Design and execution: VIZZION Architects
Structural engineer: TCA
MEP engineer: LEB-axro – Tractebel Development Engineering
General contractor: Socatra
Use: Housing
Above ground area: 3650 square metres
Below ground area: 1065 square metres
Number of levels: 1 B + GF + 4
Garage: 21 spaces
Structure: Concrete, Sicasteen blocks
Materials: Brickwork, slate roof
Completion: 1996–December 1997

Canal Front – Résidence Ribaucourt

Location: Rue de Ribaucourt 135, B-1080 Brussels, Belgium
Client: SDRB-Société de Développement de la Région de Bruxelles-Capitale
Architect: VIZZION Architects
General contractor: EGTA Contractors
Use: Housing
Above ground area: 1320 square metres
Below ground area: 220 square metres
Number of levels: 1 B + GF + 3
Structure: Concrete, masonry
Materials: Brickwork, granite, architectonic concrete, slate roof
Completion: 1995–October 1997

Canal Front – Résidence Van Meyel

Location: Rue Van Meyel 14-22, B-1080 Brussels, Belgium
Client: Van Meyel sa (Betonimmo – Investissements & Promotion)
Architect: VIZZION Architects
Structural engineer: Ellyps (Verdeyen & Moenaert)
MEP engineer: Concept Control
Quality control: Seco
General contractor: Ilegems – M&M Bouw
Use: Housing
Above ground area: 2250 square metres
Below ground area: 650 square metres
Number of levels: 1 B + GF + 4
Garage: 17 spaces
Structure: Concrete
Materials: Brickwork, granite, slate roof
Completion: August 2001–March 2003

Canal Front – Les Terrasses de l'Ecluse

Location: Rue Heyvaert – Quai de l'Industrie, B-1080 Brussels, Belgium
Client: Foncière de L'Ecluse sa (SDRB/BESIX R.E.D.)
Architect: VIZZION Architects
Execution architect: DDS & Partners Architects
Structural engineer: Ordigram
MEP engineer: Concept Control
Land surveyor: HVS
General contractor: Vanhout
Use: Housing (107 apartments)
Above ground area: 11,937 square metres
Below ground area: 4304 square metres
Number of levels: 1 B + GF + 7
Garage: 98 spaces
Structure: Concrete, masonry
Materials: Brickwork, architectonic concrete, wood
Completion: August 2008

French Consulate

Location: Place de Louvain 14, B-1000 Brussels, Belgium

Client: CEPIM-SEPEC-IBF
Architect: Michel Jaspers & VIZZION Architects
Design and execution architect: VIZZION Architects
Structural engineer: Tractebel Development
    Engineering
MEP engineer: Marcq & Roba
Quality control: AV
General contractor: Betonac-Beton
Use: Office
Above ground area: 10,644 square metres
Below ground area: 4840 square metres
Number of levels: 3 B + 2 GF + 7 + mechanical
Garage: 111 spaces
Structure: Concrete
Materials: Limestone, green granite
Completion: 1990–March 1993

Business Center Glacis

Location: Allée Scheffer/Place Glacis, L-1251
    Luxembourg, Luxembourg
Client: WACO – DIC (Deutsche Immobilien
    Chancen)
Architect: VIZZION Architects
Associate architect: Jean Petit
Project management: Emerco
Structural engineer: Simon & Christiansen
MEP engineer: Masterplan
Acoustical engineer: Venac
Security control: Secolux
General contractor: Giorgetti Carlo
Use: Office, 10 housing units, retail
Above ground area: 17,935 square metres (office),
    2190 square metres (housing), 195 square metres
    (retail)
Below ground area: 2190 square metres (office),
    635 square metres (housing)
Number of levels: 2 B + GF + 6
Garage: 135 spaces (office), 12 spaces (housing)
Structure: Concrete
Materials: Stone, granite, aluminium
Completion: March 2002–November 2004

Riverside Square

Location: De Gerlachekaai 20, B-2000 Antwerp,
    Belgium
Client: Exmar
Architect: Michel Jaspers & VIZZION Architects
Design and execution architect: VIZZION Architects
General contractor: Interbuild
Use: Office
Above ground area: 10,200 square metres
Below ground area: 2,500 square metres
Number of levels: 1 B + GF + 5 + mechanical
Structure: Concrete
Materials: Limestone, granite
Completion: 1988–September 1990

Residentie Alphee

Location: De Gerlachekaai/Schaliënstraat 1-3,
    B-2000 Antwerp, Belgium
Client: Reslea nv
Architect: Michel Jaspers & VIZZION Architects
Design and execution architect: VIZZION Architects
General contractor: Interbuild
Use: Housing
Above ground area: 5817 square metres
Number of levels: 1 B + GF + 7
Structure: Concrete
Materials: Brickwork, metal roof
Completion: 1994–January 1997

Mechelen Campus

Location: Schaliënhoevedreef 20/Oude
    Antwerpsebaan, B-2800 Mechelen, Belgium
Client: U-PLACE
Architect: VIZZION Architects
Structural engineer: Archimedes + ABIDT

MEP engineer: Eurimpro nv + STD
General contractor: M&M Bouw/Willemen/Claes
Use: 11-building office business park
Above ground area: 56,104 square metres
Below ground area: 25,377 square metres
Number of levels (tower): 1 B + GF + 13 +
    mechanical
Parking spaces: 814 (interior); 810 (exterior)
Structure: Concrete, masonry
Materials: Brickwork, aluminium window frames,
    zinc and tiles roof
Completion: August 1999–December 2005

The Walt Disney Company France Headquarters (a.k.a. Cassiopée)

Location: ZAC du centre urbain du Val d'Europe,
    Ville de Chessy, Marne-la-Vallée, France
Client: Etoiles d'Europe sas (Buelens nv – Almafin nv)
Architect: VIZZION Architects/Interfaces sarl
Quality control: Qualiconsult
General contractor: Campenon Bernard
Use: Office
Above ground area (SHOB): 12,371 square metres
Below ground area (SHOB): 5550 square metres
Number of levels: 2 B+ GF + 5 + mechanical
Parking spaces: 199 (interior), 6 (exterior)
Structure: Concrete
Materials: Limestone, plaster, aluminium, zinc roof
Completion: June 2003

Fortis Headquarters

Location: Boulevard Emile Jacqmain 53, B-1000
    Brussels, Belgium
Client: Fortis AG
Architect: VIZZION Architects & Michel Jaspers
Design architect for the façades and the public
    lobby: Michael Graves & Associates
Functional design and execution architect:
    VIZZION Architects
Structural engineer: Ingénieurs Associés sa/Atenco sa
MEP engineer: Tramar j.v. (Tractebel Development
    Engineering sa/ Marcq & Roba sprl)
Acoustical engineer: Mathys Acoustical Adviser sprl
Interiors: VIZZION Architects
Quality control: Seco
General contractor: CFE
Use: Office, 434-seat restaurant
Above ground area: 24,000 square metres
Below ground area: 14,300 square metres
Number of levels: 4 B + 1 GF + 7 + mechanical
Site area: 3865 square metres
Garage: 164 spaces
Structure: Concrete
Materials: Natural stone, copper roof
Completion: June 1999–December 2002

Jacqmain 83

Location: Boulevard Emile Jacqmain 83, B-1000
    Brussels, Belgium
Client: Fortis AG
Architect: VIZZION Architects
Structural engineer: TPF Chapeaux
Acoustical engineer: Venac
Quality control: Seco
Security coordination: SEFMEP
Contractor (carcass): Compté
Use: Office
Above ground area: 10,697 square metres
Below ground area: 1202 square metres
Number of levels: 1 B + 1 GF + 8
Site area: 1345 square metres
Structure: Concrete
Materials: Granite, Mocca Creme natural stone,
    powder-coated aluminium
Completion: 1976, original construction (architect
    A.&J. Polak)
Renovation: 2003

South Center Steel and South Center Titanium

Location: Avenue Fonsny 38/Place Broothaers 7-9,
    B-1060 Brussels, Belgium
Client (building): sm Fonsny Midi
Client (interiors): Swiss Life Belgium
Architect: VIZZION Architects
Structural engineer: Verdeyen & Moenaert
MEP engineer: Solitech
Swiss Life interiors: VIZZION Architects
Quality control: Seco
General contractor: Maurice Delens/Jacques
    Delens/CFE/Louis De Waele/Van Rymenant
Use: Office
Above ground area: 19,696 square metres
Below ground area: 8919 square metres
Number of levels: 3 B + GF + 7/10
Garage: 120 spaces
Structure: Concrete
Materials: Granite, metal, zinc roof
Completion: October 2001–September 2004
    (Steel)/2005 (Titanium)

Swiss Life (Belgium) Headquarters at South Center Steel

Location: Avenue Fonsny 38, B-1060 Brussels,
    Belgium
Client (building): sm Fonsny Midi
Client (interiors): Swiss Life
Architect: VIZZION Architects
Structural engineer: Verdeyen & Moenaert
MEP engineer: Solitech
Interiors (Swiss Life): VIZZION Architects
Quality control: Seco
General contractor: Maurice Delens/Jacques
    Delens/CFE/Louis De Waele/Van Rymenant
Use: Office
Above ground area: 13,628 square metres
Below ground area: 5262 square metres
Number of levels: 3 B + GF + 10
Garage: 69 spaces
Structure: Concrete
Materials: Granite, metal, zinc roof
Completion: October 2001–September 2004

South Center Titanium

Location: Place Broothaers 7-9, B-1060 Brussels,
    Belgium
Client: sm Fonsny Midi
Architect: VIZZION Architects
Structural engineer: Verdeyen & Moenaert
MEP engineer: Solitech
Quality control: Seco
General contractor: Maurice Delens/Jacques
    Delens/CFE/Louis De Waele/Van Rymenant
Use: Office
Above ground area: 6068 square metres
Below ground area: 2562 square metres
Number of levels: 3 B + GF + 7
Garage: 51 spaces
Structure: Concrete
Materials: Granite, metal, zinc roof
Completion: 2005

South Express (A1) – Groupe S Headquarters

Location: Avenue Fonsny 40, B-1060 Brussels,
    Belgium
Client: sm South Express (Eurobalken (Soficom
    Development) 70%, BESIX R.E.D. 10%, CFE
    10%, Sofipari 10%)
Architect: VIZZION Architects
Execution architect: DDS & Partners Architects
Structural engineer: VK Engineering (Ingénieurs
    Associés)
MEP engineer: Van Reeth
Quality control: AIB Vinçotte
General contractor: Valens/Jacques Delens/CFE/
    Louis De Waele

Use: Office
Above ground area: 10,544 square metres
Below ground area: 3633 square metres
Number of levels: 2 B + GF + 6 + mechanical
Garage: 75 spaces
Structure: Concrete
Materials: Granite, powder-coated aluminium,
zinc roof
Completion: September 2005–March 2008

South Express (A2)
Location: Avenue Fonsny 39, B-1060 Brussels,
Belgium
Client: sm South Express (Eurobalken (Soficom
Development) 70%, BESIX R.E.D. 10%, CFE
10%, Sofipari 10%)
Architect: VIZZION Architects
Execution architect: DDS & Partners Architects
Structural engineer: VK Engineering (Ingénieurs
Associés)
MEP engineer: Van Reeth
Quality control: AIB Vinçotte
General contractor: Valens/Jacques
Delens/CFE/Louis De Waele
Use: Office
Above ground area: 10,214 square metres
Below ground area: 3633 square metres
Number of levels: 2 B + GF + 6 + mechanical
Garage: 71 spaces
Structure: Concrete
Materials: Granite, powder-coated aluminium,
zinc roof
Completion: September 2005-May 2008

Housing
Joli Bois – Clos des Lipizzans
Location: Clos des Lipizzans 1-2, 3-4/Avenue des
Grands Prix, B-1150 Brussels, Belgium
Client: Fortis Real Estate
Project manager: Fortis Real Estate
Architect: VIZZION Architects
Structural engineer: TCA
MEP engineer: DTS
Landscape architect: JNC International
Quality control: AIB Vinçotte
General contractor: CEI Construct
Use: Housing (2 buildings, 39 apartments)
Above ground area: 5600 square metres
Below ground area: 3333 square metres
Number of levels: 1 B + GF + 4
Parking spaces: 65 (interior), 8 (exterior)
Structure: Concrete, masonry
Materials: Brickwork, granite, architectonic
concrete, wood
Completion: October 2002–June 2005

Joli Bois – Résidences Alezan, Balzan and Tobiano
Location: Avenue des Grands Prix 166-168/Drève
des Shetlands 2-4-6, 10-12-14, B-1150 Brussels,
Belgium
Client: Fortis Real Estate
Project manager: Fortis Real Estate
Architect: VIZZION Architects
Structural engineer: TCA
MEP engineer: VK Engineering
Landscaped architect: JNC International
Quality control: AIB Vinçotte
General contractor: Cordeel
Use: Housing (3 buildings, 87 apartments)
Above ground area: 12,700 square metres
Below ground area: 5080 square metres
Number of levels: 1 B + GF + 5
Garage: 87 spaces
Structure: Concrete, load bearing masonry

Materials: Beige and brown-grey brickwork,
granite, architectonic concrete, wood
Completion: April 2004–September 2007

Le Jardin des Fonderies
Location: Rue de Ribaucourt 137-139-141, B-
1080 Brussels, Belgium
Client: SDRB-Société de Développement de la
Région de Bruxelles
Architect: VIZZION Architects
General contractor: Socatra
Use: Housing
Above ground: 4220 square metres
Below ground: 1150 square metres
Number of levels: 1 B + GF + 4
Parking spaces: 24 spaces (interior), 11 spaces
(exterior)
Structure: Concrete, masonry, steel
Materials: Brickwork, architectonic concrete,
powder-coated aluminium
Completion: 1996–January 1998
Awards: 1998 Prix Européen Philippe Rotthier de
la Reconstruction de la Ville, mention; MIPIM
Awards 1998, winner in the residential
developments category

La Belle Chanson
Location: Avenue Jacques Brel 39-45/Rue Théodore
De Cuyper 70, B-1200 Brussels, Belgium
Client: Larebel-Woluwé sa (VIZZION Europe)
Architect: VIZZION Architects
Structural engineer: SIC sa
MEP engineer: Sotech sa
Acoustical engineer: Venac sprl
Quality control: Seco
General contractor: Heijmans – De Coene Construct
Use: Housing (50 apartments)
Above ground area: 6581 square metres
Terraces: 731 square metres
Below ground area: 2109 square metres
Number of levels: 1 B + GF + 5
Garage: 60 spaces
Site: 3321 square metres
Structure: Concrete
Materials: Brick, plaster, architectonic concrete
Completion: May 2008

Les Trois Mâts
Location: Rue Théodore De Cuyper 167-179, B-
1200 Brussels, Belgium
Client: Larebel-Woluwé sa (VIZZION Europe)
Architect: VIZZION Architects
Structural engineer: SIC sa
MEP engineer: Sotech sa
Acoustical engineer: Venac sprl
Quality control: Seco
General contractor: Franki Construct
Use: Housing (53 apartments), a crèche
Above ground area: 7015 square metres
Terraces: 926 square metres
Below ground area: 2655 square metres
Number of levels: 1 B + GF + 5
Parking spaces: 68 (interior) + 6 (exterior)
Site area: 5007 square metres
Structure: Concrete
Materials: Brick, plaster, architectonic concrete, wood
Completion: September 2008

Euro Village
Location: Rue Godecharle/Rue Wiertz, B-1050
Brussels, Belgium
Client: Skyline Projects nv
Architect: VIZZION Architects
Structural engineer: SIC
MEP engineers: Solitech
Security co-ordinator: Technix

General contractor: Louis De Waele
Use: Housing (4 buildings, 274 units)
Above ground area: 25,554 square metres
Basement area: 16,441 square metres
Number of levels: 3 B + GF + 7 to 11
Garage: 275 car spaces, 14 motorcycle spaces
Structure: Concrete
Materials: Brick, architectonic concrete
Completion: June 2004–September 2006

Villa Bozkaya
Location: Ankara, Turkey
Client: Family Bozkaya
Architect: VIZZION Architects
Use: Single-family housing
Above ground area: 600 square metres
Below ground area: 400 square metres
Number of levels: 1 B + GF + 1 + roof
Site area: 2200 square metres (ca. 72 metres x
30 metres)
External materials: Traditional coating, blue tiles,
copper roof
Internal materials: Exotic woods, Spanish marble
Completion: 2000

Ömerli
Location: Kadirova Street, Ömerli, Istanbul, Turkey
Client: VIZZION Europe
Architect: VIZZION Architects
Use: Single-family housing (81 three- and five-
room villas)
Above ground area: 23,105 square metres
Terraces: 5340 square metres
Public park: 23,932 square metres
Private gardens: 60,644 square metres
Number of levels: GF + 1
Site area: 99,323 square metres
Structure: Masonry, concrete
Completion: 2008–2010

Quai des Princes
Location: Quai des Princes, Cap d'Ail, French
Riviera, France
Client: Quai des Princes s.c.a. (VIZZION Europe)
Architect: VIZZION Architects
Use: 109 serviced apartments, restaurant, lounge–
bar, fitness centre, rooftop lagoon pool
Above building area: 20,246 square metres
Below ground area: 12,217 square metres
Number of levels: GF + 2 + rooftop
Parking spaces: 181 spaces (147 single spaces, 17
double spaces)
Site area: 5550 square metres
Structure: Concrete
Completion: 2010

Domaine du Parc
Location: Route du Luxembourg 140/Place des
Cerisiers, L-7205 Lorentzweiler (Bofferdange),
Luxembourg
Client: Immobilière Green Park sa (VIZZION Europe)
Architect: VIZZION Architects
Project manager: VIZZION Europe sa
Structural engineer: Abidt
MEP engineer: Felgen (design phase)/Sotech sa
(construction phase)
Acoustical engineer: Venac
General contractor: C.B.L.
Use: Housing (8 buildings, 105 apartments and
27 townhouses)
Above ground area: 21,355 square metres
Terraces: 4496 square metres
Below ground area: 9868 square metres
Number of levels: B + GF + 3
Site: 31,308 square metres
Structure: Concrete

Materials: Plaster, powder-coated window frames,
zinc roof
Completion: 2009

Le Domaine de Montévrain
Location: Montévrain (Plot B2), Montévrain,
Marne-la-Vallée, France
Client: sci Ile de France (Promogim)
Architect: VIZZION Architects
Use: Housing (99 apartments)
Above ground area (SHON): 6909 square metres
Below ground area: 4347 square metres
FAR: 1.23
Number of levels: 1 B + GF + 3
Garage: 147 spaces
Site area: 5626 square metres
Structure: Concrete
Materials: Natural stone, plaster, powder-coated
aluminium, powder-coated aluminium, powder-
coated steel, zinc roof, wood
Completion: April 2006

Le Parc d'Evrini
Location: Rue de Bruxelles (Plot B5), Montévrain,
Marne-la-Vallée, France
Client: snc Citalis (Cogedim)
Architect: VIZZION Architects
Operation: Citalis
Structural engineer: Soret
MEP engineers: D. Bati
Economist: Cabinet Racine
Quality control: Veritas
Use: Housing (59 apartments)
Above ground area (gross): 6660 square metres
Above ground area (net): 4130 square metres
Below ground area: 1991 square metres
FAR: 1.35
Number of levels: 1 B + GF + 3
Garage: 84 spaces
Site area: 3062 square metres
Structure: Concrete
Materials: Natural stone, plaster, powder-coated
aluminium, powder-coated steel
Completion: September 2006

Le Clos du Mail
Location: Montévrain (Plot B6), Montévrain,
Marne-la-Vallée, France
Client: snc Les Exclusives de Montévrain (Meunier)
Architect: VIZZION Architects
Operation: Meunier
Structural engineer: Soret
MEP engineer: D. Bati
Economist: Cabinet Racine
Quality control: Veritas
Use: Housing (61 apartments)
Above ground area (gross): 6459 square metres
Above ground area (net): 4006 square metres
Below ground area: 2001 square metres
Number of levels: 1 B + GF + 3
Garage: 83 spaces
Site area: 3074 square metres
FAR: 1.30
Structure: Concrete
Materials: Natural stone, plaster, powder-coated
aluminium, powder-coated steel, zinc roof, wood
Completion: September 2006

Les Jardins Victoriens
Location: Rue Marco Polo, F-77700 Serris Val
d'Europe, Marne-la-Vallée, France
Client: snc Marignan Habitat
Architect (concept and aesthetic follow-up):
VIZZION Architects
Execution architect: COTEC
Structural engineers: COTEC

MEP engineer: COTEC
Acoustical engineer: Venac
Quality control: Veritas
Contractor (carcass): Legendre
Use: Housing (86 apartments)
Above ground area: 11,513 square metres
Below ground area: 3306 square metres
Number of levels: 1 B + GF + 3/4
Parking spaces: 139
Structure: Concrete
Materials: Plaster, zinc roof
Completion: May 2002–October 2003

Shopping malls and mixed-use projects
City Center and City 2 Shopping Mall
Location: Boulevard du Jardin Botanique 20/Rue
Neuve/Rue des Cendres, B-1000 Brussels,
Belgium
Client: Citymo (Fortis Real Estate)
Architect: VIZZION Architects
Shopping mall interiors co-architect: Design
Architectural
Structural engineer: Setesco sa
Service engineer (HVAC, liquids): Atenco sa
Service engineer (electricity): Tractebel
Development Engineering
Acoustical engineer: D2S
Quality control: Seco
General contractor (City Center office B1 &
finishings B1/B2): Hochtief
General contractor (City 2 Shopping Mall/City
Center housing and offices B2): Besix/Maurice
Delens/Louis De Waele
Use: Office (30,938 square metres), retail (46,119
square metres, 103 units), housing (1652 square
metres)
Gross building area: 98,370 square metres
City Center office and retail: 39,550 square
metres, above ground area; 10,507 square metres,
below ground area
Building height: 38 metres
Atrium height: 29.50 metres, 7 levels
City 2 Shopping Mall: 27,000 square metres
City Center housing: 1652 square metres
Garage: 19,661 square metres, 450 spaces
Number of levels (office): 2 B + GF + 7
Number of levels (mall): 1 B + GF + 2
Structure: Concrete, steel for the shopping mall
newly built penthouse level
Materials: Limestone, powder-coated window
frames, powder-coated aluminium, granite
Original Bon Marché architect in 1928:
G.J. Maugue
Original City 2 architect in 1978: Aaron Chelouche
associated to Lathrop-Douglass; Marie-Bernadette
Raimbault, responsible for interiors and façades
City 2 Shopping Mall completion: October 1998–
November 1999, renovation and addition
City Center completion: 2000–June 2003, new
construction

Les Grands Prés
Location: Place des Grands Prés 1, B-7000 Mons,
Belgium
Client: Foruminvest
Architect: VIZZION Architects/Groupe ISIS
Landscape architect: AWP+E
Project Manager: Tractebel Development
Engineering
Lighting consultant: ACT-Art Concept Technology
General contractor: Lixon
Use: Shopping mall (75 retail and restaurant units)
Building area: 46,754 square metres
Height of atrium: 13 metres
Number of levels: GF + 1

Parking spaces: 2600
Site area: 23.5 hectares
Structure: Concrete
Materials: Natural stone, granite, steel and glass.
Completion: September 2003
Award: ICSC – International Council of Shopping
Centers 2005 European Awards, large new centres
category, commendation

Mowo Center
Location: Route du Luxembourg 111, L-7241
Bereldange (Walferdange), Luxembourg
Client: Cecobe sa (VIZZION Europe)
Architect: VIZZION Architects
Structural engineer: Abidt
MEP engineer: Sotech – Felgen
Acoustical engineer: Venac
Quality control: Secolux
General contractor: WUST Entreprises
Use: Retail
Building area: 5817 square metres
Number of levels: GF + 1
Parking spaces: 87
Structure: Concrete, wood (roof)
Materials: Powder-coated aluminium frames
Completion: November 2005–November 2006

Media Square
Location: Place des Carabiniers 18-18a-19, B-1040
Brussels, Belgium
Client: Benvenuta sa
Architect: VIZZION Architects
General contractor: Jacques Delens
Use: Office, housing
Above ground area: 4266 square metres, office;
1962 square metres, housing
Below ground area: 3386 square metres, office; 663
square metres, housing
Number of levels: 2 B + GF + 2 + mechanical,
office; 1 B + GF+ 3/8, housing
Office parking spaces: 84 spaces (garage); 6 spaces
(exterior)
Structure: Concrete
Materials: Stone, brick, metal and glass.
Completion: 2000–February 2003
Award: Les Règles de l'Urbanisme 2004, finalist in
the newly built ensembles harmoniously
integrated within the urban fabric category

Nile City
Location: Corniche El Nil, 11221 Cairo, Egypt
Client: Nile City Investments
Design architect and architectural execution
follow-up: VIZZION Architects
Architect of record (twin towers and shopping
mall): Etienne Watelet; I.D.S Limited and
Partners, formerly Search International
Architect of record (hotel): Etienne Watelet-I.D.S
Limited and Partners; Dar Al-Handassah
Consultants
Structural engineers: BESIX Engineering
Department; Hamza Associates
MEP engineer: Shaker Consultancy Group
Contractor: JVBO (BESIX – Orascom jv)
Use: Office, five-star hotel, luxury apartments,
shopping mall
Above ground area: 196,647 square metres
North Tower above ground area: 53,647 square
metres, office
South Tower above ground area: 54,002 square
metres, office, residences
Hotel above ground area: 52,757 square metres
Retail above ground area: 29,087 square metres
Below ground area: 62,566 square metres
Number of levels (twin towers): 4 B + GF +
mezzanine + 34

Number of levels (hotel): 1 B + GF + mezzanine + 25
Height: 143 metres (twin towers); 100 metres (hotel)
Garage: 1296 spaces
Structure: Concrete
Materials: Glass-reinforced concrete (GRC), glass, powder-coated aluminium
Completion: 1998–September 2003 (twin towers and shopping mall); 2005–June 2008 (hotel)

Green Square

Location: Boulevard Général Jacques/Boulevard du Triomphe/Chaussée de Wavre, B-1160 Brussels, Belgium
Client: Green Square sca (VIZZION Invest), Green Senior sprl (VIZZION Invest) and Green Résidence sprl (VIZZION Invest)
Client's representative: VIZZION Europe
Architect: VIZZION Europe
Structural engineer (Building A): VK Engineering sa
Structural engineer (Building B): Lesage & Paelinck sprl
MEP engineer: Sotech sa
Acoustical engineer and control: Venac
Quality control: Seco sc.
Use (Building A): Serviced apartments, residences, retail and fitness centre
Use (Building B): Apartments, retirement home, retail
Building A (front building)
Above ground area: 13,991 square metres
Below ground area: 10,827 square metres
Number of levels: 4 B + GF + 7 + mechanical level
Building B (rear building)
Above ground area: 16,685 square metres
Below ground area: 5866 square metres
Number of levels: 2 B + GF + 6
Garage: 96 spaces (Building A); 102 spaces (Building B)
Site area: 8505 square metres (7414 square metres, private land, 1091 square metres, public land)
Structure: Mixed
Materials: Metal, granite, brick, plaster, wood, wooden window frames
Completion: 2011

Studies and projects under progress
Hoek van Holland

Location: Langeweg, Hoek van Holland, The Netherlands
Client: BAM Vastgoed
Architect: VIZZION Architects
Use: Housing
Above ground area: 25,166 square metres
Below ground area: 7980 square metres
Number of levels: 1 B + GF + 10 + mechanical
Structure: Concrete
Materials: Natural stone
Competition study: 2003

Heron Plaza

Location: Avenue de la Toison d'Or 24-29, B-1050 Brussels, Belgium
Client: Heron Belgium
Architect: VIZZION Architects
Structural and MEP engineers: Tractebel Development Engineering
Acoustical engineers: Venac
Use: Hotel, housing, retail, fitness centre
Above ground area: 38,865 square metres (96 new housing units: 27,263 square metres; 12 renovated housing units: 1942 square metres; retail: 9660 square metres)
Below ground area: 10,405 square metres
Number of levels: 2 B + GF + 5
Garage: 139 spaces
Structure: Concrete

Materials: Limestone, granite, powder-coated aluminium window frames, metal, zinc roof
Study: 2001–2006

Crédit Mutuel du Nord and shopping arcade

Location: Boulevard de Waterloo 16, B-1000 Brussels, Belgium
Client: BKCP Crédit Professionnel
Client's representative: Nexity
Architect: VIZZION Architects
Use: Office, retail arcade
Above ground area: 8556 square metres
Below ground area: 4003 square metres
Number of levels: 2 B + GF + 4 + mechanical
Garage: 23 spaces
Structure: Concrete
Materials: Aluminium, metal, limestone, curved glass
Original architect in 1961: Hugo Van Kuyck
Renovation study: 2000–2005

Hôtel Royal Botanique

Location: Rue Royale 171–173/Haecht/Traversière/ Comète/Brialmont, B-1210 Brussels, Belgium
Client: Building Engineering
Architect: VIZZION Architects
Hotel operator: Rosebud Héritage sa – Rue Royale sa
Use: 150-room hotel, housing
Above ground area: 13,900 square metres, hotel; 6100 square metres, housing
Below ground area: 8000 square metres
Number of levels: 4 B + GF + 7
Parking spaces: 178 (120 + 58) interior spaces; 5 exterior spaces
Structure: Concrete
Materials: Glass and metal curtain wall, brickwork, plaster
Study: 2002–2005

Au fil de l'Eau

Location: Rue Spintay/Rue du Brou, B-4800 Verviers, Belgium
Client: Les Rives de Verviers (Foruminvest)
Architect: VIZZION Architects
Execution architect: DDS & Partners Architects
Structural and MEP engineer: Tractebel Development Engineering
Use: Shopping mall
Above ground area: 51,589 square metres
Below ground area: 48,147 square metres
Garage: 1412 spaces
Structure: Concrete
Completion: 2011

Anka Hill

Location: Ankara, Turkey
Client: VIZZION Europe
Architect: VIZZION Architects
Use: Shopping mall, entertainment and health centre, housing, hotel
Gross building area: 652,936 square metres
Shopping mall: 198,918 square metres
Entertainment and health centre: 63,000 square metres
Tower 1: 102,500 square metres, housing
Tower 2: 72,550 square metres, housing, hotel
Congress centre: 27,200 square metres
Housing for municipality: 188,768 square metres
Height: 63 storeys, 230 metres, tower 1; 40 storeys, 150 metres, tower 2; 38 storeys, 133 metres housing for the municipality
Site area: 142,299 square metres
Study: 2006

Kayseri

Location: Kayseri, Turkey
Client: VIZZION Europe
Architect: VIZZION Architects
Use: Shopping mall, hotel, congress centre, housing, entertainment, fitness centre
Above ground building area: 150,600 square metres
Below ground area: 29,200 square metres
Shopping mall: 96,800 square metres
Entertainment: 15,500 square metres
Fitness and congress facilities (hotel): 9500 square metres
Hotel (upper levels): 28,000 square metres
Residences: 30,000 square metres
Below ground garage levels: 152,800 square metres (shopping mall); 15,000 square metres (hotel)
Parking spaces: 5090 (shopping mall); 500 (hotel)
Height: 82 metres
Site area: 75,536.36 square metres
Study: 2007

Bursa shopping mall

Location: Bursa, Turkey
Client: VIZZION Europe
Architect: VIZZION Architects
Use: Shopping mall, movie theatres, wellness centre, hotel, office, housing
Gross building area: 225,295 square metres
Above ground building area: 172,997 square metres
Below ground area: 52,298 square metres
Shopping mall: 137,828 square metres
Movie theatres: 3205 square metres
Wellness centre: 2986 square metres
Hotel: 15,150 square metres
Office: 14,644 square metres
Mall residences: 34,482 square metres
Park residences: 17,000 square metres
Parking spaces: 4660
Site area: 62,100 square metres
FAR: 2.5
Study: 2007

Bursa sport centre

Location: Bursa, Turkey
Client: VIZZION Europe
Architect: VIZZION Architects
Use: 35,000-seat football and athletics stadium, 2,000-seat secondary football field, 7000-seat sports hall, Olympic-size swimming pool
Study: 2007

Şancity

Location: Cumhuriyet Avenue, Taksim, Istanbul, Turkey
Client: VIZZION Europe
Architect: VIZZION Architects
Use: Retail, theatre, conference centre, office, 52-room retirement house
Gross building area: 162,079 square metres
Shopping mall: 58,384 square metres
Theatre and conference centre: 6978 square metres
Office: 10,623 square metres
Retirement home: 3016 square metres
Parking area and shelter: 83,078 square metres,
Parking spaces: 2103
Site area: 14,760 square metres
Study: 2007

Istanbul seaside

Location: Kemerburgaz, North of Istanbul, Turkey
Client: VIZZION Europe
Architect: VIZZION Architects
Use: New city
Gross building area: 4,001,109 square metres
Housing: 1,682,282 square metres
Hotels: 622,625 square metres

Retail: 196,380 square metres
Office: 279,293 square metres
Sports: 156,888 square metres
Education: 254,456 square metres
Cultural: 105,423 square metres
Administrative: 51,500 square metres
Hospital 45,000 square metres
Wellness: 62,500 square metres
Congress centre: 544,762 square metres
Study: 2007

Istanbul 'da Haydarpaşa

Location: Istanbul, Turkey
Client: Calik Holding A.S.
Architect: VIZZION Architects
Use: Towers 1, 2, 3, housing; Towers 4, 5, office, housing; Towers 6, 7, hospitality
Gross building area: 2,218,664 square metres including 394,773 square metres of parking spaces
Housing: 583,000 square metres
Hospitality: 149,000 square metres
Hospitals and retirement house: 35,000 square metres
Office: 280,000 square metres
Retail shops: 197,000 square metres
Shopping malls: 196,000 square metres
Exhibition/Fairs: 134,000 square metres
Convention centre: 99,000 square metres
Sport centre: 14,500 square metres
Yacht club/Marina: 9,000 square metres
Museums, themed parks and other socio-cultural activities including theatres and cinemas: 6000 square metres
Height (tip of the spire): Towers 1, 2, 3: 218 metres; Tower 4: 381 metres; Tower 5: 319 metres; Towers 6, 7: 298 metres
Above ground storeys: Towers 1, 2, 3: 39; Tower 4: 74; Tower 5: 59; Towers 6, 7: 51
Basements: 7
Structure: Steel
Materials: Oxidized green copper, glass
Study: 2005

Istanbul-Levent IV

Location: Buyukdere Avenue 4, Levent, Kagithane, Istanbul, Turkey
Client: VIZZION Europe
Architect: VIZZION Architects
Use: Office
Above ground area: 24,617 (FAR: 2.5) or 29,541 square metres (FAR: 3) or 39,388 square metres (FAR: 4)
Semi-below ground area: 3621 square metres
Below ground area: 5697 square metres
Below ground parking area: 29,666 square metres
Number of levels: 9 B + GF + 30
Parking spaces: 1000
Site area: 8562.5 square metres
Useable land area: 4281 square metres
Study: 2007

Oyak Towers

Location: Istanbul, Turkey
Client: VIZZION Europe
Architect: VIZZION Architects
Use: Office, congress and fitness centre, department store
Above ground area: 29,400 (FAR: 3) or 49,000 square metres (FAR: 5)
Below ground garage: 400 spaces (FAR: 3) or 600 spaces (FAR: 5)
Number of levels: 6 B + GF + (up to) 35 + mechanical
Site area: 9800 square metres
Study: 2007

Altunizade

Location: Altunizade area, Istanbul, Turkey
Client: VIZZION Europe
Architect: VIZZION Architects
Use: Mixed-use ensemble
Above ground area: 108,452 square metres
Below ground area: 171,857 square metres
Five residential towers: 77,798 square metres
Fitness centre and a swimming pool: 6164 square metres
Cafés and restaurants: 4501 square metres
Shopping mall: 84,263 square metres
Storage and loading area: 3540 square metres
Garage: 95,441 square metres, 3181 spaces
Shelter: 8602 square metres
Number of levels (towers A/E): 8 B + GF + 21
Number of levels (towers B/D): 8 B + GF + 27
Number of levels (tower C): 8 B + GF + 30
Study: 2007

Resneli Niyazi Bey

Location: Istanbul, Turkey
Client: VIZZION Europe
Architect: VIZZION Architects
Use: Mixed-use ensemble
Above ground area: 15,423 square metres
Below ground area: 25,108 square metres
Housing: 13,200 square metres, 88 units
Garage: 7960 square metres, 180 spaces
Cellars and shelter: 800 square metres
Garden: 1000 square metres
Number of levels: 5 B + GF + 21
School: 4146 square metres including a 956-square-metre playground
Number of levels: GF + 3
Retail: 2503 square metres
Shelter: 362 square metres
Garage: 11,560 square metres, 362 spaces
Number of levels: 4 SS + GF
Site area: 4200 square metres
Study: 2007

West Bay Tower

Location: Doha, Qatar
Client: VIZZION Europe
Programme: VIZZION Europe
Architect: VIZZION Architects
Use: Mixed-use tower
Above ground area: 58,154 square metres
Below ground area: 36,960 square metres
Office (levels 36 to 56): 15,599 square metres
Apartments (levels 17 to 34): 19,776 square metres, 112 units
Hotel (levels 1 to 15): 21,205 square metres, 274 rooms
Retail (ground floor): 574 square metres
Garage: 36,960 square metres, 627 spaces
Number of levels: 7 B + GF + 57 + 4 mechanical
Height (tip of spire): 310 metres
Site area: 5280 square metres, including a 1950-square-metre park
FAR: 11
Study: 2008

Three master plans: Bequia

Location: Bequia, St. Vincent and the Grenadines
Client: VIZZION Europe
Architect: VIZZION Architects
Use: Resort
Above ground area: 8839 square metres (4050 square metres of residences (villas), 3239 square metres of common equipments (lobby, bar, restaurant, hotel), 1550 square metres of services)
Study: 2007

Three master plans: Petit Mustique

Location: Petit Mustique, St. Vincent and the Grenadines
Client: VIZZION Europe
Architect: VIZZION Architects
Use: Resort
Above ground area: 39,469 square metres (27,000 square metres of residences (hotel and villas), 4450 square metres of retail and wellness centre, 8019 square metres of staff housing and infrastructural works)
Study: 2007

Three master plans: Eden Resort

Location: Police Bay, Seychelles
Client: IRET (Robelco)
Architect: VIZZION Architects
Use: Resort
Building area: 27,000 square metres (reception building with lobby and main bar, bungalows and villas, main and beachfront restaurants, pavilion, golf clubhouse)
Site area: 93 hecatres
Study: 2006

**1979 Parc de la Villette (1),
competition study**
Paris, France
International competition, landscape design

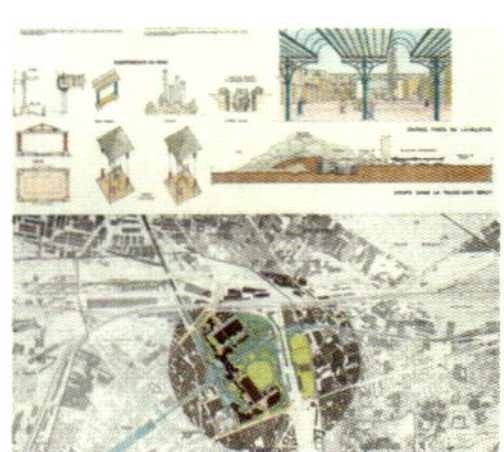

**1982 Parc de la Villette (2),
competition study**
Paris, France
International competition, landscape design for a
50-hectare site

1982 Battery Park City (3), study
New York, New York, United States
For Cooper Eckstut Associates, study for the newly
created 37-hectare waterfront

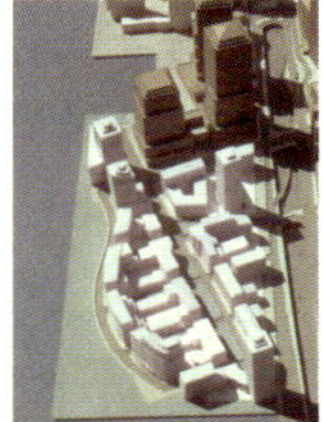

1984 Chicago (3), study
Chicago, Illinois, United States
For Cooper Eckstut Associates, new neighbourhood
landscaping

1984 Hoboken (3), study
Hoboken, New Jersey, United States
For Cooper Eckstut Associates, marina

Chronology

All figures include above and below ground areas.
The numbers in brackets following specific projects refer
to the list of partnerships on page 301.

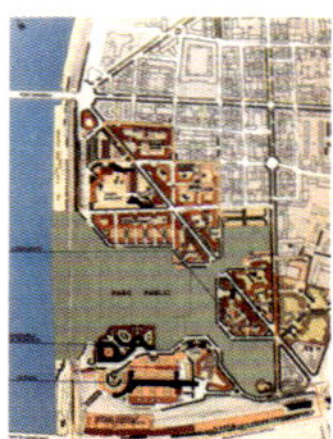

**1985 Parc des Cévennes (2),
competition study**
Paris, France
International competition, landscape design

1985 Sedan-Quai de la Régence (4)
Sedan, France
Office Public Départemental d'HLM des Ardennes,
12,000 square metres, 176 housing units

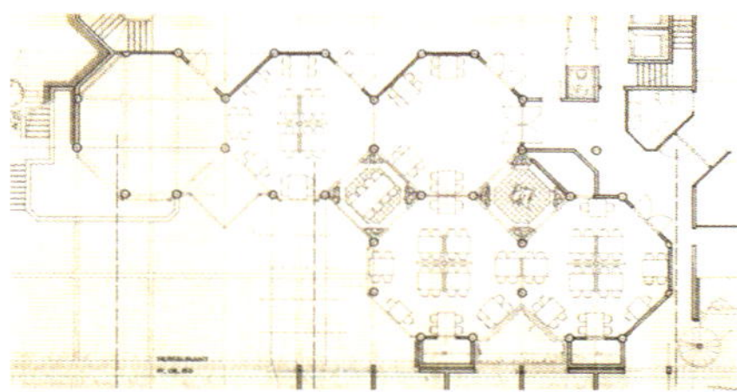

1985 Aix-la-Chapelle (5)
Aachen, Germany
13,000 square metres, 120-room spa clinic

1986 Newport (3), study
New York, New York, United States
For Cooper Eckstut Associates, marina

1986 Charleville-Mézières (4)
Charleville-Mézières, France
Mairie de Charleville-Mézières and SEAA,
8000 square metres, firemen station

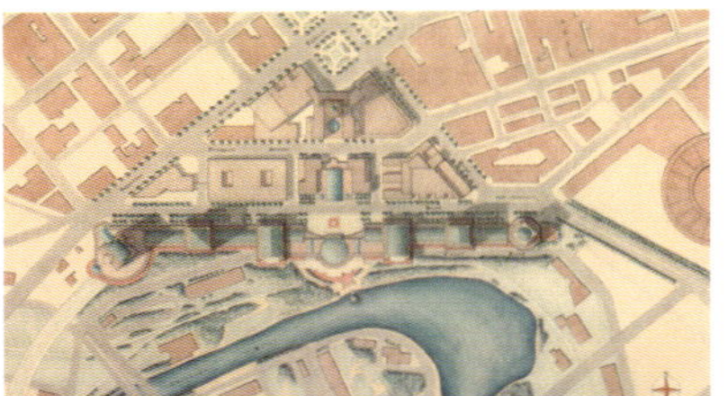

1987 Cleveland Riverfront (3)
Cleveland, Ohio, United States
For Cooper Eckstut Associates, riverfront
redevelopment urban master plan

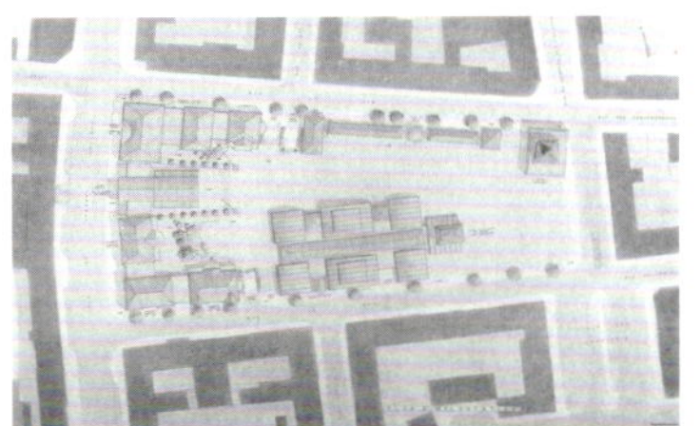

1988 Amiens (4), **competition study**
Amiens, France
City of Amiens, urban landscaping

1988 Béthune "Le Perroy" (4)
Béthune, France
Le Nouveau Logis, Office Public Départemental
d'HLM des Ardennes, 14,800 square metres, 121
housing units

1988 Papyrus
Nile River, Egypt
72-metre, 52-room cruise boat

1989 Klassis Resort Hotel
Silivri (Istanbul), Turkey
Klassis Turizm, 40,000 square metres, 308-room resort
hotel and casino, competition-winning project

1989 Tractebel Headquarters (6)
Brussels, Belgium
Tractebel, 63,000 square metres, office headquarters,
competition-winning project

1990 Radisson SAS Royal Hotel (7)
Brussels, Belgium
SAS International Hotels, 28,000 square metres,
281-room hotel

1990 Green Water Plaza (8)
Antwerp, Belgium
Naviga, 4800 square metres, office

1990 Riverside Square (8)
Antwerp, Belgium
Exmar, 12,700 square metres, office

1990 Ariane Building (6)
Brussels, Belgium
Tractebel, 36,000 square metres, office, competition-winning project

1991 Klassis Resort and Golf
Silivri (Istanbul), Turkey
Klassis Turizm, 45,500 square metres, 150-room resort hotel, 70 villas and apartments, golf course

1991–1992 PPA Molenbeek, study
Brussels, Belgium
Commune de Molenbeek-Saint-Jean, 54-hectare master plan

1992 The Regent Brussels (9)**, study**
Brussels, Belgium
Immo Grenadiers, 15,000 square metres, five-star hotel

1992 Residentie Arethusa (8)
Antwerp, Belgium
Exmar, 3800 square metres, housing

1992 Vervloet
Brussels, Belgium
Vervloet, 2200 square metres, showroom and workshops

1992–2003 Triset, study
Braine-l'Alleud, Belgium
Triset, 7290 square metres, office

1993 Mathonet at Ariane Park, study
Brussels, Belgium
SDRB, 47,500 square metres, office

1993 Banco do Brazil/Trône 14–16 (8)
Brussels, Belgium
Trooninvest, 2800 square metres, bank headquarters

1993 French Consulate (8)
Brussels, Belgium
CEPIM-SEPEC-IBF, 15,484 square metres, French Consulate

1994 Villa Palladine
Brussels, Belgium
Mutuelle Jordaens, 3572 square metres, 11-unit
apartment building

**1994 Kredietbank Headquarters, now
KBC (8)**
Brussels, Belgium
Kredietbank, 100,000 square metres, bank
headquarters, competition-winning project

**1995 Rue Royale 154–158/Vésale/
Vandermeulen (9) study**
Brussels, Belgium
Sicabel, 8208 square metres, renovation and new
construction, office and housing

**1995 Sun Assistance – Cuvelier,
Monteyne & Vanmoerkerke**
Ostend, Belgium
Cuvelier, Monteyne & Vanmoerkerke, 2038 square
metres, mixed-use office with housing

1995 Green Island – phase 1 (10)
Brussels, Belgium
NCC Group (Brustar One), 16,289 square metres,
office, MIPIM Award 2000, FIABCI 2001, special
mention

1995–2001 Porte du Lion, study
Braine-l'Alleud, Belgium
Leasinvest/Votquenne, 8134 square metres,
two office buildings

1996 Quatre-Bras
Kraainem, Belgium
Immobilière SEM, 11,000 square metres, office
renovation

1996 Résidence de l'Abbaye
Brussels, Belgium
DHB, 5495 square metres, housing, Les Règles d'Or
de l'Urbanisme awards 2004, finalist

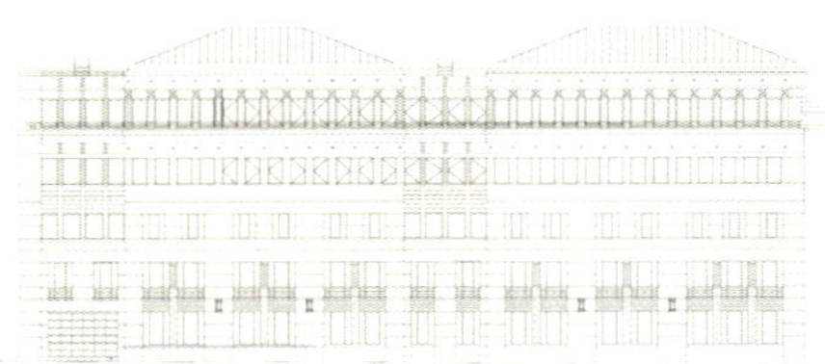

1996 ACKB (8)
Brussels, Belgium
Kredietbank, 3500 square metres, office renovation

1996 Chaussée de Ninove
Brussels, Belgium
Dheedene Develop, 4285 square metres, retail

1997 Lloyd George 7 (11), formerly Zurich Assurances Headquarters
Brussels, Belgium
Zurich Assurances, 23,500 square metres, office renovation

1997 Archimedes (8)
Antwerp, Belgium
Reslea, 3791 square metres, office

1997 Residentie Alphee (8)
Antwerp, Belgium
Reslea, 5817 square metres, housing

1997 Impératrice
Brussels, Belgium
Immo JASPE-Immo SEM-LCEBE, 14,000 square metres, office renovation

1997 Law Courts (8)
Tongeren, Belgium
Regie der Gebouwen, 6548 square metres, law courts

1997 Ribaucourt
Brussels, Belgium
SDRB, 1540 square metres, housing, Les Règles d'Or de l'Urbanisme awards 2004, finalist

1997 Loi 62
Brussels, Belgium
Fortis/Compagnie Immobilière de Belgique, 9900 square metres, office renovation

1997 Résidence le Lorrain (8)
Brussels, Belgium
NCC Group (Eurobalken), 4715 square metres, housing

1997–1999 Argent 18–22, study
Brussels, Belgium
GIB Immo, 12,676 square metres, office renovation

1997–2004 Porte Jacqmain, study
Brussels, Belgium
Banimmo/Buelens, 23,000 square metres, office

1997–2004 Porte Jacqmain, study,
Brussels, Belgium
Banimmo/Buelens, 8300 square metres, housing

1998 Astra Gardens (12)
Diegem, Belgium
Buelens Real Estate/IBC Vastgoed, 7664 square
metres, business park

1998 Belliard 9–11
Brussels, Belgium
Eden Blue sa, 8350 square metres, office renovation

1998 Le Jardin des Fonderies
Brussels, Belgium
SDRB, 5370 square metres, transformation of an industrial building
into housing units, 1998 Prix Européen Philippe Rotthier de la
Reconstruction de la Ville, mention, MIPIM Award 1998

1998 Résidence du Cloître
Brussels, Belgium
DHB, 3415 square metres, housing, Les Règles d'Or
de l'Urbanisme awards 2004, finalist

1998 Green Island – phase 2 (10)
Brussels, Belgium
NCC Group (Eurobalken), 35,020 square metres,
office, MIPIM Award 2000, FIABCI 2001, special
mention

1999 Hôtel Saint James, study
Monaco, Principality of Monaco
Société des Bains de Mer, 40,922 square metres,
hotel

1999 Ibis Brussels Airport
Diegem, Belgium
Accor, 4384 square metres, hotel transformation and
addition

1999 US Army
Brussels, Belgium
Copropriété chaussée de Louvain, 9918 square
metres, defence

1999 Alhambra (13)
Brussels, Belgium
All Build, 23,827 square metres, mixed-use office
and housing

1999 Communautés (8)
Brussels, Belgium
Betonimmo (Besix Group), 30,280 square metres,
office

1999 Novotel Brussels Centre Tour Noire
Brussels, Belgium
Accor Hotels Belgium, 15,336 square metres,
217-room hotel

1999 Rue Royale 132 (8)
Brussels, Belgium
Fonds de Sécurité d'Existence des Ouvriers de la
Construction, 10,100 square metres, office

1999 City 2 Shopping Mall
Brussels, Belgium
Fortis Real Estate, 27,000 square metres, renovation
and extension of Brussels's largest downtown
shopping mall

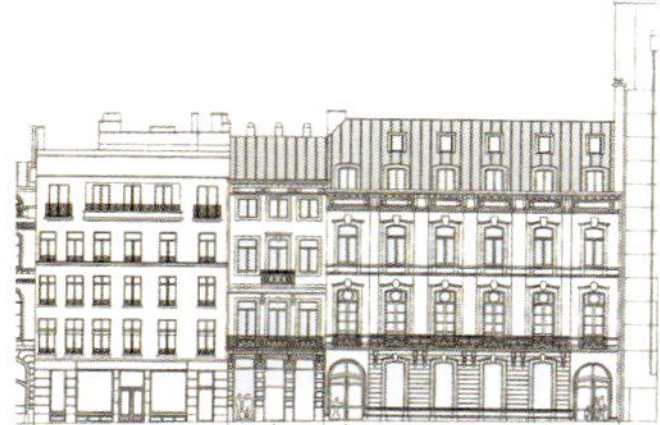

1999 Le Faubourg d'Egmont
Brussels, Belgium
Faubourg d'Egmont, 3584 square metres, high-end
mixed-use project comprising retail, office and housing

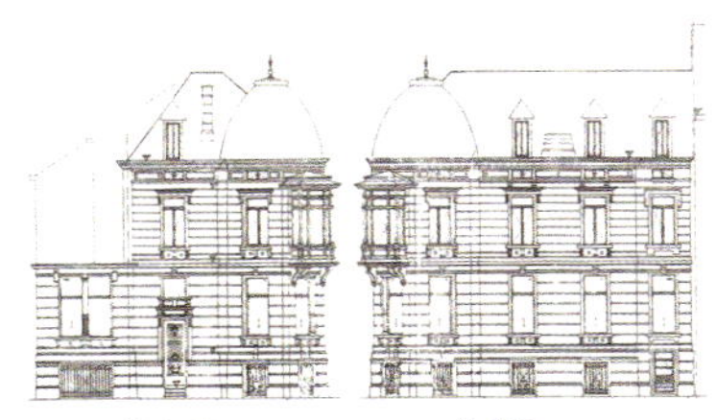

1999 Liverpool
Brussels, Belgium
Commune de Molenbeek-Saint-Jean, 567 square
metres, office renovation

1999–2001 Hôtel de Paris, study
Monaco, Principality of Monaco
Société des Bains de Mer, 52,821 square metres,
hotel reconstruction

2000 HLSCC Culinary Arts Centre, study
Tortola, British Virgin Islands
H. Lavity Stoutt Community College, 6161 square
metres, higher school, meeting rooms and restaurant;
with Mirsand Town Planning & Arch. LTDA

2000 Povarskaya Moscow Hotel, study
Moscow, Russia
Mosrybhoz/Petrolenenergo-Invest, 11,500 square
metres, hotel study

2000 Strastnoy Moscow Hotel, study
Moscow, Russia
Mosrybhoz/Petrolenenergo-Invest, 18,000 square
metres, hotel study

2000 Joseph II 40
Brussels, Belgium
Jomo (Insignia Belgium), 10,591 square metres,
office renovation

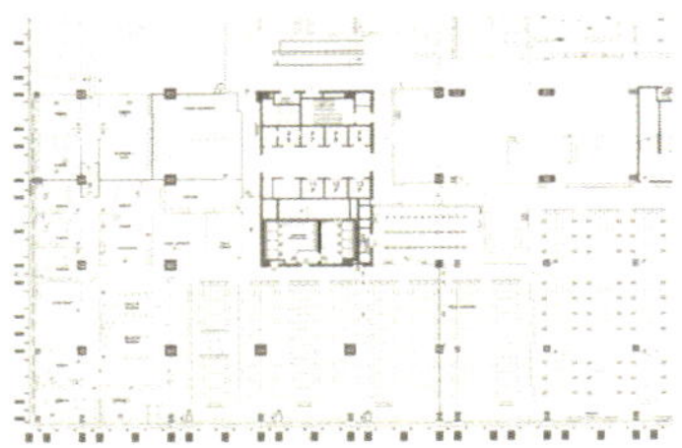

2000 Fortis/Montagne du Parc 3
Brussels, Belgium
Fortis, 1000 square metres, office renovation

2000 Hôtel Barsey, now Warwick Barsey Hotel
Brussels, Belgium
Hôtel Barsey, renovation

2000 Dexia Management Headquarters
Brussels, Belgium
Copropriété 1 Square de Meeûs/Dexia Bank, 7905
square metres, financial headquarters, renovation

2000 Villa Bozkaya
Ankara, Turkey
Mr and Mrs Bozkaya, 800 square metres, villa

2000 Empereur Center (14)
Brussels, Belgium
Clairière et Promotion, 14,500 square metres, office

2000 Delwart-Baie
Brussels, Belgium
EGTA, 7132 square metres, housing

2000 Loi 91
Brussels, Belgium
Cavens, 1821 square metres, office renovation

2000 Exki-Porte de Namur
Brussels, Belgium
Greenfield's, 190 square metres, natural product
themed fast food

2000 Les Semailles-Château
Brussels, Belgium
JCX, 1415 square metres, office renovation

2000–2001 Parvis des Brigittines, study
Brussels, Belgium
Brigittines, 5441 square metres, hotel

2000–2005 Waterloo 16, studies
Brussels, Belgium
BKCP Crédit Professionnel/Nexity, 12,559 square metres, office renovation with a new retail arcade

2001 East Side II, study
Contern, Luxembourg
Société immobilière de Contern, 10,685 square metres, office

2001 Baeck
Brussels, Belgium
Dheedene Construct/Immo Decade, 7586 square metres, housing

2001 Résidence les Erables
Brussels, Belgium
Burco, 9112 square metres, housing

2001 Brigittines, study
Brussels, Belgium
Socatra (Brigittines), 15,800 square metres, mixed-use housing and hotel

2001 Brigittines
Brussels, Belgium
Socatra (Brigittines), 1200 square metres, housing

2001 AVN Walcourt
Brussels, Belgium
BPI, 3560 square metres, office

2001 Galilée Building/Dexia Bank
Brussels, Belgium
Dexia Bank, 51,770 square metres, office renovation, competition-winning project

2001 Admiral Building (8)
Brussels, Belgium
Betonimmo (Besix Group) – Investissements & Promotion (CFE Group), 32,500 square metres, office

2001 Eudip Three
Brussels, Belgium
European District Properties Three (Banimmo),
25,410 square metres, office renovation

2001 Exki - Rue Neuve
Brussels, Belgium
Exki, 325 square metres, natural product themed
fast food

2001 Industrie 10
Brussels, Belgium
Allfin, 4488 square metres, office renovation

2001 Scandic Bruges
Bruges, Belgium
Scandic, 6684 square metres, hotel

2001–2004 Cureghem, study
Brussels, Belgium
Artim, 28,077 square metres, office and housing

2001–2006 Heron Plaza, study
Brussels, Belgium
Heron Belgium, 49,270 square metres, hotel,
housing, retail arcade

2002 and still under progress   Brussels Technopark (15)
Brussels, Belgium
I.D.I.M., 81,778 square metres, office business park

2002 Casino Anspach, competition study
Brussels, Belgium
Eurocasino, 11,200 square metres, casino

2002 Rijswijk-BAM, competition study
Rijswijk, The Netherlands
BAM Vastgoed, 43,688 square metres, housing

2002 Rijswijk-HKW, competition study
Rijswijk, The Netherlands
BAM Vastgoed, 43,924 square metres, housing,
renovation and new construction

2002 East Side I, study
Contern, Luxembourg
Société immobilière de Contern, 11,800 square metres, office

2002 Montoyer 63, study
Brussels, Belgium
Leasinvest, 10,257 square metres, office renovation

2002 Belliard 14–18
Brussels, Belgium
International Real Estate, 6624 square metres, office renovation

2002 P&V HDP
Brussels, Belgium
P&V, 3524 square metres, office renovation

2002 Résidence de l'Ermitage
Brussels, Belgium
DHB/SDRB, 7976 square metres, housing

2002 PPAS Porte de Ninove
Brussels, Belgium
Commune de Molenbeek-Saint-Jean, urban planning

2002 Arts 51–52
Brussels, Belgium
Fundibel (HPG–Hugenholtz Property Group Belgium), 8490 square metres, office renovation

2002 Trône 4
Brussels, Belgium
Immobilière SEM, 4057 square metres, office renovation

2002 Belliard 60–62
Brussels, Belgium
STAM Europe-Land of Bade-Wurtenberg, 6594 square metres, office renovation

2002 Fortis Headquarters (16)
Brussels, Belgium
Fortis, 38,300 square metres, financial headquarters, competition–winning project

2002 P&V Building
Brussels, Belgium
P&V, 1115 square metres, main entrance atrium lobby

2002–2005 Hôtel Royale Botanique, study
Brussels, Belgium
Building Engineering, 25,500 square metres,
150-room hotel and housing

2002–2006 Meeûs 23/Luxembourg, study
Brussels, Belgium
Belgian European Properties, 12,732 square metres,
office renovation and housing

**2003 Casino Madeleine, competition
study**
Brussels, Belgium
Eurocasino, 4225 square metres, casino

**2003 Hoek van Holland, competition
study**
Hoek van Holland, the Netherlands
BAM Vastgoed, 33,146 square metres, housing

2003 Moreau-Goyave, study
Goyave, Guadeloupe
Caraïbes Développement, 22,600 square metres,
housing

2003 Office Kiev, study
Kiev, Russia
GAP Insaat, 36,000 square metres, office renovation

2003 Porte de Ninove, study
Brussels, Belgium
Watan, 29,536 square metres, two office buildings

2003 Ulens 21–27, study
Brussels, Belgium
Herpain, 8916 square metres, office

2003 Wassenaar, study
Wassenaar, the Netherlands
BAM Vastgoed, 8800 square metres, housing
renovation

2003 Media Square
Brussels, Belgium
Benvenuta, 10,277 square metres, mixed-use project comprising office, apartments and a townhouse, Les Règles d'Or de l'Urbanisme awards 2004, finalist

2003 Etap Hotel Brussels Airport
Diegem, Belgium
Etap Hotel, 4756 square metres, 187-room hotel

2003 Montoyer 70
Brussels, Belgium
Allfin, 5545 square metres, office renovation

2003 Park Avenue
Brussels, Belgium
Robelco, 15,240 square metres, office renovation

2003 Van Meyel 14–22
Brussels, Belgium
Van Meyel (Betonimmo – Investissements & Promotion), 2900 square metres, housing

2003 Boulevard Emile Jacqmain
Brussels, Belgium
Ville de Bruxelles, downtown boulevard landscaping

2003 Disney Europe/Cassiopée (17)
Chessy, Marne-la-Vallée, France
Etoiles d'Europe (Buelens – Almafin), 17,921 square metres, Disney Europe headquarters

2003 Nile City (18)
Cairo, Egypt
Nile City Investments, 206,048 square metres, mixed-use twin towers above a shopping mall

2003 City Center
Brussels, Belgium
Fortis, 71,370 square metres, mixed-use office, housing and shopping mall

2003 Les Grands Prés (19)
Mons, Belgium
Foruminvest, 46,754 square metres, shopping mall, ICSC International Council of the Shopping Centers Awards 2005, commendation

2003 Les Jardins Victoriens
Serris-Val d'Europe, France
Marignan Habitat, 14,819 square metres,
86 apartments

2003 Soficom Headquarters/
Brugmann 27
Brussels, Belgium
Soficom, 5978 square metres, office renovation

2003 Fortis/Jacqmain 83
Brussels, Belgium
Fortis AG, 11,899 square metres, office renovation

2004 Espace Pétrusse (20), study
Luxembourg, Luxembourg
Accor, 51,400 square metres, mixed-use ensemble
comprising offices, hotel and housing

2004 Hameau du Bailly, study
Marne-la-Vallée, France
VIZZION Europe, 80,371 square metres, large-scale
urban ensemble

2004 Auderghem 22–28
Brussels, Belgium
Cofinimmo, 9738 square metres, office renovation

2004 Belliard 68
Brussels, Belgium
Fundibel (HPG–Hugenholtz Property Group
Belgium), 8737 square metres, office renovation

2004 Strato
Brussels, Belgium
Immogrim/LCEBE, 13,004 square metres, office
renovation

2004–2007 P&V/Frankrijklei 39
(21 for phase 2)
Antwerp, Belgium
P&V, 6500 square metres, office renovation

2004 Belliard 12
Brussels, Belgium
Comentri (Gillion), 5550 square metres, office
renovation

2004 The Center House
Brussels, Belgium
Allfin, 6680 square metres, office renovation and
new construction, seven apartments

**2004 Dream Castle Hotel at Disneyland
Resort Paris**
Marne-la-Vallée, France
UBX Development (PORR), 27,042 square metres,
400-room resort hotel

2004 South Center Steel
Brussels, Belgium
Fonsny Midi, 18,890 square metres, office

2004 Tabellion
Brussels, Belgium
Immomax-Newcobel (Socatra), 6640 square metres,
housing

2004 Rue de Namur 80
Brussels, Belgium
Taldec, 1081 square metres, transformation of an
office building into housing units with retail

2004 Business Center Glacis (22)
Luxembourg, Luxembourg
Waco-DIC, 23,145 square metres, mixed-use
building comprising office and housing

**2005 Hilton Brussels at Heron Plaza,
study**
Brussels, Belgium
Heron Belgium, 14,300 square metres, hotel

2005 Istanbul 'da Haydarpaşa, study
Istanbul, Turkey
Çalık Holding A.Ş., 2,218,664 square metres,
housing, hotels, hospitals, retirement house, office,
retail shops, shopping malls, exhibitions and fairs,
convention centre, sports centre, yacht club, marina,
museums, themed parks and other socio-cultural
activities including theatres and cinemas

2005 South Center Titanium
Brussels, Belgium
Fonsny Midi, 8630 square metres, office

2005 Swiss Life (Belgium)
Brussels, Belgium
Swiss Life (Belgium), insurance headquarters
interiors

2005 Lavallée
Brussels, Belgium
I.L.D.W.D.-Allfin, 22,193 square metres, office

2005 The Pavilion (23)
Brussels, Belgium
Robelco, 25,814 square metres, office renovation,
façades design

2005 Joli Bois-Clos des Lipizzans
Brussels, Belgium
Fortis Real Estate, 8933 square metres, 39 apartments

2005 Les Manoirs du Jonc
Brussels, Belgium
DDS Invest, 3912 square metres, two apartment
buildings, renovation and new construction

2005 Monte-Carlo Bay Hotel & Resort
Monaco, Principality of Monaco
Société des Bains de Mer, 68,400 square metres,
334-room resort hotel and casino, competition-
winning project, MIPIM Awards 2006, finalist

2005 Luxembourg 40
Brussels, Belgium
Belgian European Properties, 13,274 square metres,
office

2005 Mechelen Campus
Mechelen, Belgium
U-PLACE, 81,481 square metres, 11-building office
business park

2006 BILC, competition study
Brussels, Belgium
BILC, 56,917 square metres, logistics centre and
workshops

2006 Parc des Chartreux, competition study
Fouquières-Lès-Béthune, France
VIZZION Architects-Tractebel-VIZZION Europe, 80-hectare site, 144,000 square metres, large-scale urban ensemble, winning project in 2006 of a town planning bidding organised by the Communauté des communes de Noeux et environs

2006 ORA, study
Istanbul, Turkey
Duruhan, 59,000-square-metre site, outlet centre (41,000 square metres), hotels (150 and 270 rooms), performance arena (4000 seats), congress centre (18,500 square metres), theme park (9400 square metres), car park (90,000 square metres)

2006 Ali Sami Yen, study
Istanbul, Turkey
VIZZION Europe, 36,768-square-metre site, 105,000 square metres, office (70,000 square metres), hotel (20,000 square metres) and retail (15,000 square metres)

2006 Beşiktaş, study
Istanbul, Turkey
VIZZION Europe, 53,950 square metres, office (30,000 square metres), department store (10,000 square metres) and car park (13,950 square metres)

2006 Anka Hill, study
Ankara, Turkey
VIZZION Europe, 652,936 square metres, hotel, shopping mall, entertainment and health centre, housing, hotel

2006 Caddebostan, study
Istanbul, Turkey
VIZZION Europe, 21,378 square metres, luxury apartment buildings

2006 Ankara Gaziosmanpaşa, study
Ankara, Turkey
VIZZION Europe, 54,000-square-metre site, 70,200 square metres, housing (54,000 square metres) with car park (16,200 square metres)

2006 Doğan Henkel, study
Istanbul, Turkey
VIZZION Europe, 81,000-square-metre site, 232,000 square metres, housing, hotel, congress centre, fitness centre, shopping mall, leisure and entertainment, car park

2006 Doğan Hilton, study
Istanbul, Turkey
VIZZION Europe, 223,805 square metres, shopping mall (166,342 square metres), conference centre (10,424 square metres), hotel (18,534 square metres), serviced apartments (17,592 square metres), housing (10,913 square metres)

2006 Doğan Hürriyet, study
Istanbul, Turkey
VIZZION Europe, 54,733-square-metre site, 190,000 square metres, office (110,000 square metres), shopping mall (75,000 square metres), sport and leisure venues (5000 square metres)

2006 Doğan Ömerli Lake, study
Istanbul, Turkey
VIZZION Europe, 2,238,211-square-metre site, 800 villas, retail, sports centre, recreation centre

2006 Eden Resort, study
Police Bay, Seychelles
IRET (Robelco), 27,000 square metres, resort

2006 Efes, study
Izmir, Turkey
VIZZION Europe, 279,000-square-metre site, hotels (51,326 square metres), communal facilities (16,139 square metres), 180-unit hillside housing (27,720 square metres)

2006 Entre-les-Deux-Portes, study
Brussels, Belgium
TD Immo Invest bvba (Prowinko België), 37,911 square metres, mixed-use project comprising hotel, housing and retail

2006 Esentepe, study
Istanbul, Turkey
VIZZION Europe, 14,992-square-metre site, 90,199 square metres, housing (38,434 square metres), retail (15,000 square metres), hotel (6765 square metres) and car park (30,000 square metres)

2006 FB Borsa, study
Istanbul, Turkey
VIZZION Europe, 2884-square-metre site, 4150 square metres, luxury apartments, restaurant and car park

2006 Istanbul 'da Haydarpaşa, study
Istanbul, Turkey
Çalık Holding A.Ş., 2,682,000-square-metre mixed-use ensemble

2006 Istanbul-Levent IV, study
Istanbul, Turkey
VIZZION Europe, 49,000 square metres,
office project

2006 Izmit AVM, study
Kocaelli, Turkey
VIZZION Europe, 137,213-square-metre site,
mixed-use ensemble comprising a shopping mall
and housing

2006 Maslak 02, study
Istanbul, Turkey
VIZZION Europe, 500,000-square-metre site,
mixed-use ensemble comprising a congress centre,
office, a hotel, residences and lofts

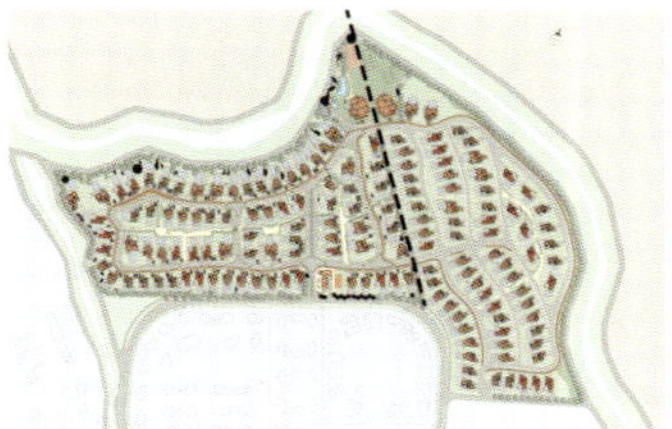

2006 Ömerli 02, study
Istanbul, Turkey
VIZZION Europe, 88,852-square-metre site, luxury
villas, social club

2006 Radisson SAS EU Brussels Hotel
Brussels, Belgium
Nexity II.G., 9858 square metres, 149-room hotel

2006 Arlon 63–65
Brussels, Belgium
Cerbux Invest, 1871 square metres, office renovation

2006 City Garden
Brussels, Belgium
Nexity Belgium, 12,074 square metres, office

2006 Le Domaine de Montévrain
Montévrain, Marne-la-Vallée, France
Ile de France (Promogim), 11,256 square metres,
housing around a landscaped garden

2006 Le Genève
Brussels, Belgium
Office Léopold III (HPG-Hugenholtz Property
Group Belgium), 26,300 square metres, office
renovation

2006 Montoyer 75
Brussels, Belgium
P&V Assurances, 11,357 square metres, office
renovation

2006 Avenue du Bois de la Cambre
Brussels, Belgium
Taldec, 1105 square metres, apartment building

2006 Mowo Center
Bereldange, Luxembourg
Cecobe (VIZZION Europe), 5817 square metres, retail

2006 Etuve
Brussels, Belgium
Bluehill (Groupe Liégeois), 8690 square metres, transformation of an office building into housing units

2006 Euro Village
Brussels, Belgium
Skyline Projects, 41,995 square metres, four buildings comprising 274 apartments

2006–2009 De Boeck (21 for phases 2–5)
Brussels, Belgium
Bruxelloise de Rénovation-SDRB, 13,937 square metres, five apartment buildings, 84 units

2006 Le Clos du Mail
Montévrain, Marne-la-Vallée, France
Les Exclusives de Montévrain, 8460 square metres, 61 apartments

2007 Altunizade, study
Istanbul, Turkey
VIZZION Europe, 280,309 square metres, mixed-use ensemble comprising five residential towers, fitness centre, swimming pool, cafés and restaurants, shopping mall, garage and shelter

2006 Le Parc d'Evrini
Montévrain, Marne-la-Vallée, France
Citalis (Cogedim), 8651 square metres, 59 apartments

2007 Bequia, study
Bequia, St. Vincent and the Grenadines
VIZZION Europe, 8839 square metres, housing ensemble (villas) with common equipments such as lobby, bar, restaurant and hotel

2007 Bursa shopping mall and sport centre, study
Bursa, Turkey
VIZZION Europe, 225,295 square metres, shopping mall (137,828 square metres), movie theatres (3205 square metres), wellness centre (2986 square metres), hotel (15,150 square metres), office (14,644 square metres), mall residences (34,482 square metres), park residences (17,000 square metres), parking spaces (4660)

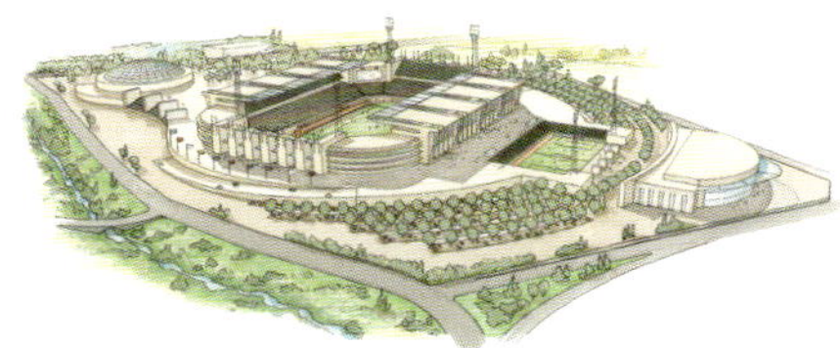

2007 Bursa sport centre, study
Bursa, Turkey
VIZZION Europe, 35,000-seat football and athletics stadium, 2,000-seat secondary football field, 7000-seat sports hall (mini-foot, basketball, tennis), olympic swimming pool

2007 Hilton Istanbul Fashion Shopping Mall, study
Istanbul, Turkey
VIZZION Europe, 223,805 square metres, shopping mall, conference centre, hotel, serviced apartments, housing

2007 Istanbul seaside, study
North of Istanbul, Turkey
VIZZION Europe, 4,001,109 square metres, new city comprising all urban functions

2007 Kayseri, study
Kayseri, Turkey
VIZZION Europe, 165,000 square metres, mixed-use ensemble comprising shopping mall, hotel and housing

2007 La Plantation, study
Bordeaux, France
VIZZION Europe, 221,000 square metres, business park, housing, hotel and gold club house

2007 Oyak Towers, study
Istanbul, Turkey
VIZZION Europe, 29,400 to 49,000 square metres, 16- to 37-storey office project

2007 Mayens de l'Ours, study
Les Agettes, Veysonnaz, Switzerland
VIZZION Europe, 42,885 square metres, resort comprising a hotel, 237 housing units and retail

2007 Mercator, study
Brussels, Belgium
VIZZION Europe, 21,500 square metres, office renovation

2007 Petit Mustique, study
Petit Mustique, St. Vincent and the Grenadines
VIZZION Europe, 39,469 square metres, hotel, villas, retail and wellness centre

2007 Resneli Niyazi Bey, study
Istanbul, Turkey
VIZZION Europe, 40,531 square metres, mixed-use ensemble comprising a school, retail, housing, garage and shelter

2007 Şancity, study
Istanbul, Turkey
VIZZION Europe, 162,079 square metres, shopping mall with cultural leisure and entertainment venues

2007 Westminster Hotel, study
Nice, France
VIZZION Europe, 10-storey hotel

2007 White Star Hotel & Resort, study
Méribel, France
VIZZION Europe, five-star resort hotel

2007 Coppens 2–6 (21)
Brussels, Belgium
Goddard Lloyd, 1229 square metres, apartment building, seven units

2007 Le Belliard
Brussels, Belgium
P&V Assurances, 22,743 square metres, office renovation

2007 Joli Bois-Résidences Alezan, Balzan and Tobiano
Brussels, Belgium
Fortis Real Estate, 17,780 square metres, three buildings comprising 87 apartments

2007 The Lounge (21)
Brussels, Belgium
Skyline Projects, 4221 square metres, 10 apartments, 46 serviced apartments, garden

2007 Hôtel Merode
Brussels, Belgium
Sogemad, 3958 square metres, office and housing renovation

2007 Regency Office
Brussels, Belgium
Sogemad, 6983 square metres, office

2008 West Bay Tower, study
Doha, Qatar
VIZZION Europe, 95,114 square metres, 310-metre
mixed-use tower

2008 Total Gas Station (21)
Mons Grands Prés, Belgium
Total, 120 square metres, gas station

2008 Kempinski Hotel Duke's Palace (21)
Bruges, Belgium
Royal Center (P&V), 16,420 square metres, 95-room
five-star hotel

**2008 South Express A1 – Groupe S
Headquarters (21)**
Brussels, Belgium
South Express (Eurobalken (Soficom Development)
70%, BESIX R.E.D. 10%, CFE 10%, Sofipari 10%),
14,177 square metres, office

2008 La Belle Chanson
Brussels, Belgium
Larebel-Woluwé (VIZZION Europe),
8690 square metres, 50 apartments

2008 Relais Spa (21), Val d'Europe
Marne-la-Vallée, France
Groenhaven, 20,242 square metres, serviced
apartments and retail

2008 South Express A2 (21)
Brussels, Belgium
South Express (Eurobalken (Soficom Development)
70%, BESIX R.E.D. 10%, CFE 10%, Sofipari 10%),
13,847 square metres, office

2008 The Fairmont Cairo at Nile City (24)
Cairo, Egypt
Nile City Investments, 53,165 square metres,
552-room, five-star hotel

2008 Les Terrasses de l'Ecluse (21)
Brussels, Belgium
Foncière de l'Ecluse (SDRB and BESIX R.E.D.),
16,241 square metres, 107 apartments

2008 Les Trois Mâts
Brussels, Belgium
Larebel-Woluwé (VIZZION Europe), 9670 square
metres, 53 apartments and a creche

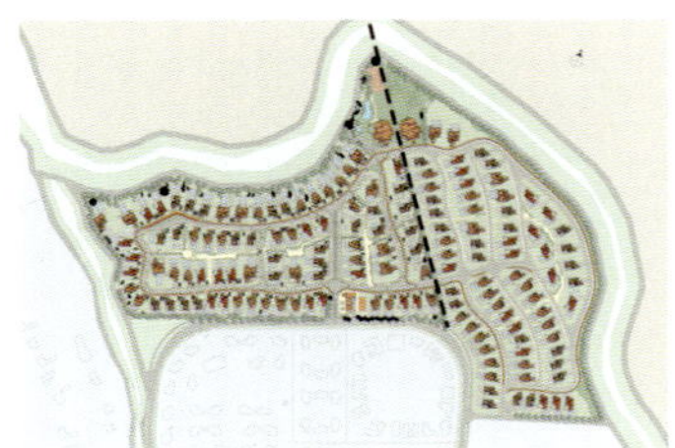

2008–2010 Ömerli
Istanbul, Turkey
VIZZION Europe, 23,105 square metres, 81 luxury villas,
social club, supermarket with a 23,932-square-metre
public park and 60,644 square metres of private gardens

2009 Atrium Gardens (21)
Brussels, Belgium
Skyline Projects, 8993 square metres,
three apartment buildings, 64 units

2009 De Gerlache (21)
Brussels, Belgium
City Projects, 8500 square metres,
two apartment buildings, 63 units

2009 Nautea (21)
Brussels, Belgium
Watan sa (BESIX R.E.D.), 30,387 square metres,
two office buildings

2009 Route d'Arlon
Luxembourg, Luxembourg
VIZZION Europe, 17,607 square metres, housing
with retail units

2009 Brugmann Court (21)
Brussels, Belgium
Brugmann Court (Wilma Project Development/BPI),
19,485 square metres, 7 apartment buildings, 86 units

2009 Domaine du Parc
Lorentzweiler (Bofferdange), Luxembourg
Immobilière Green Park (VIZZION Europe),
31,223 square metres, housing ensemble comprising
eight buildings (105 apartments) and 27 townhouses

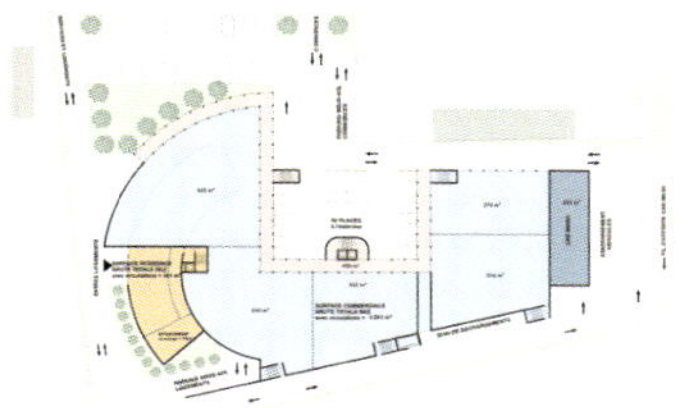

2009 Tousalon
Walferdange, Luxembourg
VIZZION Europe, 16,003 square metres, retail,
housing, office

2009 Brugmann Square
Brussels, Belgium
Brugmann Square (VIZZION Europe), 6570 square
metres, housing, renovation

2010 Horizon
Brussels, Belgium
Immobilière Horizon (VIZZION Europe),
1360 square metres, housing

2010 Quai des Princes
Cap d'Ail, France
Quai des Princes (VIZZION Europe), 32,463
square metres, 109 high-end serviced apartments
on the French riviera near Monte-Carlo

2011 Au fil de l'Eau (21)
Verviers, Belgium
Foruminvest, 99,736 square metres, 113-unit
shopping mall

2011 Green Square
Brussels, Belgium
Green Square (VIZZION Invest), Green Senior sprl
(VIZZION Invest) and Green Résidence sprl
(VIZZION Invest), 47,369 square metres, mixed-use
ensemble comprising apartments, serviced
apartments, retirement home, retail, fitness centre
and community services

2012 Le Parc
Villars-sur-Ollon, Switzerland
Domaine du Parc Holding Development, 71,046
square metres, 34 chalets, two serviced residences
and six apartment buildings

(1) Landscape design in collaboration with Robert & Reichen
(2) Landscape design in collaboration with JNC International
(3) For Cooper Eckstut Associates
(4) In collaboration with Cabinet AUSIA sarl
(5) In collaboration with M. Teich
(6) Bureau d'Architecture M. Jaspers & Partners and Dirk Bontinck, architects;
     VIZZION Architects, design architect
(7) Bureau d'Architecture M. Jaspers & Partners, architect; VIZZION
     Architects, design and execution architect
(8) Michel Jaspers & VIZZION Architects, architects; VIZZION Architects,
     design and execution architect
(9) Michel Jaspers & VIZZION Architects, architects; VIZZION Architects,
     design architect
(10) VIZZION Architects & Michel Jaspers, architects; VIZZION Architects,
     design and execution architect
(11) In collaboration with ELD partnership, project manager
(12) In collaboration with ASSAR
(13) In collaboration with Michel Jaspers according to ARC building permit
(14) Architect: François Schilling sa; ARC sa and VIZZION Architects
(15) In collaboration with Archi+I
(16) Michael Graves & Associates, design architect for the façades and the lobby;
     VIZZION Architects & Michel Jaspers, architects; VIZZION Architects,
     functional design and execution architect
(17) In collaboration with Interfaces sarl
(18) Architect of record: Etienne Watelet-I.D.S Limited and Partners
(19) In collaboration with Groupe ISIS
(20) In collaboration with architect Marc Werner
(21) Execution by DDS & Partners Architects
(22) In collaboration with Jean Petit
(23) Architect: Archi 2000; façades designed by VIZZION Architects
(24) Architect of record: Etienne Watelet-I.D.S Limited and Partners;
     Dar Al-Handassah Consultants

Credits

Index